The Moscow Yiddish Theater

THE MOSCOW YIDDISH THEATER

ART ON STAGE IN THE TIME OF REVOLUTION

BENJAMIN HARSHAV

Documents translated by Benjamin
and Barbara Harshav

Yale University Press

New Haven and London

Publication is made possible with the help of a generous grant from the
Lucius N. Littauer Foundation.

Frontispiece: Costume design by Itshak Rabinovich for *A Feast in Kasrilevke,* based on
a work by Sholem-Aleichem. Performed in 1926 at the Belorussian State Yiddish
Theater, Minsk.

Designed by Nancy Ovedovitz and set in Monotype Joanna type by Duke &
Company, Devon, Pennsylvania. Printed in the United States of America.

Library of Congress Cataloging-in-Publication Data
Harshav, Benjamin, 1928–
The Moscow Yiddish Theater : art on stage in the time of revolution / Benjamin
Harshav ; documents translated by Benjamin and Barbara Harshav.
p.   cm.
Includes bibliographical references.
Includes translations into English from German, Hebrew, Russian, and Yiddish.
ISBN 978-0-300-11513-0 (alk. paper)
1. Moskovskii gosudarstvennyi evreiskii teatr—History. 2. Theater, Yiddish—
Russia (Federation)—Moscow—History—20th century. I. Title.
PN3035.H38 2007
792.089′92404731—dc22   2007019926

A catalogue record for this book is available from the British Library.

The paper in this book meets the guidelines for permanence and durability
of the Committee on Production Guidelines for Book Longevity of the Council
on Library Resources.

10 9 8 7 6 5 4 3 2 1

Contents

Prelude

Yiddish theater is first of all a theater in general, a temple of shining art and joyous creation—a temple where the prayer is chanted in the Yiddish language. We say: The tasks of world theater serve us as the tasks of our theater, and only language distinguishes us from others.—Director A. Granovsky

The Moscow Yiddish theater (1918–1949) was born out of space and out of time. Out of space, because it happened outside the former Pale of Settlement, where over five million Jews lived and spoke their own language; out of time, because it did not grow out of any organic development but emerged out of the blue, in a surreal moment, in the middle of World War I, and among privileged, Russian-speaking Jews who admired Russian and European cultural models. The originators, the Jewish Theater Society in Petrograd (1916), were intent on building a modern, secular Jewish culture, with a theater alongside literature, art, and music, a theater on the highest levels of the innovative theaters of Europe. Director A. Granovsky, twenty-eight years old, was a disciple of Max Reinhardt's in Germany and projected a new conception of theater—in tacit dialogue with the most original theaters in Russia and Germany and akin to the avant-garde in painting and in poetry.

Some critics assumed it was the Communist October Revolution of 1917 that provoked the revolution in art and provided the impetus for this theater as well. But the history of culture is more complex than that. Like all other revolutionary art movements in Russia—Cubo-Futurism, Rayonism, Suprematism, "Non-Objective" (abstract) painting, Meyerhold's theater—the Yiddish theater was born before the Revolution. Even its first programmatic brochure, actually published after the Revolution, was couched in national rather than Communist language. For several years, it seemed to the avant-garde artists that their slogans of revolution and "throwing the past overboard from the ship of modernity"—as the Russian Futurist manifesto proclaims

—matched similar words in Soviet political jargon. Even the aesthetics of mass scenes and the rejection of individualism and psychologism could, on the surface, be presented as Communist collectivism. Furthermore, by nationalizing the theater, the government provided it with a budget and with existence (meager though it was). But the Communist regime also distorted, politicized, and crushed the modern arts. When the Futurist Mayakovsky wrote an innovative long poem in praise of the Revolution, 150,000,000 (one hundred and fifty million was the population of Russia), the leader Lenin himself, who had rather bourgeois tastes in literature, wrote a note to Commissar of Enlightenment Lunacharsky ordering him to give Mayakovsky only a small quantity of paper to print the poem.

The Moscow Yiddish theater also created a mythological Jewish space—a lost fictional world based on the classics of modern Yiddish fiction—and an enchanting typology of Jewish characters. Only through a grotesque mirror or political negation of the past could the theater evoke this powerful bygone but symbolic world in the Soviet context. If we peel off the agitprop banalities, this may be its lasting contribution to an anti-Broadway Jewish theatrical myth. The totality of the stage experience made the performances unforgettable.

Preface

The Moscow State Yiddish Theater (GOSET) no longer exists, and the "air" (as its director A. Granovsky would have said) of that time is very distant from our own. No videos preserve the performances for us, hence the importance of the memoirs, manifestos, essays, arguments, and eyewitness accounts translated here.

Part I of this book deals with the history and aesthetics of the Yiddish theater and the avant-garde painter Marc Chagall's role in it. Part II provides a mosaic of texts that opens up a many-sided view of this theater, its emergence, methods, and significance, Chagall's role in the transformation of the theater, and the theater's role vis-à-vis the lost Jewish past, and it includes two of the three short pieces staged at the first Moscow performance, *A Sholem-Aleichem Evening.* Part II also includes two brief books in their entirety: a programmatic brochure issued in Yiddish at the opening of the theater in Petrograd and a book on the Yiddish theater published in German in Berlin in 1928. An unusual perspective on the disappearing Jewish world is provided by such assimilated Jews or semi-Jews as the Russian poet Osip Mandelshtam and the Russian Formalist Viktor Shklovsky. These documents provide a vivid image of the theater in the context of its time. It gives voice to people who observed the theater directly, during the performances, and who took part in the debates about the ways of the modern theater in general and GOSET in particular. The illustrations provide a third dimension to the theater's reconstruction.

In recent years, with new archival material, GOSET has become the topic of many studies. Unknown details of Soviet chicanery, intrigue, brainwashing, and the vicissitudes of the party line have been clarified. What fueled this scholarly vogue were two political topics: the history of this theater as a minimalist Jewish institution under the conditions of Soviet political pressures and terror and the tragic end of a genius actor, the second director of the theater, Solomon Mikhoels.

The new Jewish art theater was conceived in 1916 and born in 1918. In the 1920s, and especially after 1928, the theater increasingly became a lying, boring, subservient Soviet agitprop institution that existed, with no audience, for purely propaganda reasons. Paraphrasing the contents of individual plays is a profanation of Granovsky's conception of theater as multimedia art, where music, acrobatics, choreography, folklore, and the individual Word rather than an ideological narrative are dominant. After protracted Soviet laundering, not much of the originality or the avant-garde remained in the theater. For most of its years, this Yiddish theater was as interesting as socialist realist literature: it was merely a political phenomenon and an example of artists in a totalitarian state, meandering between censorship and short-lived liberalizations, and Jews in a cosmopolitan atmosphere. It was no longer the same theater that had been admired in its youth (even though the same persons worked there). Since most of the external facts have been clarified, I shall focus on the artistic content, the aesthetics of this theater, and its meteoric rise in the 1920s.

The origins of this book are in my long essay "Postmodernism and Fictional Worlds in Painting," accompanied by a selection of texts and documents in English translation and published in the Guggenheim Museum catalogue *Marc Chagall and the Jewish Theater* (New York, 1992), edited by Jennifer Blessing et al. (it is long out of print). Most of that book (pp. 15–204) was written or translated by me. The Guggenheim Museum sent me to Moscow, where I did research in several archives, notably the A. A. Bakhrushin State Central Theatre Museum and the Central State Archive for Literature and Art (TsGALI, later renamed the Russian State Archive for Literature and Art [RGALI]). This was followed by a long essay in Hebrew: Benjamin Harshav, "Marc Chagall: Painting, Theater, World," *Alpayim*, no. 8 (Fall 1993), pp. 9–97. Then came a book on Chagall's life, Benjamin Harshav, *Marc Chagall and His Times: A Documentary Narrative* (Stanford, Calif.: Stanford University Press, 2004), and a book on his art, Benjamin Harshav, *Marc Chagall and the Lost Jewish World: The Nature of Chagall's Art and Iconography* (New York: Rizzoli, 2006).

It is important to mention here that Chagall's authentic autobiography was published as "Eygns" (My Own World, 1925) and translated into English as chapter 2 in my book *Marc Chagall and His Times*. The later *My Life* (1932), though expanded, contains many unjustified changes.

My deep gratitude goes to Anthony Calnek, then Vice President for Communications at the Guggenheim Museum in New York, who initiated my Chagall explorations. I thank the Guggenheim Museum for allowing me to reproduce parts of my original essay and the translations of texts published in the Guggenheim Museum catalogue *Marc Chagall and the Jewish Theater*. I am profoundly grateful to my editors Nitsa Drori-Peremen at *Alpayim*, Ellen Cohen at Rizzoli, and Jonathan Brent at Yale University Press. The final text of the book owes a great deal to Mary Pasti for her sharp eyes and sense of language.

The Tretyakov Gallery in Moscow and the A. A. Bakhrushin State Central Theatre Museum provided invaluable images that bring the Yiddish theater to life. The readers of this book will be grateful for this contribution, as am I.

I am also grateful to the Rifkind Fund of the Judaic Studies Program at Yale University for their support of my research in recent years and to my assistant Michal Herzberg for her intelligent help.

I THE YIDDISH AVANT-GARDE THEATER

CHAPTER ONE The Yiddish Art Theater

One paradox of twentieth-century culture was the contrasts and contradictions between, on the one hand, trends of democratization, the "revolt of the masses," mass education, and mass media and, on the other hand, the emergence of small social nuclei of the avant-garde, which blasted tradition and promoted radically new conceptions and a new discourse of culture and politics. Such nuclei were the Italian Futurists, the Russian Cubo-Futurists, the French Surrealists, the Yiddish Expressionists, and Lenin's Bolsheviks in exile in Switzerland. Typically, such small, iconoclastic, and innovative coteries concentrated around a leader who was the prophet of an ideology and who often acquired quasi-dictatorial powers. (In the Yiddish theater, the chief actor, Solomon Mikhoels, called the director, A. Granovsky, "our leader" and talked of "the magical power of our leader"—his words were gospel.)[1] After a short period of exuberance, some of those nuclei moved from the periphery to the center of the culture (or the state); others dissolved in an eclectic cultural discourse, embraced by wider circles.

Such a nucleus of the avant-garde was the Yiddish Chamber Theater (Idisher Kamer Teatr—in short: AKT in Yiddish or EKT in Russian),[2] created in Petrograd (former St. Petersburg) in 1918. It emerged in an assimilated Russian-Jewish environment in the Russian capital and was reborn in Moscow in 1920–1921, notably under the influence of the avant-garde artist Marc Chagall. Granovsky's new theater tried to span the gap between the slogans of mass culture and the aesthetics of the elitist nucleus. It staged symbolic mass performances that still maintained the aura of an elitist avant-garde.

The Yiddish Chamber Theater emerged at the intersection of two revolutions and participated in both: (1) the upheaval in the nature and format of the theater and the struggle for a new poetics of theater (especially in Germany and Russia) and (2) the Modern Jewish Revolution, with its grand leap from the primitive and obsolete shtetl (small town) into cultural modernity.[3]

A significant point is the double use of the word "Yiddish." In Yiddish as in Russian, the word means both the Yiddish language and the Jewish nation. Hence, "building a Yiddish culture" also means "Jewish nation building." And "Yiddish theater" also means "Jewish theater."[4] Indeed, the highly stylized and experimental multimedia experience on the stage overcame mere formalism with the embodiment of a new, not just Yiddish but Jewish "mythology." Yet we could not simply call it "Jewish" because another Jewish theater emerged at the time in Moscow, HaBima, which produced plays in Hebrew. Throughout this book I opted for the variant that is contextually most appropriate, but the other meaning must be simultaneously kept in mind.

THE FAME OF THE YIDDISH AVANT-GARDE THEATER

The Moscow Yiddish theater, later known as GOSET (Gosudarstvenny Evreysky Teatr), was a modest actors' studio in Petrograd in 1919. It moved to Moscow in November 1920, and by the mid-1920s it was one of the most exciting companies in Russia and, indeed, in Europe. On a visit to Russia, the English theater critic Huntley Carter, who wrote several books on the Russian and German theater, said, "The work of GOSET has no equal in Europe."[5] And the German theater critic Alfons Goldschmidt, after visiting Moscow in 1925, wrote, "The Moscow State Yiddish Theater, directed by Granovsky in ensemble with the actors, embodies at least the beginning of something entirely new, while the Western European theater, in its degeneration, looks in vain for new forms."

When the Moscow Yiddish theater came to Berlin's Theater des Westens in 1928, the awe-inspiring theater critic Alfred Kerr began his essay with these words:

> This is great art. Great art.
>
> External image and soul-shaking. The sound of words, the sound of blood, the sound of color, the sound of images. There are calls, voices, questions, shouts, choruses. It is enjoyment and horror . . . and in the end, human communion.
>
> That is, of course, pantomime with movement into eternity. Something wonderful.
>
> (Great art.)[6]

This is not only multimedia theater but human communion. For the German Jews in the audience, who could understand only some words but could respond to this carefully choreographed *Gesamtkunstwerk* (the Wagnerian ideal of a total, multimedia theatrical event), it was, indeed, pantomime—words were not needed to understand it—but it was, further, "pantomime with movement into eternity." It is interesting to note that those critics, like the authors of the German book on the Yiddish theater included in this volume, were all assimilated "non-Jewish Jews." Their experience seems to have evoked something deep in their consciousness. As Peter Gay has noted, all six theater critics in the Berlin newspapers during the Weimar Republic were Jews.

In 1935, after the stunning performance of Solomon Mikhoels as King Lear, the distinguished Shakespearean scholar Gordon Craig wrote in the London *Times*: "Only now, after having returned from the Theater Festival in Moscow, do I understand why we have no Lear worthy of the name in Britain. The reason is quite simple: we have no actor like Mikhoels."

Theater critics were not usually sentimental or nostalgic intellectuals but highly critical writers. Similar superlatives were expressed both by visitors to Russia and by Western theater critics during the troupe's tour of Western Europe in 1928. After all the formal inventions of the first quarter of the century, in theater as in art, the avant-garde theater seemed to have exhausted its innovations; this new company filled a need at a moment of crisis. Furthermore, for the left-leaning intellectuals, it represented the new culture created in the wake of the Russian Revolution as well as the miraculous rebirth of the Jews, the most oppressed nation in Russia.

YIDDISH CULTURE AND YIDDISH THEATER

Why a theater in Yiddish?

It may be difficult to grasp today that more than half of world Jewry lived in Russia in the nineteenth century. They lived mostly in hundreds of shtetls, where they constituted two-thirds of the population, or in larger cities, where they made up half or a third of the population (most Christians lived in villages). Yet the Jews had no national or cultural autonomy and no civil rights. In the census of 1897, almost 98 percent of the Jews declared Yiddish as their language. A meaningful Yiddish literature emerged toward the end of the nineteenth century. And because Yiddish was the language of the masses and of intellectuals alike, the advancement of a modern Jewish culture could be done only in that language. (Hebrew was primarily the written language of the Jewish religious library.)

Toward the end of the tsarist regime in Russia, new ideas were circulating among the new class of Jewish intellectuals concerning the organized creation and promotion of a full-fledged, secular, and modern national culture for the more than five million Jews in Russia. After the democratic Revolution of February 1917, when Jews were granted civil rights and suddenly could move to the centers of Russia, it was only natural that they tried to implement those ideas and continued doing so under the new, Communist regime. Thus, in 1918, in Ukraine's capital of Kiev, there emerged an umbrella organization, Kultur-Lige (Culture League), devoted to Yiddish national, secular culture. Their program declared:

> Kultur-Lige stands on three pillars: Yiddish education for the people, Yiddish literature, and Jewish art. The goal of Kultur-Lige is to make our masses intelligent and make our intelligentsia Jewish. [. . .]
>
> The goal of Kultur-Lige is to help create a new Yiddish secular culture in the Yiddish language, in Jewish national forms, with the vital forces of the broadest Jewish masses, in the spirit of the Jewish working masses, in harmony with their ideal of the future.
>
> The working field of Kultur-Lige is the whole field of the new secular culture: the child before school and in school, education for the young and the adult Jew, Yiddish literature, Jewish art.[7]

The stamp issued by Kultur-Lige bore the inscription "Mendele, Peretz, Sholem-Aleichem"—naming the three great Yiddish fiction writers at the turn of the twentieth century. All three died during World War I, closing a historical chapter and securing their status as the three "classical" writers of modern Yiddish literature. Theirs was a complex literature, rich and nuanced in its language, that reached the highest European standards and yet was rooted in the world of East European Jewry. Deeply involved in understanding Jewish existence and unfolding a peculiarly Jewish iconography and typology of characters, their work formed a dignified foundation for a modern, secular, truly Jewish literature and culture. Chagall was influenced by these three classical writers and included their names in his mural *Introduction to the Yiddish Theater*.

Kultur-Lige emerged during the Russian Civil War (1918–1921), when Kiev itself was shifting from one power to another. The war, and the exterminating pogroms of 1919 in Ukraine (when about a hundred thousand Jews were slaughtered and many more were exiled from their towns), were hard on the Kiev center; but its ideas were shared by other centers of the young Jewish intelligentsia in Russia and in the reestablished Polish Republic.

On November 9, 1916, with Russia still under the tsarist regime, a Jewish Theater Society was founded in Petrograd (as St. Petersburg was renamed). Under the tsars,

Jews were not allowed into the capitals of Russia, except for some privileged, rich, and well-educated Jews, who obtained permits of residence. As a result, among more than five million Russian Jews, only twenty-five thousand lived in the capital, St. Petersburg, and six thousand in Moscow. During World War I, however, the strictures were relaxed, and in 1916 an exhibition of art by Russian Jews was arranged in Moscow. (Marc Chagall had a large hall for his paintings, although legally he was not supposed to stay in Moscow.) A wave of national awareness and pride gave rise to new Jewish organizations, such as the Jewish Theater Society, the Society for the Promotion of Art among Jews, the Hebrew schools network Tarbut, and its Yiddish counterpart, Kultur-Lige. The crowning achievement was the sixteen-volume *Evreyskaya Entsiklopediya* (Jewish Encyclopedia) in Russian, published before the Revolution.

After the Bolshevik Revolution of October 1917, Communist propaganda claimed that Communism gave equal rights to the Jews. In fact, the Soviets had no choice but to continue the liberation of the Jews begun after the democratic Revolution of February 1917. Thus, the theater was a result of "bourgeois" efforts by the Jewish Theater Society to create a Yiddish theater; only later did the Soviet regime take over, as it took over and nationalized many other enterprises. Yet, to this day, some critics repeat the cliché promoted by the Communists between the wars that it was the October Revolution that generated revolutionary art and theater. Of course, the Revolution supplied an impetus and a discourse to the new forms of art. The same is true for all other arts and poetry in Russia: most modernist trends in Russian literature and art (Futurism, Acmeism, Suprematism, and so on) emerged around 1910–1912. They were not products of the political revolution but its predecessors.

The two Revolutions of 1917 disrupted all work in the capital, but the emerging cultural powers supported the rehabilitation of the Jews as part of the new policy of elevating those oppressed by the tsarist regime. On November 29, 1918, the journal *Zhizn Iskusstva* (The Life of Art) announced the establishment of a "Yiddish [or: Jewish] Workers' Theater" in Petrograd, affiliated with the theater and performance department of the People's Commissariat of Enlightenment (Culture and Education). The Jewish Theater Society implemented that decision and published a programmatic brochure in Yiddish for the first performance.[8] In February 1919, a theater studio was established, and Aleksey (Aleksandr) Granovsky, who had studied theater in Russia and in Germany and was an assistant to the celebrated theater director Max Reinhardt, was appointed director of the Artistic Division. After five months of intensive studies,

Logo of the Yiddish Chamber Theater in its Petrograd period, designed by Mstislav Dobuzhinsky, a disciple of the World of Art movement. The initials of the Yiddish Chamber Theater appear in Yiddish and Russian.

the studio was transformed into the Yiddish Chamber Theater. Performances began on July 3, 1919.

The theater's logo, drawn by Mstislav Dobuzhinsky, an uninspired second-generation member of the premodern aestheticist World of Art movement, indicated the theater's pre-Revolutionary origins. It incorporated the Jewish national symbol, the seven-branched menora, and the letters AKT, the initials of Yiddish Chamber Theater in Yiddish. No trace of the key word "Workers" in the name of the theater remained. And no trace of "Soviet," "Communism," "Bolsheviks," "proletariat," and so forth. In the eyes of the Jewish Theater Society, the task was "again to build the national, cultural life": "Isn't it strange, frightening? Jews, who have contributed the best artists, who have given the most splendid flowers to the universal altar of art, don't have their own theater to speak Yiddish with them? . . . No! Such a theater must be. This is demanded by the honor and dignity of the Jewish people, this is demanded by our national culture . . . The new Yiddish Theater Society promised to create such a theater, a theater for us." The chairman, Lev Levidov, saw the promise in the new Yiddish Chamber Theater: "We see here young, capable people, who love with body and soul their theater, their language, the idea of our own national theater."[9]

Yet Director Granovsky's emphasis was quite different. "We say: Yiddish theater is first of all a theater in general, a temple of shining art and joyous creation—a temple where the prayer is chanted in the Yiddish language. We say: *The tasks of world theater serve us as the tasks of our theater, and only language distinguishes us from others* [emphasis added]." [10] That is, in a dialectical argument, if you want a national Jewish theater, it must be on the cutting edge of world theater as an art and contribute to it. Hence the aesthetic program developed by Granovsky in the context of both German and Russian theater innovations in the beginning of the twentieth century.

But Petrograd was not the best place for Yiddish theater, because its small Jewish community before the Revolutions consisted of largely Russified, privileged Jews, with no Yiddish-speaking masses. Thus, between July 7 and August 22, 1919, the company gave performances in the nearest Jewish center in the Pale of Settlement—Vitebsk (Granovsky's wife was from Vitebsk), where Marc Chagall was then Plenipotentiary on Matters of Art in Vitebsk City and Province and founder of the People's Art College. As far as we know, Chagall showed no special interest in this theater when it visited Vitebsk, for he was immersed in making sets for all the performances of the Theater of Revolutionary Satire, TeRevSat, which performed in Russian in Vitebsk and at the nearby front of the Civil War.

During the short period spent in Petrograd, the Yiddish Chamber Theater included the works of Yiddish and non-Yiddish authors alike, producing such plays as Maurice Maeterlinck's *The Blind*, Sholem Asch's *Sin* and *Amnon and Tamar*, A. Vayter's *Before Dawn*, and Karl Gutzkow's *Uriel Acosta*. The stage decorations by Petrograd artists were gloomy Symbolist-Expressionist paintings, without Chagall's cheerful optimism and colorful anti-Realism.

Karl Gutzkow (1811–1878) was a German playwright. The protagonist of his play, Uriel Acosta (a historical figure, 1585–1640), was born a Marrano (a Christian of Jewish origin) in Portugal but went to Amsterdam, returned to Judaism, had himself circumcised at the age of twenty-six, then wrote antireligious tracts, was excommunicated by the rabbis, recanted, and eventually shot himself with a revolver. The dilemma of whether one can be a Jew and secular at the same time was of acute interest to that secular Jewish generation.

For lack of heating materials in Petrograd, the theater was closed for the 1919–1920 season, yet rehearsals continued, giving Granovsky the chance to educate and form an entirely new kind of well-trained and integrated repertory troupe.

A parallel initiative, however small, was taken in Moscow. In September 1918 the Jewish Commissariat of the Soviet government founded a theater section as part of its Enlightenment Department. According to its chairman, Ber Orshansky, the call for actors met with little response because the Jewish intelligentsia did not support Soviet power and "sabotaged" the enterprise.[11] Instead, the department gathered young and politically trustworthy people with no theater experience. For entirely different reasons, the Petrograd studio also wanted inexperienced students: to avoid contaminating the new theatricality with people who had acquired melodramatic habits in the lower-class Yiddish folk theater. Whether the "sin" was political or artistic, the result was the same. An independent actors' studio was founded in Moscow in 1919, which also included actors of the Vitebsk Yiddish theater studio.

In 1920 the Soviet capital moved from Petrograd to the old Russian capital of Moscow. On April 1, 1920, the government authority chaired by Anatoly Lunacharsky ordered the Yiddish Chamber Theater transferred from Petrograd to Moscow. When Granovsky's theater arrived in November 1920 (with only eight of the original students), it merged with the Moscow actors' studio as well as with some actors from the Vilna Troupe, a recently formed Yiddish art theater. Granovsky was appointed director.

In 1921, Granovsky's theater, like many other cultural institutions, was appropriated by the state, and it was renamed GOSEKT (State Yiddish Chamber Theater). Its name changed several times: Studio of the Yiddish Workers Theater, Studio of the State Yiddish Chamber Theater, State Yiddish Chamber Theater (GOSEKT). Finally, in 1924, it was renamed State Yiddish Theater (GOSET), the name by which it existed between 1924 and 1949, when it was brutally liquidated. In Yiddish, the name was Moskver Idisher [Yidisher] Melukhisher Teatr (MIMT). In Germany in 1928 it appeared as the State Yiddish Academic Theater.

The Yiddish theater was located in a confiscated house, built in 1902, owned by a Jewish merchant, L. I. Gurevich, who fled during the Revolution (tiles with Stars of David are still embedded in the floor). The large living room on the second floor was turned into an auditorium with ninety seats, and the attached kitchen became a stage. The actors and their families lived on the third and first floors.

The art critic Abram Efros, literary director of the theater, brought Chagall to Granovsky and persuaded Granovsky to invite Chagall to paint the stage backdrop. Efros admired Chagall's work and, with the art critic Yakov Tugendhold, wrote a book entitled *Marc Chagall's Art*, published in Moscow in 1918.

Performances in Moscow began on January 1, 1921, in the ninety-seat hall with Chagall's murals on all the walls. A year later, the theater moved from "Chagall's box" to a larger auditorium, containing five hundred seats. Chagall's murals, which had been painted on Dutch linen sheets, stayed behind in the old place, which turned into an actors' studio; but after 1925 they were displayed in the foyer of the new auditorium.

Two magical slogans guided the new Yiddish theater and gave it immense prestige: "theater as Art" and "theater of the State." Finally, Jews could have an "art theater" (not unlike Stanislavsky's Moscow Art Theater) echoing the most advanced of the other arts—painting, literature, dance, music—and separate from the kitschy Yiddish entertainment stage. And this theater was supported by the State itself—the alien State that had been the enemy of the Jews for two thousand years! The Yiddish name for the theater sounded even better—Moskver Idisher *Melukhisher* Teatr (literally: Moscow Yiddish *Royal* Theater). It is hard to imagine the dignity and pride of its supporters. Their tangible hope for a new secular and elite Jewish national culture, and the revolutionary spirit that inspired this enterprise, made those involved open to the trends of both political revolution and the avant-garde in art.

In his Yiddish productions, Granovsky wanted the Jewish subject matter to represent general human values: the Yiddish plays were to be submerged in a general repertory. Yet as director of the Yiddish theater, he felt a special mission, which included both raising the Jewish masses to a high cultural level and creating a national Jewish secular culture. In the archives of the theater, there is a document dating from 1920 or 1921, handwritten in Russian (probably by Granovsky), formulating the goals and organizational structure of GOSEKT. The first section reads:

General Principles
- GOSEKT is the first and only attempt to create a permanent performing-arts theater for the Jewish nation.
- Because of political conditions, it was hitherto impossible to establish such a theater.
- Geographically, Moscow was selected as the cultural and artistic center of the life of the whole Republic.
- Unlike all other nationalities inhabiting Russia, the Jews are the only ones who have no territory of their own.

This was the succinct ideology of a political-cultural program, from which the organizational framework followed. To keep a theater of such importance alive, personnel at all levels had to be trained. As Granovsky saw it, there were to be three separate units: a School of Stage Art, to "train the personnel of actors and directors, who are

Sketch of Aleksey Granovsky by Marc Chagall, probably made in Paris in 1928.

totally lacking in the Yiddish theater"; a Studio, "a laboratory to develop the forms of the Yiddish theater"; and the Theater itself, "for the broad masses." The primacy here is given not to performance but to working out the detailed forms of the new theater in the experimental laboratory cum "Studio."

GRANOVSKY AND THEATER AS ART

The new art of the Yiddish theater was achieved in two stages owing to two original artists: the director Aleksey Granovsky and the painter Marc Chagall.

Aleksey (or Aleksandr) Granovsky was born Abraham Azarkh in Moscow in 1890. Since Moscow was out of bounds for most Jews, his parents must have been well-off, well educated, and Russian speaking. It was said that he knew no Yiddish before he heard it from his actors. That may be an exaggeration for a Jew growing up in Riga; Granovsky didn't talk much anyway. To claim "I don't know Yiddish" was a matter of social snobbery among assimilated Jews, implying: I am a man of the big world.

In 1891, thirty thousand of Moscow's Jews were expelled; only five thousand remained. Granovsky's family settled in Riga (the present capital of Latvia), then the third largest city of Russia. Riga has a long German tradition but had been under Russian rule for two centuries. There he studied both Russian and German language and culture and through them the culture of Western Europe. At that time, Riga, at the intersection of several empires and cultures, produced such intellectuals as the film director Sergey Eisenstein (two years older than Granovsky), whose Jewish father converted to Lutheranism and became the city architect of Riga, and Solomon (Shloyme) Vovsi/Vofsi (pseudonym: Mikhoels), who, like Granovsky, was born in 1890.

In 1910, Granovsky began studying theater in St. Petersburg, and from 1911 to 1914 he studied in Germany at the Munich Theater Academy, where he worked for a season as an assistant to Max Reinhardt, one.of the luminaries of the modern stage. In 1917, Granovsky studied film directing in Sweden. Back in Petrograd in 1918, he joined the new Theater of Tragedy, which was supported by such prominent intellectuals as Maksim Gorky and Aleksandr Blok and was devoted to promoting classical drama for the masses. There, he directed Sophocles' *Oedipus Rex* and Shakespeare's *Macbeth* in Russian. He also directed two operas, Charles Gounod's *Faust* and Nikolay Rimsky-Korsakov's *Sadko*, and the famous German-language production of Vladimir Mayakovsky's Futurist play *Mystery Bouffe*, performed for the Third Congress of the Communist International (Comintern). Yet, like many intellectuals of Jewish origin, he abandoned (or found no place in) the general theater and moved into Jewish culture. Then he built a Yiddish theater of his own. Similar transformations occurred to Chagall, Efros, Altman, and others, but eventually they all reverted to the general culture.

Granovsky and his mentors believed in the creation of Yiddish theater as *Art*. The Jewish cultural renaissance of the preceding forty years had been concentrated in textual arts, literature, and ideology; the intellectuals argued that to become a full-fledged culture, the Jewish nation needed music, plastic arts, and theater as well. Since theater was accepted only as an art in the most modern sense, they recognized no earlier Jewish theatrical tradition.

Granovsky learned from Max Reinhardt the staging of mass scenes—a key type of performance after the Revolution, now supported by a new social ideology. When Granovsky developed his theater, he didn't have Reinhardt's twenty thousand extras, but he could imitate a mass scene by orchestrating the interactions between the actors. He erected a unified "total work of art" (Wagner's *Gesamtkunstwerk*) using two devices:

he brought all the arts—music, literature, folklore, dance—together to create one, total effect, and he gathered all the actors into one integrated human body that could converge on a "spot" or suddenly fall apart. In Reinhardt's conception the director was the decisive force in the theater. But Chagall thought otherwise. Eventually the director Granovsky and the artist Chagall clashed when Granovsky said: "Who is the Director here: you or I?"[12]

Reinhardt staged plays from many cultures and periods. He had no theory except for the principle that every theme, every play, demands its own form. When Granovsky came to Reinhardt, during World War I, Reinhardt was the most prestigious director in the German theater scene. But Granovsky came into his own in a more radical age, after the Revolution, at a time of new theater trends. He was a contemporary of the anti-illusionists (Bertolt Brecht) and political playwrights (Erwin Piscator) and developed a rigorous theory of theater as a formal and sacred art.

Granovsky began from absolute zero. As Abram Efros put it, "Granovsky had to build on an empty space. He was his own ancestor."[13]

Ever since the Greco-Roman period in Palestine, theater had been banned in Judaism, probably because it epitomized the joys and debauchery of heathen culture. Naturally, there were a few exceptions: several Hebrew dramas were written and performed in post-Renaissance Italy; and for centuries there were popular entertainments in Yiddish, notably the Purim-shpil, enacting the story of Esther and other historical legends. Nevertheless, theater in the modern European sense was almost nonexistent in Yiddish or Hebrew.

In 1876, Abraham Goldfaden launched a Yiddish theater in the interstices between Russia and Romania to provide entertainment and some moral teaching to the masses, but in 1883 the Russian government banned all theater in "jargon" (the derogatory name for Yiddish). The ban was lifted between 1905 and 1910 but renewed after this five-year window until the 1917 Revolutions. Yiddish popular theater, primarily lower-class melodrama (such as Franz Kafka saw and admired in Prague in 1910), struggled for its life in exile in London and New York. But Granovsky, like most highbrow Yiddish writers and cultural activists of his time, would have nothing to do with it. Thus, the writer Mark Rivesman said about Goldfaden: "He had absolutely no idea of theater art in the European sense of the word."[14] Among Yiddish intellectuals, New York's celebrated Second Avenue Yiddish theater was considered kitschy and degrading to Yiddish culture.

During the 1905–1910 period, when Yiddish theater was legal in Russia, there were important beginnings: good literary and theatrical plays on contemporary topics were written by Perets Hirshbeyn and Dovid Pinsky; plays by Gorky, Gerhard Hauptmann, Shakespeare, and Friedrich von Schiller, translated into literary Yiddish, were performed; celebrated actors emerged, notably Ester-Rokhl Kaminsky, who made a strong impact on young Mikhoels during her performances in Riga. Granovsky and his contemporaries rejected that theater too because it was individualistic, psychological, and literary rather than theatrical. It was alien to Reinhardt's and Granovsky's conceptions of mass theater. In the eyes of the Communist regime, those Yiddish playwrights were "petit bourgeois" writers. And young, Russian-speaking Granovsky probably knew little about them anyway; they were too parochial for this snobbish disciple of Reinhardt's. Furthermore, this conception of mass theater and the distancing from the brooding, hesitant individual, the "superfluous people" of Russian literature, coalesced with the principles of the new, socialist aesthetics.

Like Chagall in art, Granovsky adopted some of the most recent developments in theater technique in Europe while simultaneously reaching back to the most refined classics of Yiddish fiction.

GRANOVSKY'S SYSTEM

In 1918, when Granovsky undertook his mission, he announced the search for candidates to train as actors for the new theater. There were only two preconditions: the candidate must have no previous experience with theater and could not be older than twenty-seven. (Granovsky himself was twenty-eight.) This selection process coincided with the political selection process for the Yiddish theater studio in Moscow, which barred anybody with "Old World" conventions or customs. Granovsky made an exception for Shloyme Vovsi, an intellectual who had studied law at Petrograd University but was Granovsky's age. Vovsi had a "monkey-face" so ugly that Granovsky found him beautiful. From the beginning—and under his new stage name, Mikhoels (son of Michael)—he was Granovsky's right-hand man and his conduit to the other actors.

In the first programmatic publication of the Yiddish Theater Society in Petrograd in 1919, the star actor Shloyme Mikhoels described the political situation: "Outside, the revolutionary wave raged. Human eyes and too-human thoughts, scared and scattered, were blinking in the chaos of destruction and the chaos of becoming . . . At a time when worlds sank, cracked, and changed into new worlds, a miracle occurred, perhaps still small, but very big and meaningful for us Jews—the Yiddish theater was born."[15]

Granovsky trained his actors ab ovo, utilizing the best resources of the avant-garde theater and professionals in all disciplines. With the support of Jewish institutions, he hired some of the best Russian teachers who stayed in the starving capital to instruct the actors in music, rhythm and dance, gesture, "plastic movement," and acting techniques. The actors also intensively studied Yiddish literature, language, folklore, and folk songs. Each actor was to master all theater arts and to be in precise command of his body and voice. The system was similar in part to Vsevolod Meyerhold's "Biomechanics"; it prepared the actors to be as agile as acrobats (the circus was an inspiration for the theater, as it had been for Meyerhold and Eisenstein, Marc Chagall and Rainer Maria Rilke). The stress fell on language, music, and folklore as they related to the Jewish fictional world they reenacted. A rich, modern Yiddish language was an avant-garde achievement in itself. Not formed until the twentieth century, it telescoped the cultural past, which in other languages went back all the way to the Renaissance, in one fell swoop.

Mikhoels described the mood of the students: "Two feelings struggled in our hearts: the great will to create on the stage in the Jewish world and the internal doubt in our own strength . . . Indeed, who were we?—lonely dreamers with fuzzy strivings; what did we bring with us—except for oppressed and tense limbs and internal constriction, complete ignorance and helplessness in stage work and stage technique?—nothing . . . Yet one thing each of us had—an ardent will and readiness for sacrifice . . . And our leader told us it was enough."[16]

Granovsky did not separate form from content. For him, "Man" was but one of the elements of a stage production, along with the script, the music, the sets, and the lighting. But, as Mikhoels wrote, "We could only give ourselves, the Jew . . . to give the stage *Man* with a capital 'M,' man in general—this became our goal." The teaching and rehearsals were conducted in Russian, although the texts were in Yiddish, and Granovsky learned some Yiddish from the actors' speech. A typical *Yekke* (East European nickname for a culturally German Jew), assimilated to what Jews understood as high-culture German manners, Granovsky had an ideal of silence—a state that was alien to the talkative Eastern European Jews who were his actors and audiences. According to Mikhoels, he taught that the Word is the greatest weapon of stage creation. Its value lies not only in speech but in silence . . . The normal state is silence . . . The Word is a whole event, a supernormal state of Man . . . The intervals of silence between the phrases and moods in human utterances are the background from which the great, meaningful Word emerges . . .

. . . A movement must be logically articulated into its basic elements as a complex algebraic formula is broken down into its simple multipliers.

The normal state [of Man] is static . . . The movement is an event, a supernormal state . . . Every move must start from the static state, which is the main background from which the meaningful movement emerges.[17]

The theater performance was a work of art, a radical, densely orchestrated multimedia event that had nothing to do with Stanislavsky's psychological realism. When every element was drilled to perfection, rehearsals began. Granovsky devoted between 150 and 250 rehearsals to each production, chiseling every move and every word or half word. No wonder the actors who remained with the troupe admired their director. "For us," Mikhoels wrote, "he is the highest authority and the last word," for "we studio pupils see what is still concealed from everybody . . . We see the labor filled with sacrifice, the love of art and the people, and the rich content filled with ideas, which breathes in his work!"[18]

A note handwritten by Granovsky provides a key to the director's exposition of a play. The symbols were used to score the actors' scripts.

I	pause
II	long pause
I:I	long pause and change of mood
→	merging
word underlined	foregrounding
Ω	modulating a word
↓	end of mood
↑	beginning of mood
Mus	music
———	music continues
F.M.	end of music

Modulation of movement and voice, shifts of mood and dynamics, gave life to the ensemble. It was between words and movement that the art of the ensemble was located. The text, like the actor, was treated as a means to the goal—the total performance—and the shorter the text the better. Granovsky sought a total effect, involving every move of a multimedia polyphony and involving every spectator in every move. Performances were so rich because they articulated each separate medium into a myriad of tiny steps, each one foregrounded and meaningful. He said: "I consider stage art an independent and sovereign domain. Therefore, all elements constituting a finished performance—the man, the script, the music, the sets, and the lighting—must be subordinate to a single steadfast thought and the completed score of the production."[19]

Granovsky saw the theater as a temple, a performance as a religious experience, and stage action as a choir action: "Every type, everybody's movement, everybody's acting, painting, every role of individuality in the play, is only a part of the architectonic whole . . . Our artistic goal is the play as a whole . . . And the value and significance of the smallest role is great in its relation to the whole dramatic construct . . . One false performance of a word, or a move, not just of the central figure in a play but of the smallest and most overshadowed, can corrupt and cheapen the whole artistic image."[20]

The shrewd Austrian Jewish writer Joseph Roth, referring to Granovsky's theater, couched a similar idea in more philosophical terms: "the transformation of the accidental into the design of destiny."[21]

A play was to become a multilayered, internally cohesive, autonomous, and ideal object of art. This was Granovsky's theory as crystallized in the first months of his studio. He refined this vision throughout his tenure at the Yiddish theater, choreographing a polyphonic and dynamic, constantly surprising performance. He was "mathematically" precise and pedantically meticulous about every detail. Although the Moscow Yiddish theater did not stage many productions, almost every one was a cultural event. But already during the preparations for the first Moscow performance, a new force burst onto the stage, contributing a fictional world of Yiddish literature and folklore and a network of surreal devices: the art and personality of Marc Chagall.

A prominent Russian drama critic and theater professional observed: "When one sees this 'Jewish acting,' one cannot fail to be struck by the emotional appeal and rapidity of movement, the intensity of speech and vigor of the gestures. In its early productions, when the old repertory was being revised, poor Jews in tattered garments and comical masks or rich Jews—in frock-coats and stately, old-fashioned robes with colorful trimmings—would dart and dance about on the curious platforms and crooked staircases, in an ecstasy of delight. They were the Jews of the poorer slums. They would stand for a moment in solemn stillness, like monuments, before dashing away into the hum of the marketplace, or springing from one platform to another, or rushing down a flight of stairs and away."[22]

In the context of the polyphonic productions, the importance of language was diminished and condensed. The greatest successes of the theater occurred with audiences who hardly understood Yiddish; many Russians attended performances in Moscow (in later years, using earphones and simultaneous translations), and German audiences perhaps understood some of the words. A story about HaBima, the parallel Moscow Hebrew theater that used similar sources of Yiddish folklore, is telling, although that theater was still influenced by Stanislavsky's method. The actor and director Mikhail Chekhov once visited a rehearsal directed by Stanislavsky's disciple Evgeny Vakhtangov, the director of HaBima. Chekhov, who did not know Hebrew (neither, for that matter, did Vakhtangov), said to him, "I understood it all except for one scene." Vakhtangov continued to work on that scene, and on his next visit Chekhov understood it perfectly. A scene was not effective as theater art if a viewer needed the words. The lack of a language common to the theater and the audiences encouraged Granovsky's virtuoso treatment of the nonverbal aspects of this *Gesamtkunstwerk*.

For the same reason, ideology was unimportant as well. Like Mayakovsky and Meyerhold, Granovsky, though slowly, was willing to incorporate a socialist propaganda message in whatever play he staged—what counted to him was not the message but the effectiveness of the play's impact on the spectator. Indeed, ideology was almost an excuse for producing a play. As soon as the troupe performed in Western Europe in 1928, Granovsky was accused by Commissar of Enlightenment Lunacharsky of neglecting socialist ideology, and the theater was summoned back to Moscow. (Granovsky, fortunately, remained in the West.)

FICTIONAL WORLD

The Yiddish theater's greatness did not rest solely on Granovsky's polyphonic approach, nor on his mathematically calculated scores and directing. It derived rather from the fusion of these formal ideas with the surreal deformations of reality and evocation of a Jewish fictional world, created by modern Yiddish literature and elevated to a level of art by Marc Chagall.[23] As in Chagall's work itself, another language was superimposed on the languages of avant-garde theater: a powerful, time-forged, fictional universe, with a series of generalized but unique types. That world was deformed, made grotesque, stood on its head—yet was revitalized in a new, theatrical mythology.[24]

Other Russian directors of the time merged leftist art with ideological slogans, but politicized ideology is flimsy and transient, whereas a fictional world with unique prototypical characters remains in the imagination of the spectator, whether introduced with admiration or derision, or both. The ideologies that were attached to GOSET's productions were easily forgotten: "They come to curse and find themselves blessing," as one critic put it.[25] The characterizations of the old Jewish world were intended to condemn it, but the types and situations remained powerful, material, and vivid, whereas the political statements easily evaporated. Indeed, such estranged or semi-Jews as the poet Osip Mandelshtam and the Formalist critic Viktor Shklovsky saw in the Yiddish theater's productions the vitality (and tragic end) of the shtetl world and paid no attention to the obvious Soviet message.

This fictional world was raised to the level of a timeless myth through Granovsky's rhythm of "spots," which broke down the continuities of character and plot as if they were the subject matter of an Analytic Cubist painting. It was Chagall who taught him to depart from realism and continuity of space and time and to embrace simultaneity of action on several levels—for which not Chagall but his Constructivist followers, the artists Itshak Rabichev, Natan Altman, Itshak Rabinovich, built multilevel stages.

Chagall and Granovsky were polar opposites: the former was emotional, "childish," "crazy," the very embodiment of the awakening folk type from the Jewish Pale of Settlement; the latter was rational, Europeanized, German trained and assimilated, mostly silent, precise, and disciplined. They met at the very beginning of the Yiddish theater in Moscow, for a production of three negligible skits, yet the collision of these two willful originals changed the course of the theater.

One critic bluntly asked about Granovsky: "This alien Goy will build a Jewish theater?" Of course, Granovsky was no "Goy" (Gentile), but so he appeared in the eyes of the Yiddish-speaking, talkative, Eastern European Jews. The program for a Petrograd performance of the Yiddish Chamber Theater carried a notice, written in quasi-German, yet in Yiddish letters, that typifies Granovsky's attitude: "Das publikum wert gebeten entzagen zikh fun aplodismentn um tsu behalten di gantskeyt fun ayndruk." (The audience is requested to refrain from applauding to preserve the wholeness [totality] of the impression.) *Entzagen* (in German: *entsagen*) is not a Yiddish word.

Granovsky's productions in Petrograd might have been perfect, but no one remembered them. It was only after Chagall's influence on the theater that a stunning effect was achieved—*A Sholem-Aleichem Evening* was performed three hundred times in the first five years. After Chagall's departure, Granovsky revived another thematically Jewish play, first performed in Petrograd: *Uriel Acosta,* by the nineteenth-century German playwright Karl Gutzkow, but in Moscow, too, it was a boring flop that endangered the very existence of the theater. Only a return to *Sholem-Aleichem,* as seen through Chagallian eyes, brought the Yiddish theater back to popular attention. For Chagall, *Sholem-Aleichem* was not a comedy routine, a laughing matter, but true Modernist art. For the audiences, here was their quintessential Jewish identity.

The vital link between Granovsky and Chagall was Mikhoels. Shloyme Vovsi/Vofsi (Solomon Mikhoels) was born on March 4, 1890, in Dvinsk, midway between Chagall's Yiddish Vitebsk and Granovsky's Russian Riga. His father was a forest merchant and owned an estate. Before the Revolution, Dvinsk belonged to Vitebsk Province, and after 1918 it was incorporated into Latvia (and renamed Daugavpils). Thus it came to be affiliated with two different cultural worlds and shared features of both—hence Mikhoels's closeness to the emotive, rich Yiddish folklore, on the one hand, and his admiration for Europe's precise and sophisticated culture, on the other. Mikhoels found a common language with, and admiration for, both Chagall and Granovsky. As one of eight sons of a rich merchant, he received a traditional Jewish education until the age of fifteen and was steeped in Jewish learning and literature. Like Chagall's parents, his family adhered to the Lithuanian (Byelorussian) brand of Hasidism, ChaBaD, typified by emotionalism, warmth, and joy, as well as admiration for learning.

In western Lithuania, where Mikhoels was born, a rich man's way of life was also influenced by the Haskala (Jewish "Enlightenment") and by an admiration for Russian and German culture. When his father went bankrupt, the family moved to Riga, where Mikhoels graduated from a science-oriented Russian high school in 1908. He married a daughter of Yehuda-Leyb Kantor, a rabbi, doctor, *maskil* (secular intellectual), Hebrew poet, and editor of a Russian newspaper in St. Petersburg, *Russky Evrey* (The Russian Jew).

After being rejected by St. Petersburg University because he was a Jew, Mikhoels studied in Kiev. Finally, in 1915, he was admitted to the law school of Petrograd University, and graduated in 1918. Yet his attraction to acting and his commitment to Jewish culture led him to Granovsky's budding studio rather than the practice of law.

He became the lead actor in most of Granovsky's plays. As an actor, Mikhoels combined his intellectual powers, a restrained, disciplined emotionalism, and the skills he had learned under Granovsky's tutelage to create one celebrated role after another. The essence of his art, however, came from Chagall: the painter was the source of the tragicomic perception of the absurdity of Jewish (and general human) existence, evoked through a demonstrative anti-Realism.

Almost from the beginning, the aloof Granovsky charged Mikhoels with conducting the daily work of the troupe. Mikhoels was stage director, and before each production he announced a competition for each role. Mikhoels read to the actors from the recently published *Evreyskaya Entsiklopediya* (Jewish Encyclopedia) in Russian. His enthusiastic "conversion" to Chagall converted the theater as a whole. (See Chagall's memoirs about his work in the theater and about his first encounter with Mikhoels, in Chapter 3.) Under Mikhoels's guidance, the actors—all of whom came from towns in the Pale of Settlement—recovered the gestures, movements, intonations, and sensibilities of the Jewish shtetl world from their childhood memories. Mikhoels and his counterpart, Benjamin Zuskin (another western Lithuanian), worked together to bring to light the subtle connotations and gestures of the disappearing Jewish world. This was knowledge no teacher could provide; it was the source of the emotive depth and existential irony that the actors brought with them, which was then stylized and refined by Granovsky's system. Granovsky embraced the Jewish fictional world, its gestures and characters, and integrated it into his polyphonic conception, creating theater productions closer to a mythological happening than to a Formalist performance.

The "crazy," "spinning," unreal characters of classic Yiddish literature were social types representing a codified, stereotypical society; they were quintessential prototypes rather than psychologically refined individuals. This is why the theater went back to the classics rather than dealing with the early twentieth-century Yiddish literature of individualism and impressionism.

A Sholem-Aleichem Evening was based on character types familiar from Yiddish literature and folklore. The central character of *Agents*[26] is Menakhem-Mendel Yakenhoz, mirrored fourfold, a symbolic character based on Sholem-Aleichem's book by that name who is as proverbial and popular in Yiddish discourse as Hamlet is in English. Menakhem-Mendel is the prototype of a shlemiel, who seesaws between soaring fantasy and searing failure. A shtetl type, he attempts all Jewish *luft-parnoses* ("professions of the air"), such as matchmaking (shlemiel that he is, he brings together "a wall with a

Scene from At Night in the Old Marketplace: A Tragic Carnival *by Y.-L. Peretz, 1925. Adaptation: Yikhezkel Dobrushin. Director: Aleksey Granovsky. Set design: Robert Falk. Music: Aleksandr Krein.*

wall," a bride with a bride) and stock market speculation (with much the same success). *Agents* provides only abbreviated glimpses of Menakhem-Mendel, but no full-fledged presentation was needed—just an evocation of the type, which the spectators no doubt knew. Menakhem-Mendel, acted by Mikhoels, was also the central figure of the Yiddish theater's play 200,000—*A Musical Comedy* (based on Sholem-Aleichem's *The Winning Ticket*) and its later version, titled simply *Menakhem-Mendel*. In 1925 he became the hero of the film *Jewish Luck,* which boasted Granovsky as director, Lev Pulver as composer, Isaac Babel as screenwriter, Edward Tisse (Eisenstein's cameraman) as cinematographer, and Mikhoels, Zuskin, and the cast of the Yiddish theater as actors; even the train compartment by Chagall used for the stage production was adopted and became the trademark of the film.

Other variants of the same fictional world were brilliantly conceived for plays based on Goldfaden's *Sorceress,* Y.-L. Peretz's *At Night in the Old Marketplace,* and Mendele Moykher

Scene from At Night in the Old Marketplace.

Sforim's *The Travels of Benjamin the Third*. The texts were treated nonchalantly, shortened and augmented, mixed in with other works by the same authors.[27] What Granovsky kept intact were the grotesque and "philosophical" characters, meditating about the ways of God's world, and the messy yet symbolic situations.

SOCIAL ANALYSIS

In an interview given in Berlin in April 1928, Mikhoels formulated the "method of scenic social analysis": "Instead of the individual's moods, half words, half tones—explicit, burgeoning social feelings; instead of isolated heroes with private, purely subjective, limited experiences—joyful mass movements, with their noise, their dancing on the ruins of the old, their great social hopes and rational activities; instead of types—social figures that convey the breadth of large human masses, of human collectives; instead

Scene from At Night in the Old Marketplace.

of family conflicts, instead of 'Chekhovism,' instead of sadness and melancholy—large social contradictions that create the background for all the action on the stage."[28]

No doubt, part of this language was due to the fact that Mikhoels then toed the Communist Party line—he subordinated the Granovsky system to Soviet collectivist slogans—yet part of it was due to a true theatrical vision, which had excited European audiences.

The ideological conflict was described by Mikhoels thus: "Looking for the means to reveal most sharply and conspicuously the tragic content of past Jewish life, which is condemned to disappear in our country, the theater showed a great diversity in evoking new stimuli in its development. To hone the characters, to perfect the stage devices, to uncover new social kernels hidden in the atrocious, often-anecdotal classical figures—this was our continuing path. *Isn't tragicomedy one of the phenomena typical of our contemporary epoch?* [emphasis added]."[29]

This ideological conflict, combined with the artistic tensions within the polyphonic art, produced new, hybrid genres: Peretz's *At Night in the Old Marketplace* was dubbed "A

Scene from At Night in the Old Marketplace.

Tragic Carnival"; Mendele's *The Travels of Benjamin the Third*, "A Touching Epic"; Sholem-Aleichem's 200,000, "A Musical Comedy"; Jules Romains's *Trouhadec*, "An Eccentric Operetta."

The hybrid genres represent Mikhoels's vision of the modern world and Jewish destiny as a tragicomedy. And he refers to the actors of his theater as "Comedians," in the sense of the commedia dell'arte or the itinerant comedians in *Hamlet*—creating an oxymoron. The brochure *Yiddish Chamber Theater*, published on the theater's first tour outside Moscow, the tour of Jewish Ukraine in 1924, is filled with proletarian and revolutionary phraseology. But Mikhoels, in an article called "Our Comedians' Parade in Ukraine," evokes the waves of horrifying pogroms against Jews in Ukraine in 1919.

The basic oxymoron is, "The comedians of the Jewish theater travel over the ruins of Jewish Ukraine," but he concludes with the obligatory Soviet optimism:

Not tears but joy.
And joy and joy we carry over the ruins of Jewish Ukraine. [Emphasis added.][30]

Scene from At Night in the Old Marketplace.

   This tragicomic sense of humanity and Jewish destiny gave Mikhoels his unique actor's force: His grotesque or comical types carry a deep, sad overtone of tragedy. And the tragic character of King Lear is wrapped in the language and gestures of comedy. This is, of course, a Shakespearean feature as well, but Mikhoels drew it from his own life and times. According to all accounts, Lear was his greatest role as an actor; he gave a truly brilliant, tortured, and unique performance.

CHAGALL'S IMPACT

Granovsky did not mind being eclectic. He harnessed any and all devices of the contemporary Russian and European avant-garde theater for his new concept: a "Surrealist" perception of the fictional world, projected in Jewish literature and refracted through the polyphonic and tragicomic, kinetic and musical, rationally calculated and intuitive multimedia event. A historian of the avant-garde theater in Soviet Russia wrote:

Solomon Mikhoels in the leading role in
At Night in the Old Marketplace.

At the same time it is obvious from early accounts of their work [Granovsky's theater] that while they borrowed much from Meyerhold—his system of biomechanics, for instance— they had nothing in common with his intellectualization of theatrical form. They held his theories but expressed them with more drama and play of mood. Particularly is this seen in their stage settings. They believed that the decor should evolve images in the minds of the audiences—but they approached the mind through the senses. Their settings were always highly functional—look, for instance, at the settings for Goldfaden's *The Sorceress: An Eccentric Jewish Play,* three-dimensional combinations of planes, ladders and platforms arranged in a staccato picture that stabs the mind into an awareness of incoherent pain. The idea of the structure is pure Meyerhold—the carrying out of the idea has the stamp of ecstasy, mystery and unfathomable sadness. A great contribution was made by such expressionists as the artists Chagall and Rabichev, and later by Natan Altman, Rabinovich and Falk. They lit up the stage with a series of vivid pictures, always three-dimensional and mobile, which seemed to have a life of their own, which harmonized with and enhanced the grotesquerie of the stylized movements and which underlined the inherent color and richness in the Jewish character.[31]

This could almost be a description of Chagall's art. Chagall left the Yiddish theater after its first production, yet the artists that succeeded him were his admirers and disciples. Moreover, he influenced the conception of the theater as a whole, as various accounts report. An unexpected witness was the Labor Zionist leader David Ben-Gurion, who came from Eretz-Israel to visit Moscow in 1923. In the "war of the languages," the Palestinian David Ben-Gurion came down on the side of the Hebrew HaBima rather than the Yiddish theater, which commits two "sins": the acting is both Yiddish and "leftist." Of the Yiddish theater's production of 200,000, he recorded in his diary: "They sit on roofs, ledges, and stairs, don't walk but hop, don't go up but clamber, don't come down but tumble and leap—Sholem-Aleichem is unrecognizable."[32] The set was Rabichev's, yet this is clearly the description of a Chagallian placement of characters and a Chagallian conception of "groundless" space. Of course, Chagall's reading of Sholem-Aleichem's topsy-turvy world was absolutely correct. Ben-Gurion was never known for his appreciation of literature or art, but he registered what he saw.

The German critic Max Osborn also visited Moscow in 1923, and on his return he wrote an essay on Chagall. He described 200,000 in this way:

> The curtain goes up and you see a strange chaos of houses, intertwined in a Cubist manner, rising one above the other on different levels. Intersecting one another at sharp angles, they either stand below wide roofs or suddenly appear without a roof altogether, like a man taking off his hat, and display all their internal secrets. Here and there, bridges and passageways are drawn; wide streets rise and fall diagonally. Meyerhold's Constructivist stage is embodied here in original variants. The Cubist linear play of these forms is complemented and enriched by Cézanne colors. Your eye perceives a fantastic interpretation of a Jewish-Russian small town, presented in the narrow confines of a stage in an unusually joyful and charming formula. Before the spectator's eye, everything can happen simultaneously: the events in the tailor shop, scenes among the populace of the *shtetl* who accompany the play and [take] the experiences of the main characters as their own—a picturesque, machine-like, mimic-acrobatic choir.
>
> When the news arrives about the tailor's unexpected great win of a huge sum, setting the whole town into an unusual excitement, suddenly, high above the roof of one building appears the figure of a Jew with a red beard and a green greatcoat, with a sack on his back and a staff in his hand. Instinctively I said aloud: "Chagall!" And suddenly everything became clear: this is the world of Chagall. From him, everything emerged: the young artist-decorator Rabichev's creations, Granovsky's constructions, and the accompanying music of the composer Pulver. The latter, with unusual expressiveness, embodied Oriental motifs, ancient Jewish images, and Russian songs in operatic melodies, with trumpets and kettledrums.[33]

Later, in Mikhoels's dressing room, Osborn learned that, indeed, "Marc Chagall had played a decisive role in the development of the whole stage art of the Yiddish Chamber Theater; that, in this circle, he was considered the great originator and inspiration." He also learned that "Chagall's box" was preserved like a temple in the "House of Yiddish Theater Art" (as the former small theater was called).

> It is no accident that painting exerted such an influence on the stage, no whim of a theater director attracted by the work of an artist. It was a stronger force, an inner necessity. Always, when the personality and the school of a master truly find a clear and strong expression for the cultural spirit of the time—the stage is captivated by it—and only then is it captivated . . . Like no one else in the young Russia of our days, Chagall has the stunning power of transforming the elements of an exceedingly rich and profound artistic folk culture into colorful, dreamy visions that strike our imagination.[34]

In August 1918, Chagall was appointed by Commissar of Enlightenment Lunacharsky himself to be the Plenipotentiary on Matters of Art in Vitebsk City and Province.[35] Chagall built a unique People's Art College and invited some of the best artists of the day to teach in this bastion of "Leftist" art. Among the invited were the Suprematists El (Eliezer) Lissitzky and Kazimir Malevich, who launched a new art movement, Affirmers of the New Art (UNOVIS). Their art now focused on abstract shapes, compositions of rectangles and triangles of various colors. This seemed to be more radical than Chagall's still figurative deformations of reality, and the students shifted to the left. Chagall was a whimsical and disorganized leader, and he was, in fact, pushed out of his own college. With his wife and daughter, he left for Moscow, where he accepted the invitation to paint the decorations for the first Moscow performance of three short dramatic pieces by Sholem-Aleichem.

Chagall immersed himself feverishly in the work. In the course of forty days in November–December 1919 he furnished the stages for the three plays and painted the sets, the curtains, the murals that covered all the walls, the frieze under the ceiling, and even the actors' clothes and faces. Instead of putting a painting in a theater, he enclosed the whole theater in a painting—hence its name "Chagall's box." Granovsky said, "Who is the Director here: you or I?"—and never hired him again. Efros had to keep the lights on before the play and explain to the audience what the murals meant and why the actors looked frozen on the stage and revived in the murals. Efros correctly set the quarrel between artist and director for the domination of the play in the historical context of the Russian theater.[36]

THE HEBREW HABIMA

Parallel to the Yiddish theater, a Hebrew theater was established in Moscow. Monti Ja-kobs, the theater critic of the prestigious German newspaper *Vossische Zeitung*, began his review of the Yiddish theater's 200,000 thus: "As at HaBima, the same *furor judaicum*, it is a play that pulls the spectator out of his seat and draws him into the strong rhythm emanating from the stage." This is not the place to discuss HaBima at length, but a few words are in order, for the two theaters are often mentioned together.

A group of young people gathered before World War I in Bialystok to create a new kind of *bima* (the Hebrew word for "stage"; *ha* is the article) in order to perform in the budding spoken Hebrew language. In 1918, arriving in Moscow, they received the patronage of the great Stanislavsky, and HaBima became one of the four studios attached to his Moscow Art Theater. The young Vakhtangov, Stanislavsky's most famous disciple, became HaBima's director. In November 1918, HaBima was recognized as a Soviet state theater. With *The Eternal Jew*, *The Dybbuk*, and other plays, HaBima enters general theater history; its 1926 tour of Europe was a great triumph, especially in Germany, then the center of European theater.

Hebrew was the language of the holy books and the Jewish religious library (as Cha-gall said of HaBima: "The actors don't act but pray"),[37] but during the Modern Jewish Revolution it rapidly expanded its genres into secular literature, politics, and science. Turning a language of religious texts into a spoken language that dealt with mundane and secular topics was not easy, yet toward the end of the nineteenth century such a language began to crystallize, and between 1906 and 1913 the first Hebrew-speaking social cells emerged in Palestine. HaBima was an early attempt at speaking the biblical language on stage (most of its own actors knew no Hebrew beforehand). Thus two Jewish theaters in Moscow, in two languages, were established as Soviet state theaters in the first years after the October Revolution.

Soon the "war of the languages" was raging. Those who wanted to revive Yiddish culture in Russia saw Hebrew as a religious vestige of bygone times, not the language of the masses. Kultur-Lige's programmatic brochure exemplifies the conflict. It attacks the parallel Hebrew school organization Tarbut as being "Zionist-Rabbinical" and promot-ing Eretz-Israel: "A land where Jews don't live they call our land; a language Jews don't speak they call our language." The Evsektsya (the Jewish Section of the Communist Party) battled the recognition of HaBima; its leader, Semen Dimandshteyn, claimed that HaBima was "a whim of the Jewish bourgeoisie; the money of the Revolutionary power should not be allowed to support a theater the peasants and workers don't want." But some of the most illustrious Russian intellectuals of the day (and, as Efros put it, the anti-Semites) supported the new phenomenon that used the lofty and pure biblical language. Maksim Gorky and the world-famous singer Fyodor Chaliapin wept during its performances. Leaders of the Russian intelligentsia wrote a letter to Lenin on its behalf, and the commissar of nationalities—Stalin himself—overruled the Yiddish Evsektsya and saved the Hebrew HaBima.

In January 1926, the Moscow State Theater HaBima departed on its spectacular tour of Western Europe and the United States.[38] Most of the troupe did not return to Russia and instead reestablished HaBima in Tel Aviv, where eventually it became the Israeli National Theater.

Both HaBima and GOSET drew on the achievements of the Russian avant-garde theater, although HaBima, still in the Stanislavsky tradition, was more conservative and expressionistic. Both derived their strength from the same collective Jewish folk tradition, expressed in mass ensemble scenes and the multimedia polyphony of music, dance, sets, and stage scenes. The Hebrew HaBima, too, drew on the Yiddish literary tradition translated into Hebrew (notably, Dovid Pinsky's *The Eternal Jew* and Solomon An-sky's *The Dybbuk*). The solemn language of the still-far-from-colloquial and biblical Hebrew influenced the pathos and the elevated, heroic national style of HaBima; it did not have the humor, irony, or flexibility of moods typical of popular Yiddish. Though emanating from the same national milieu, HaBima fostered the Hebrew genre of high tragedy, oriented toward a utopian dream, while GOSET showcased the Yiddish genre of comedy and looked the tragic end of a culture straight in the eye.

A SOVIET THEATER

In 1927, in recognition of their artistic contributions, Granovsky, Mikhoels, and Zuskin were awarded the title of People's Artist of the USSR. They were co-opted to the system. GOSET had to bend over backward to adapt to ever-changing ideological and political demands. Indeed, it served propaganda purposes in the USSR and abroad. Jewish traditional images were merged with the so-called Soviet internationalism (which had forcibly put pigs on the new Jewish collective farms). Almost from the beginning of the regime, political engagement was more pervasive in the jittery Jewish sector than elsewhere. The program of the spectacle *Carnival of Yiddish Comedians* included: "Thieves' songs from Odessa and Warsaw; a Negro performance, 'Java Celebes'; the Jewish King Lear in Pensa; Klezmer songs; three loves—Negro, American, Hasidic; street songs from Vilna; Hasidic songs and dances; 'Matchmaking'—an unusual operetta; American songs in Jewish style; six Jewish acrobats; the Marseillaise" (according to the playbill of May 12, 1923). What the Jewish comedians in Russia knew of "Negro love," and how such love is related to the Indonesian islands Java and Celebes, is hard to imagine; and the "Marseillaise" is a rather comical ending to a "third world" folk carnival.

The theater wanted to put on plays and was willing to pay any intellectual price to do so. It was typical of the Russian intelligentsia at the time that they used the Party-line rhetoric at every occasion. It would be hard for the speakers themselves to sort out what they really believed in, what they paid lip service to, and what they said out of conformism or pressure. The Jewish theater was a Soviet institution, after all.

Even as early as 1924, in the collection of essays published for the theater's tour of the devastated Jewish Ukraine, we read in the opening article:

> The chamber theater conquered the proletarian and hard-working milieu. There is no laborer, no hard-working person, who just observed the theater and didn't speak about it with excitement. On the contrary, you can feel the contempt and partial boycott of the Jewish bourgeoisie, the clerics, and to some extent also the old Jewish actors. And it is quite clear why the chamber theater pours the last spade of earth on old bourgeois mores, on the old mold, and creates not just a mood but a will to a productive working life.
>
> The Zionist, the Jewish rich man,[39] squirms with his ugly grimace; the *shtrayml* [fur hat], the synagogue, hurls dead curses and excommunications. But all the simple folk storm around enthusiastically, eager to fight; the wide masses are filled with joy and revolutionary ecstasies.
>
> The Yiddish Chamber Theater is a political-cultural force. No doubt it is becoming the revolutionary people's theater.
>
> No doubt![40]

And even Mikhoels, who clearly is still in shock over the pogroms in Ukraine in 1919, writes: "To the march of the October victory, with energetic creative pathos, the comedians of the Yiddish Chamber Theater march in a parade over Ukraine."[41]

Finally, the theater was allowed to go abroad. On April 7, 1928, GOSET performed 200,000 in Berlin. More than forty reviews were published in Germany. Its reception surpassed anything other Russian theaters experienced, and a book about GOSET was published in German with the participation of such prominent writers as the Communist

and poet Ernst Toller, the novelist Joseph Roth, and the theater critic Alfons Goldschmidt.[42] Berlin was the center of innovative theater. As many reviews indicated,
"Granovsky was received in Berlin as a new theatrical messiah, a more innovative and
revolutionary director than Meyerhold, Reinhardt and Piscator."[43]

GOSET traveled throughout Germany and visited Vienna and Paris; but from the
beginning, the center suspected Granovsky's intentions, and toward the end of the
year Lunacharsky condemned the direction of the theater, and it was forced to return
to Russia. Granovsky stayed in the West. After several unsuccessful attempts, he had
a considerable success directing Arnold Zweig's *Sergeant Grisha*, produced in Berlin in
1930, and he also made several German films. With the rise of the Nazis, he fled to
France and faded into oblivion. On March 11, 1937, at the age of forty-seven, he died
in Paris, one of the most original theater directors of the century. About the same
time, the great innovator Meyerhold, who had sold his soul to the Communists, was
tortured to death in a Soviet prison.

In 1928, when Granovsky remained in the West, Mikhoels became the director of
GOSET. He enjoyed great fame in Russia and was accepted in Moscow's high society.
He continued performing Jewish plays, insisting that this was the task of the Yiddish
theater, that classical and Russian plays were better performed in the Russian Chamber
Theater next door, directed by Aleksandr Tairov (Kornblit).

But pressures and criticism were incessant. During the purges of the 1930s, Stalin's
henchman Lazar Kaganovich came to a performance. He inspired terror in the director
and actors, screaming that it was a shame to show such crippled Jews: "Look at me.
I am a Jew. My father was also like this: tall, broad, healthy."[44] Mikhoels immediately
started rehearsing a drama about a strong Jewish type "from the people," Moyshe
Kulbak's *Boytre;* but soon enough Kulbak himself was arrested and liquidated, and his
plays were banned.

EPILOGUE

During World War II, Mikhoels was appointed chairman of the newly established Jewish
Anti-Fascist Committee in Moscow. It was the first time that Stalin's regime recognized
one worldwide Jewish nation and a Soviet institution that spoke for all Soviet Jews.
Mikhoels and the Yiddish poet Itsik Fefer visited the United States in 1943 to solicit
international aid and Jewish contributions in the war against Hitler.

But in 1948, Mikhoels was lured from Moscow to Minsk, where he was brutally murdered on Stalin's orders. Most Yiddish writers, actors, and activists were arrested; some were shot, others tortured. The theater was closed, along with the last Yiddish newspaper and the last Yiddish publishing house in Soviet Russia.

Chagall (in 1922) and Granovsky (in 1928) left Soviet Russia for Western Europe and could not be safely mentioned in Russia during the Soviet period. During the purges of 1937, Chagall's murals were hidden under the stage. In 1949 or 1950 they found their way to the Tretyakov Gallery in Moscow. One version has it that the Liquidation Commission of the theater gave the murals to the gallery in 1950;[45] another version, prevalent in Moscow art circles, is that the last artistic director of the theater, the painter Aleksandr Tyshler, when he saw that all was lost, carried the canvases there on his back. Yet another version has it that the murals of the Yiddish theater were hidden in the cellar of an inactive church, a closed storage area of the Tretyakov Gallery, and were opened only in 1973 for Chagall's signature.

Perhaps all three versions are true. The canvases (not the paintings) were restored in 1989 and shown in many exhibitions around the world. The Tretyakov conservators did a careful, professional job of preparing the canvases in 1991 for transport to Germany and later to other countries.[46] They deliberately did not attempt to restore the original colors, instead "letting time do what time does," as Mr. Aleksey Kovalev explained to me. A venerable approach, but in this case "time" had too much of a human face.

Stage mock-ups and costume designs from throughout the theater's brief history wound up in the A. A. Bakhrushin State Central Theatre Museum in Moscow, where they were sealed in a storage room along with the archives of the Russian Chamber Theater, directed by Aleksandr Tairov (Kornblit). Both theaters were liquidated. A fire presumably broke out at the Bakhrushin—only in this room—and the set designs, packed in a very tight ball, bound with ropes, were burned around the edges. The documents also suffered a layer of water damage: somebody must have tried to extinguish the fire with water. To this day, the causes and facts of that destruction have not been fully disclosed. Traces of those actions can be seen on the margins of several illustrations in this book.

CHAPTER TWO

Chagall's Theater Murals

INTERPRETATION OF CHAGALL'S IMAGERY

The murals Chagall made for the State Yiddish Chamber Theater in Moscow in 1920 were a landmark for both the painter and the theater.[1] The theater was transformed from a small actors' studio, producing traditional plays, albeit in a new manner, into one embracing Chagall's anti-Realist and polyphonic conception of Modern art, combined with his vision of the "Modernist" Yiddish classical writer Sholem-Aleichem and the vitality of topsy-turvy Jewish existence.

In July 1914, after four years in Paris, Marc Chagall (1887–1985) returned to Russia. In August 1918, he was appointed by the commissar of enlightenment, A. Lunacharsky, to the post of Plenipotentiary on Matters of Art in Vitebsk City and Province. Chagall plunged into an array of activities, including the founding of a People's Art College (not "Academy"—he hated academies), where he invited some of the most original modern artists to serve as professors, including Kazimir Malevich, founder of the abstract trend of Suprematism, and Chagall's former "disciple" El Lissitzky, who "converted" to the new "Non-Objective Art." Chagall argued against the party bosses in Vitebsk in the name of Leftist art. He claimed that Revolutionary art was not art by and about proletarians but a revolution in the history of art, parallel to the social revolution. The Suprematists, however, more radical than Chagall, swayed the revolutionary students and pushed him out of his college. So, in the summer of 1920, Chagall went to Moscow with his wife and daughter and taught outside the capital in Malakhorka, in a Jewish colony for orphans of the 1919 pogroms in Ukraine. In November 1920 he accepted an offer to paint the backdrop for three short pieces by Sholem-Aleichem, staged in the new Yiddish Chamber Theater, which had moved with the Soviet capital from Petrograd to Moscow.

A Total Painting Environment

Abram Efros, the perspicacious Russian art critic who co-wrote in Russian the first book on Chagall's art (*Marc Chagall's Art* [1918], with Yakov Tugendhold; German edition: Berlin, 1921), was appointed artistic director of the theater. He persuaded the director, Aleksey Granovsky, to invite Chagall to design the stage sets for the first production.

Aleksandr Tairov (whose Jewish name was Kornblit), the innovative director of the Russian Chamber Theater in Moscow, had promoted a new conception of the artist's function: rather than painting the backdrop alone, the artist would construct the whole three-dimensional stage. But Chagall went beyond that, embracing the entire auditorium in a painting ensemble. Within forty days, in November–December 1920, he painted an eight-meter-long canvas, *Introduction to the Yiddish Theater*, hung on the long left wall. On the opposite wall, between three windows, he placed four tall images of the Four Arts that participated in the new total theater: *Music, Dance, Drama,* and *Literature.* A long frieze under the ceiling, *The Wedding Table,* tied together the Four Arts while illustrating Sholem Aleichem's one-act *Mazl-Tov* ("Congratulations!"—as at a wedding). And in the back, facing the audience as they left the theater, was a cosmopolitan, almost translucent square painting, *Love on the Stage.* Chagall also designed the constructed stage, the furniture, and the curtains and painted the costumes and the faces of the actors. Thus, instead of a painting inside a theater, the audience experienced a theater performance within a Chagallian four-wall painterly space. It was soon nicknamed "Chagall's box."

Chagall hated any naturalistic disturbance and pitched a temper tantrum when Director Granovsky, in the Stanislavskyan tradition, hung a real towel on the stage. Chagall even painted the rags that were bought in the market to make costumes, and covered the actors' bodies and faces with colorful dots and miniature drawings. As Efros tells it:

> He obviously considered the spectator a fly, which would soar out of its chair, sit on Mikhoels's hat, and observe with the thousand tiny crystals of its fly's eye what he, Chagall, had conjured up there. [. . .]
>
> [. . .] On the day of the premiere, just before Mikhoels's entrance on the stage, he clutched the actor's shoulder and frenziedly thrust his brush at him as at a mannequin, daubing dots on his costume and painting tiny birds and pigs no opera glass could observe on his visored cap, despite repeated, anxious summonses to the stage.[2]

Marc Chagall with Solomon Mikhoels as Reb Alter in Mazl-Tov, by Sholem-Aleichem, during rehearsals for the opening of the Yiddish theater, Moscow, 1921.

The actors were thus perceived as moving Chagallian figures. This coincided with Granovsky's theory that the normal human state is silence, and that actors should pop up out of the silence and fall back into it. To Chagall, the actors merely provided another degree of animation in the space. Efros wrote of the production of *A Sholem-Aleichem Evening*: "The best places were those in which Granovsky executed his system of 'dots' and the actors froze in mid-movement and mid-gesture, from one moment to the next. The narrative line was turned into an assembly of dots."[3]

But this was contrary to the usual conception of theater as a three-dimensional, dynamic art. Efros shrewdly understood the problem: "The wholeness of the spectator's impression was complete. When the curtain rose, Chagall's wall panels and the decorations and actors on the stage simply mirrored each other. But the nature of this ensemble was so untheatrical that one might have asked, Why turn off the light in the auditorium, and why do these Chagallian beings move and speak on the stage rather than stand unmoving and silent as on his canvases?"[4]

The stage and the walls mirrored each other because Chagall used images of the actors for his painted carnival. Chagall would not abide by the traditional three-dimensionality of the theater any more than he would limit himself to two dimensions in painting. On his long mural, within a two-dimensional surface, he rendered figures as both two-dimensional (Mikhoels's flat torso in blue shirt, no. 22 on the Map below) and three-dimensional (his legs in black pants). We may call it: two-and-a-half dimensional art. The images are often presented in a *multiplanar perspective*; that is, individual figures or groups and geometric forms appear each on their own plane, sometimes two-dimensional and sometimes three-dimensional, and the planes are stacked behind or beside or on top of each other, with no realistic continuity between them. Chagall often used geometrical shapes in his paintings, especially flat, monochromatic rectangles and triangles in the Suprematist style, but he always tended to see them as real objects in a three-dimensional world, that a person could climb under or fly above. His own wife and child peep out from between two flat color stripes in *Introduction to the Yiddish Theater* (no. 45), and the major figures of the painted theater leap above geometric space altogether. Yet without the geometrical shapes underneath, they would have been floating in groundless space.

The Polyphonic Canvas

As the audience entered the theater and looked at the huge mural on the left wall, *Introduction to the Yiddish* [Jewish] *Theater*, a powerful sweeping movement carried them forward and upward; yet the movement was constantly impeded by groups of figures, bizarre activities, and ever-changing painterly events, making it a long journey indeed. In many of Chagall's early paintings, the figures—lovers, a rooster, a fish, the Wandering Jew—hover over the unreal scenery, overcoming the force of gravity. But in *Introduction* there is no such setting at all, no earth, no continuity of houses, streets, or town. The figures are simply floating in abstract space. And their limbs are often floating apart. The authority of space is transferred from representations of the fictional world to another stratum: geometric areas formed by Suprematist-like stripes and Orphic-like circles. The rectangular shapes, moving diagonally upward and downward, make a powerful unifying frame in the shape of a flattened **w**.

The movement forward and upward is further reinforced by the band of human figures that occupies precisely half the height of the mural and moves slowly from its lower to its upper half. This colorful band represents the story of this theater, whereas the paler images and vignettes in grisaille on the margins, scattered all around, represent

Chagall's personal world. The whole painting is framed on each side by a cow and a human figure in a red shirt.

Chagall rarely painted canvases larger than the sweep of his arms (unless he designed a mock-up, to be enlarged tenfold and executed by masters at making stained glass windows, mosaics, or tapestries). In the Moscow Yiddish theater, however, the size of the wall was given, and the proportion of height to length was close to 1:3. Chagall resolved the problem by dividing the long mural into three parts, organized around three circles (rings of a circus?) that move upward from left to right and gradually increase in diameter. The circles set off three functional groups of human figures: the management of the theater, the musicians, and the comedians.

Within each human grouping, there is no realistic space but rather a conceptual conjunction that unites them. We cannot imagine, for example, an actual scene in which Chagall, touching Granovsky with his palette, is carried in Efros's arms. The scene is rather a realization of the dead metaphor "Efros brought Chagall to Granovsky" (no. 6).[5]

The use of Suprematist elements in the midst of this lively world is, of course, a profanation. Malevich sought to achieve "a 'desert' in which no object could be perceived but feeling" in order to rediscover pure art, "not obscured by the accumulation of 'things,'" hence called "Non-Objective Art."[6] And along comes Chagall, using flat, monochromatic forms as a floor to climb under and as a ground for his human figures to walk on and to float above!

One of the first objects that strikes us is the strong black diagonal stripe at the center of the canvas, moving forward and upward (no. 18). We recognize this gesture in other post-Revolutionary paintings by Chagall, echoing Mayakovsky's poem "Left March" (with the refrain *Levoy! Levoy! Levoy!*—"Left Foot Forward!"). In the right half of the painting is a parallel move: the faint pastel stripes, though oriented downward, are stacked so that as a band of colors they also move upward, parallel to the black stripe.

From group to group, perspectives are often inverted—for example, some miniature figures (small size usually implies that we are seeing them at a distance) appear not beyond but before the larger figures. The same ambiguity permeates Chagall's treatment of time. The near past—preparations for the production, the performances themselves—as well as allusions and reminders of the Jewish religious and folkloristic deep past are all presented simultaneously in the present. In a typical postmodernist gesture, Chagall blurs the logical boundary between object-language (describing the presented objects) and metalanguage (describing the painter's own life and language).

In sum, space, time, and perspective are all evoked in the painting and are presented in discontinuous, disrupted bursts. The spectator's position is not taken for granted either. Chagall was furious that chairs were placed in the auditorium (of a theater!), thus fixing the place of the spectators. As in a museum, he expected spectators to go back and forth from mural to mural. The spectators' distance needs to be variable: to grasp the whole, we must stand at the opposite wall; to understand the activities of the human groups, we need a middle view, far enough away to perceive a third of the canvas but close enough to recognize the figures; and to read the minute inscriptions and ornaments on the actors' heads, we must press our noses up to the canvas.

Introduction is characterized by a gay celebration of colors: some are bold and saturated (in the left half of the painting); some are pale and ornamented (mostly toward the right).[7] Color, though by and large subordinated to the boundaries of figures and geometric bodies, occasionally revolts against the domination of spatial form. Thus, the yellow on the margins of the middle circle flows over the geometric boundary into the space above, where it becomes a background for little sketched figures (nos. 27–28); similarly, in the lower-right triangle, the diffuse orange, though contained in geometric boundaries, permeates the fiddler, bird, and synagogue in the background, as if merging all the disproportionate objects in one level of color and depth (nos. 51–52); and in the lower-right corner, several colored stripes cover the indecent scene of a boy urinating on a pig (no. 53).

Each major element of the painting—human and animal figures, geometrical shapes, and color—is subordinated to other elements in parts of the canvas and asserts its dominance in other parts. Where one element is interrupted, another takes over. The paucity of materials available to Chagall in the Moscow winter of 1920 is evident, but he employed anything he could lay his hands on. The mural was painted on thin "Dutch bed sheets," bought in the black market and sewn together. He used gouaches, mixed kaolin with paint and water, applied sawdust and pencil. Sometimes he left the dripping or mopped-up paint stains as part of the texture. He dipped lace in paint, pressed it to the canvas, then removed it, leaving its impression on the canvas (for example, on the dress of the female dancer in Dance), and drew similar tiny patterns with a brush.

The Art of Comedy

Chagall's "supernatural" perception of both art and life (in 1912, Apollinaire called Chagall's early art "surnaturel," even before he coined the label "Surrealism"), his turning away from the realism, psychologism, and impressionism that still reigned in the Russian theater, his unsentimental emphasis on the vitality of traditional Jewish folk culture—these traits infected the spirit of the theater and influenced its later achievements.

The importance of Chagall's role in the theater lay in his embracing the genre of the carnivalesque (as later formulated by the Russian cultural critic Mikhail Bakhtin),[8] the topsy-turvy world that had reigned in medieval fairs. It was precisely through the carnival that Chagall was able to introduce the old, abandoned, and subverted Jewish world as the tangible substance of a work of art. This enabled the theater to fill its productions with a fictional world populated by rich archetypes, flesh-and-blood popular characters, and outlandish figures and encompassing widely shared jokes and an inimitable language endearing to its users. And although the characters were grotesque and out of touch with reality, they also were inspired by flights of fantasy and poetry and by an ahistorical sense of absurd and comic human dignity.

By turning that fictional world upside down, Chagall saved it from extinction. Later the Yiddish theater could be either sentimental or politically obnoxious and rudely critical, even anti-Semitic (showing the "Yid" in full bloom, as Efros described it);[9] yet the materiality and vitality of the lost Jewish world was preserved, and resounded in the minds of the spectators, including gentiles, assimilated Jews, and Communists in Russia and in Western Europe. The traditional Jewish world, fictionalized in Yiddish literature, could be resurrected on the Soviet stage only in the genre of comedy.

An Art of Three Times

The whole auditorium, "Chagall's box," could be viewed in light of Efros's understanding of Chagall and the Yiddish theater as an art sprung from nowhere, with no history or tradition, therefore an "art of three times," encompassing its own present, past, and future. It is a celebration of Chagall's and the actors' generation as they enact the past to extract its folk spirit, joy, and artistic values for the present. It is a procession onward and upward, to an unknown future, which they will reach by turning their world upside down. Yet the figures in the last group on the right of the long wall, are not looking to the future but back to the present, to the performance itself.

This perception of Jewish culture entailed a foreboding of its own disaster. Secular Jewish culture, to which Chagall, Efros, and the new Yiddish theater contributed, was imported from general European culture. It was a utopian effort to create a culture of "three times." But secular Jewish culture had no true past—it had to borrow one from the religious tradition; and it had no true future of its own—it borrowed one from the Russian Revolution. Eventually it was wiped out by that same Revolution.

THE ICONOGRAPHY OF CHAGALL'S THEATER PAINTINGS

Introduction to the Yiddish Theater

This long mural presents the history of the new Yiddish theater as Chagall's autobiographical narrative. The word "introduction" means both the physical movement of the audience toward the stage (from left to right, i.e., in the Russian direction, opposite to the direction of Yiddish writing) and the ideological introduction to a new kind of theater. The interpretations here follow the numbers on the accompanying Map of *Introduction*, moving from left to right.[10] (For color reproductions of the art discussed here, see the illustrations following page 58.)

1–2. In white and gray, we see the beginnings of the Yiddish Workers Theater in the white nights of Petrograd in 1918–1919. There were no Jewish masses, let alone workers, in Petrograd, hence no Yiddish audience for a "workers" theater. The meaning is carried by two realizations of Yiddish idioms: the director is looking for light, perhaps drinking light and enlightenment (the theater was appointed and subsidized by the Commissariat of Enlightenment), but the light is artificial—he is "talking to the lamp" (in Yiddish: *redt tsum lomp; a lomp* is a *glomp,* i.e., dumb, cannot respond). The worker is "talking to the wall" (*redt tsu der vant*)—a wall is opaque, gives no response, no resonance. Either way, the images mean: you are talking in vain.

2. The isolated proletarian audience (the figure wearing a worker's cap) of the Yiddish Workers Theater is eagerly waiting to applaud. Yet the audience encounters a void, a wall. Into this gray background area (continued in ever-darker gray areas in the upper left of the mural) a colorful theater narrative is introduced.

3. A green animal ("cow") bursts onto the scene and takes on the play with its horns. For the October celebrations in Vitebsk, on November 8, 1918 (according to the new Soviet calendar), Chagall painted a green cow, as he tells us, indicating the new, anti-academic and anti-Realist, revolutionary art; his students copied the green cow

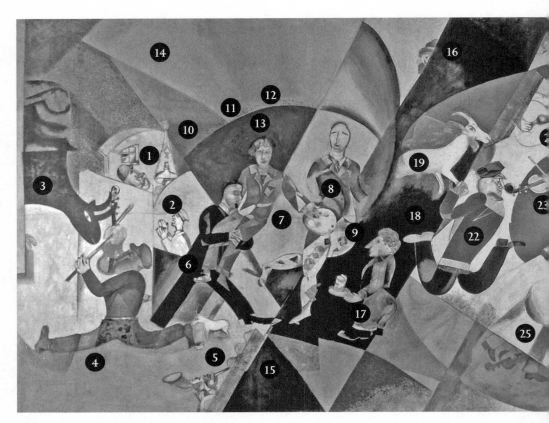

Map of Introduction to the Yiddish Theater *by Marc Chagall, 1920.*

and hung it all over the city (note the split in the middle of the cow, as if it is painted on two pieces of cardboard). Whether the story is true or not doesn't matter. Chagall retold it as part of his private mythology (and so did Efros). The Communist bosses did not like it: "Why is the cow green? What has that to do with Marx and Lenin?" (*My Life*).[11] Chagall often used bright or saturated green as a challenge to realism: in his first theater work, in the Petrograd cabaret Comedians' Resting Place, he painted the faces of all the actors green; his own face is green in *I and the Village,* and so are the faces of "the Green Jew" (the revered preacher of Slutsk) in the painting of that name (1914) and the violinist in the panel *Music* on the opposite wall of the Moscow Yiddish theater. In his autobiography Chagall wrote: "I often said that I was not an artist, but

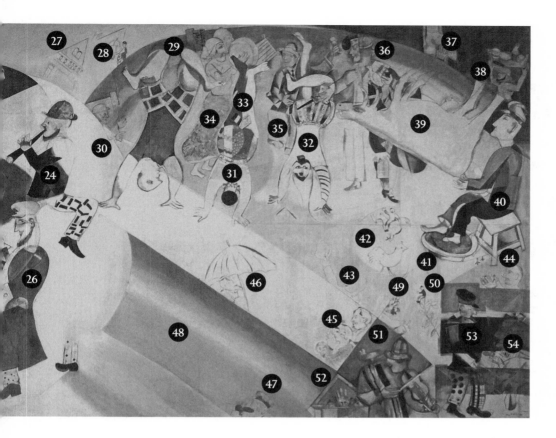

some kind of a cow. I thought of placing [the cow] on my calling card."[12] Here the painted cow represents avant-garde art and Chagall's impact on the new theater.

4. The leading actor, Shloyme Mikhoels, came to Chagall to learn the nature of modern art. In Yiddish, as in other languages, to play the violin and to act on a stage take the same verb, "to play" (*shpiln*); hence the violin is a metaphor for acting: if your fiddle is broken and you cannot *shpil* (play) it, you cannot *shpil* (act).[13] The broken fiddle indicates the impasse Mikhoels saw in the old style of acting, and the gesture of offering it to the animal implies his willingness to learn. As Chagall explains in his autobiography, his avant-garde art transformed the lead actor Mikhoels and, through him, the entire group to overcome the "familiar psychological realism." Mikhoels

performs an acrobatic act, as taught in Granovsky's studio. The folk ornament on his pants indicates Mikhoels's link to popular culture and his fondness for Yiddish folklore, which he taught to the actors.

5. The young goat may indicate that Mikhoels is a naïve "baby," curious about the new, "green" art. A popular Yiddish lullaby starts: *Unter shloymeles vigele / shteyt a shney-vays tsigele* (Under little Shloyme's [or any other name's] cradle / stands a snow-white kid).

6. Abram Efros, artistic director of the Yiddish Chamber Theater in Moscow, who brought Chagall to the director, Granovsky. Here he brings him literally, a realization of the metaphor. Efros strides determinedly, left foot forward (as in Mayakovsky's topical poem "Left March").

7. Marc Chagall, in semi-Constructivist working clothes, is pointing out to Granovsky the palette of his new art.

8. Aleksey (Aleksandr) Granovsky, director of the Yiddish Chamber Theater. Assimilated to Russian and German culture, he wears formal European attire; but he is dancing a quadrille and has folk ornaments on his legs, along with several Stars of David, complete or broken down into triangles (see no. 9).

9. Star of David, representing the Jewish national mission that Granovsky undertook. The triangles on his left leg are shards of Stars of David.

10. The texts in the murals, all in Yiddish, are transcribed here in bold letters. When Chagall uses the traditional, "square" letters, they are rendered here in capital letters; when he writes in longhand, using "written" or cursive letters, they are rendered here in lowercase letters. If the words are inverted in the original, they are underscored here.

At number 10 a Yiddish inscription appears on top of the first circle, written with traditional "square" Hebrew letters. It is conspicuously placed above the red arc that brings together the three dominant figures of the theater. The study for *Introduction* presents their names unambiguously: **IKSVONARG LAGASH EFROS**. The first two words are inverted; when read in the opposite direction, they read GRANOVSKI SHAGAL. The third word is straightforward: EFROS. In the completed mural, however, this becomes more complex. Efros's name, originating from the Hebrew Bible, is usually spelled in Yiddish as in Hebrew (consonants only): APRT אפרת; but here we have the new Soviet Yiddish spelling—without any Hebrew and with all the vowels: EFROS עפּראָס. Efros's revolutionary stride underlines the message: "Energy! Stride with your left foot forward!" (as in Mayakovsky's "Left March"). "Revolution!" (In the state? In the theater? In art?)

On the final canvas the names are distorted further. Of LAGASH, all that remains is **...AG...SH,** with vestiges of letters in between; and even EFROS has only **EF...S,** with paler outlines of the rest. Inside the words, however, in place of the missing letters, there are tiny drawings: Chagall painting at his easel and the professorial Efros reading a book. Thus, Chagall combined two systems, letters and ideograms, and two cultures, Jewish and Russian, to represent his protagonists.

11. **LAGASH** לאגאש. The name "Chagall" inverted, as if to read the Yiddish letters in the Russian direction, from left to right. Here the name is presented with dual media: instead of the second "A" we get an iconic representation of the painter, his body in the form of the missing Hebrew letter "A" (alef א).

12. The inverted name of Granovsky. In the study, when read in Yiddish from right to left, the name appears in full, IKSVONARG יקסװאָנאַרג, and includes Hebrew vowel markers, as in traditional Yiddish books. When read in the inverted, "Russian" direction it reads GRANOVSKI.[14] In the final mural, however, the name is distorted: **IKTIKTUNARG** יקטיקטונארג. When read in the inverted direction, it says "Granu . . ."; seeing the figure, we know who it is—the rest is redundant. When, however, we read the name in the Jewish direction (from right to left), we get **IKT** twice (in Yiddish, the graphic shape of a printed "s" ס is easily changed into "т" ט). These are the Russian initials of "Jewish Chamber Theater" spelled "Evreysky Kamerny Teatr" in Russian and transcribed in Yiddish: Ievreysky Kamerny Teatr, יעװרעיסקי קאמערני טעאטר. Again, this is a kind of dual naming—the man and the acronym of his theater mirror the linguistic duality (or, should I say, trilingualism: Yiddish letters, Russian direction, Hebrew vowels).[15]

Chagall's unusual spelling, with most Yiddish letters arranged in reverse, from left to right, indicates the direction of the reader's walk along the canvas toward the stage. The shift in the direction of writing may also indicate the new, European direction that Yiddish culture was taking.

13. Behind Chagall, on a red, Revolutionary background, appear the Tablets with the Ten Commandments (abbreviated) and various synagogue objects and ornaments: in the upper right, a lion; in the lower left, a Constructivist rendering of a synagogue *bima* (platform from which the Torah is read). These indicate the traditional Jewish ritual art that stands behind him. Under the Tablets is Chagall's ubiquitous umbrella—in Yiddish, *shirem*—as if he is saying: *Zol undz got bashiremen,* "May God protect us" (literally: "umbrella us"—i.e., "take us under his umbrella"; see also no. 28).

14. Areas of autonomous colors, as if radiating from an event: a huge rainbow after

the Flood, yet representing neither the sky nor the order of colors in a rainbow (see also the dove at no. 39 and the rainbow at no. 48).

15. Someone blowing a *shofar* (ram's horn), emerging from a wooden synagogue ornament, as if heralding the new year, the new time.

16. Half a head peeping out from under the black stripe to observe the new scene. It may be the head of the *shofar* blower (no. 15).

17. According to Chagall's autobiographical accounts, the janitor Efraim served him milk mixed with water while he was working on the murals. Both liquids can be seen in the glass.

18. A black stripe in a Suprematist shape. This one parallels Efros's rectangular leg (no. 6) and marches upward and toward the stage. Yet its two-dimensionality is undermined and ironized from above and below.

19. The goat, the cheapest milk-giving animal to keep, is a symbol of Jewish shtetl poverty. Like the goats Chagall painted on both sides of the theater curtain, this goat opens the show.

20. Above the second circle, from under the black stripe, emerges a winged angel with trumpet, announcing the event.

21. Drummer. The play begins: playing music as a metaphor for playing (acting) on a stage. Here the klezmer band, composed of traditional Jewish musicians, includes a drummer, a violinist, a clarinetist, and a cimbalom player. The musicians are elated and defy realism; their limbs are scattered above and below the geometrical planes.

22. Mikhoels performing his acrobatics, his right hand holding and leading Chagall's goat. On his white belt are subtle drawings of shtetl images; a lace pattern is below it. Little figures drawn by Chagall are also on Mikhoels's chest and throat.

23. Violinist in formal attire with a clown's hat. His head flew skyward, and his legs may be at number 25.

24. Clarinet player. On his pants, above each of the black stripes, are Yiddish inscriptions, in cursive letters to indicate intimacy (otherwise, Chagall uses printed letters). The inscriptions amount to a list of Chagall's family members. At birth, children were given Yiddish names and were so registered on the Russian birth certificates. Yet in daily life siblings called each other and their peers by Russian names. Here, however, Chagall mostly reverts to the original Yiddish names: **feyge ite** (mother), **yhzkl** (father [*yikhezkel* in Hebrew], **mshe** (Moyshe, Chagall's Hebrew name), **blanh** (sister Bella-Anna—Anyuta), **roze mariyaske** (sisters), **zisle** (sister Zina), **leyke mane** (the twin

sisters Liza and Manya), **berte** (Marc's wife), **ide** (Chagall's daughter, Ida), **mnahem mendl** (Menakhem-Mendel, grandfather, spelled half in Hebrew, half in Yiddish), **ba** (unfinished), **basheve** (grandmother), **avrhm neyah** (uncles Avrohom, Noyakh = Abraham and Noah, as pronounced in Chagall's Litvak Yiddish dialect).

25. Violinist in a tailcoat, climbing under the square plane.

26. Cimbalom player. Some identify him as Lev Pulver, a major composer and the musical director of the Moscow Yiddish Theater, but in 1920 he was not yet around.

27. Facade of the Petrograd synagogue where Chagall was invited to paint murals for a school. Granovsky saw the theater as a temple of modern culture, a substitute for religion: "Yiddish theater is [. . .] a temple of shining art [. . .] a temple where the prayer is chanted in the Yiddish language."[16]

28. Little figure with umbrella, representing Chagall in his satisfied state (see also no. 46). Umbrella in Yiddish is *shirem*; the figure is *bashiremt*, "protected by destiny" (literally: "covered with an umbrella"). The Hebrew source reads: "May God *sheymer u-matsil zayn*" (May God guard and save). SheyMER / ShiREM is an anagram (protector/umbrella).

29. A collage of newspapers or posters with headline letters. In pale letters: **BAVEGUNG** (movement; also: cultural or political movement); in bold letters: **IDISHE K**[ULTUR] (Yiddish culture movement)[17] and [TEA]**TR,** spelled as in Russian. Chagall refers apparently to the Yiddish cultural movement Kultur-Lige, which organized Yiddish schools and supported Yiddish literature, art, and other cultural matters. Chagall joined the Moscow chapter and participated in the Moscow exhibition of three artists.

30–33. The three clowns still wear religious insignia but stand the old Jewish world on its head, topsy-turvy, as in Sholem-Aleichem's fiction. The old religious Jew on their left seems to chastise them with a pointing finger.

31. Religious Jew in skullcap, turned clown. On his belt, a Star of David ornament and an inscription in Yiddish cursive letters: **ikh bin akrob**[at] (I am an acrobat).

32. Jew in the most solemn moment of prayer, wearing phylacteries and standing on his hands. Stars of David appear among the geometrical figures on the clown's pants. Around his waist, in cursive letters, is the Yiddish inscription **ikh balavezekh ikh** ("I frolic I," or "I play pranks, am mischievous, have fun").[18]

33. Between the middle clown's legs is a printed message listing the three classical Yiddish writers as celebrated by Kultur-Lige and printed on their stamp **MEND**[ELE] **ABRAMOVICH PERETZ SHOLEM-ALEICHEM,** as well as the names of two younger writers, friends of Chagall: **BIL** [BAL-MAKHSHOVES(?)] [DER] **NIS**[TER]. It was modern Yiddish

Scene from Uriel Acosta *by Karl Gutzkow. Set design: Natan Altman.*

literature that showed the vitality of Jewish folk life and saved its images in a secular age by turning the austere religious world into a source of folklore and culture. Rather than being a coarse gesture, the note seems to be a banner raised above the overturning of the old, religious world. Or maybe Chagall had no other place to stick the note on top of the acrobatic show.

34. Two actors, playing the tambourine and the lyre. The first, dancing barefoot, has been identified as the actor Sara Rotboym.

35. Figure in formal dress, toasting the performance. The figure is sometimes identified as Benjamin Zuskin, the second most important actor of this theater, but Zuskin apparently joined the theater later.

36. Dual figure probably representing Uriel Acosta. The German playwright Karl Gutzkow's drama *Uriel Acosta* was performed in Granovsky's theater in Petrograd and was being prepared for a new production in Moscow. Acosta's dilemma of how to be

a free and thinking Jew without being religious was close to the situation of Chagall and the secular Yiddish theater. The revolver, the Spanish attire, and the circumcision scene (see no. 37) support this hypothesis. The duality and ambivalence are also expressed in the double face, male/female shoes, black/white half-figures, classical-aristocratic/modern-folk dress, and the gender ambivalence of a "feminine" figure undergoing circumcision (see no. 37).

The two half-faces of Uriel Acosta are of the painters Natan Altman and probably David Shterenberg (including his bulbous nose and little moustache). Shterenberg was head of IZO, the Section for Graphic Arts of the People's Commissariat of Enlightenment; and Altman, a member of the IZO board. They organized a branch of Kultur-Lige artists in Moscow (and, later, an exhibition for the "three," including Marc Chagall). Chagall saw them both as ambivalent between Jewish and general culture.

37. Two hands hold an instrument of circumcision. This fits the identification of the figure at number 36 as Uriel Acosta, who underwent circumcision in his twenties. It could also indicate the Jewification of the new art. The body, seemingly of a pregnant woman, appears later in Chagall's portrayals of Jesus Christ (for example, *Resurrection,* 1937–1948) and may contribute to the ambivalence expressed in Acosta's figure.

38. The waiter, bringing food to the celebration, looks like photographs of El Lissitzky at the time. Chagall, furious with Lissitzky's "betrayal" by joining Suprematism, teaches him a lesson in real art. This is a realization of the idiom Er *meg undz badinen* (He may be our servant), meaning "He is not of our class; he has plenty to learn."

39. Chagall's cow is happy, frolicking upside down like the inverted Jewish world. It ran out of its green "blood" (or Chagall ran out of paint, as he later complained when asked why he left the Soviet Union). Its avant-garde mission is fulfilled, and its horns are crowned with a dove, signaling that the Flood is over (see also the rainbow, nos. 14, 48).

40. The identity of this figure is disputed. It is probably the director Granovsky, resting satisfied after the performance. Soaking one's feet in a bowl of cold water is both a way to rest after long labor and a means to keep alert (practiced by religious Jews while studying all night).

41. In spite of the joy, the whole project stands "on chicken legs" (*oyf hinershe fislekh*), that is, on a shaky foundation.

42. Yet chickens are domestic animals, one of Chagall's emblems of the Jewish world. In the enclave connected to the chicken feet we see a Jew riding on a rooster with another Chagall emblem, a fish, in its mouth.

43–44. Ovations from the audience.

45. Berta (the future Bella) Chagall, Chagall's wife, and their daughter, Ida, along with Yikhezkel Dobrushin, Yiddish writer and literary dramaturge of the theater, come to greet Chagall.

46. Happy Marc Chagall, protected by destiny (*bashiremt*, "covered with an umbrella"; see no. 28).

47. Perhaps, in view of Chagall's new art: the enemies may shut up (literally: "block their mouths!" *farshtop zey dos moyl*—a Yiddish idiom). The figure seems to be Malevich, paralleling Lissitzky in number 38.

48. Another area of the rainbow after the Flood (see nos. 14, 39).

49. Chagall's parents, emerging from the past to greet Marc, who sits on a treetop.

50. Marc Chagall, as a religious boy in a hat, greeting his parents. He sits like a free bird on a tree (the Yiddish idiom: *fray vi a foygl*, "as free as a bird").

51. Is it Chagall himself as a happy boy practicing his art and preoccupied with music/art (Yiddish idiom: "his head is in the music"), with the dove on his shoulder after the Flood (see no. 39)?

52. Emblem of Jewish architecture, as in a synagogue (see no. 27) or on a grave-stone monument, with a hand-inscribed PN (*po nikbar*, "Here is buried"), as on Jewish gravestones. The PN may also mean "Here is buried the old Jewish world" (Lissitzky used this hand with PN in a famous poster). In triangles on both sides, the letters AT (for "Yiddish theater"), reading in the Russian direction, left to right, symbolize the new "Temple of Art" that Granovsky planned to erect in the Yiddish theater.

53. Circumcised boy peeing on a pig before the shaken old world. To Jews a pig is "unclean," taboo; and here it represents the gentile world. The hat, part of the high school uniform (as in Chagall's painting *I and the Village*), and the clown's pants apparently represent the boy Marc himself, dreaming to excel even though he is a mere Jew, as the Yiddish idiom says: *oyf tselokhes ale sonim* (in spite of all the enemies [who are denigrating the Jews]). This is not an anti-Christian statement, as some have suggested, but an expression of Jewish pride and achievement, using folk stereotypes of a divided world.

Introduction is Chagall's celebration of the new Jewish art, both in painting and in the-ater. In his manifesto "Leaves from My Notebook" (published in Yiddish in Moscow in 1922), Chagall wrote: "For myself I know quite well what this little nation can achieve. Unfortunately, I am too modest and cannot say aloud what it can achieve . . . When it wanted to—it showed Christ and Christianity. When it wished—it gave [the world] Marx and Socialism. Can it be that it won't show the world some art? It will! Kill me if not."[19] Because of the chauvinistic message, he cannot say it aloud (that is, it can be published only in a Yiddish journal), hence the images in the lower right corner of the painting are painted over or crossed out with blue and green stripes. Yet, as a true cosmopolitan, in the manifesto he speaks not of Jewish but of universal *Art*.

54. Family house in Lyozno, where his grandfather climbed on the roof and ate sweet carrot stew (*tsimes*), according to the idiom *Meshugener, arop fun dakh*, "Crazy man [i.e., creative genius], get off the roof!"—an image repeated in Chagall's paintings. The ladder is there, but the crazy/creative man went off the roof to create great art.

The Four Arts

While still in Petrograd, Granovsky provided his actors with the best Russian teachers of music, rhythm and dance, "plastic movement," literature, and song. Chagall's contribution was to bring to this polyphony of arts the vibrant expressions and images of the Eastern European Jewish world, thus providing the formalist avant-garde art and theater with a fictional world, a "myth" of its own.

But Chagall had a physical constraint—three tall windows on the right-hand wall— so he could place only four images between them. The four arts that Chagall painted there represent the traditional folkloristic equivalents to Music, Dance, Drama, and Literature. These traditional figures were linked to significant events in Jewish ritualized life and were conducted in the mundane language, Yiddish, on the margins of the Hebrew ritual texts. Indeed, in his memoirs of 1928, Chagall calls the Four Arts not by their general names but by the names of the traditional Jewish professions associated with them: "klezmers [folk musicians], a wedding jester, women dancers, a Torah scribe."[20]

The *Music* ("klezmer") figure is a transformation of the fiddler who sits on the roof in *The Dead Man* (1908) via *The Violinist* of 1912–1913. In *Music*, however, he is tall (adapted to the high wall of the mural) and looms over the little houses and the church of the Russian provincial town. The two rows of houses create horizontal depth between them, yet, in its vertical rise, the towering figure connects the rows in a perspectival paradox. The patterns of the musician's *talis* (prayer shawl) under the coat are translated into geometrical forms and are continued in the asymmetrically checkered pants: in Chagall's eyes, Jewish tradition provides geometrical forms; thus religious form and

Cubist invention are on one continuum. In the upper right, Malevich's famous black square is quoted, stood on its edge among the clouds, and the Chagall-child is hovering above the music like a little angel. A Chagallian animal on the lower left is enchanted by the music (see the parallel in *Literature*), and a little man in the upper left between the houses is raising his arms in appreciation of it. This romantic gesture of powerful, soaring music is ironized on the upper left by a little boy defecating behind a fence, as described in Chagall's original autobiography.[21] Like the musician himself, many vignettes here are quotations from earlier works and verbal images by Chagall, including the abandoned ladder, the free bird on the treetop, the mother in the window, the little Lyozno church.

Dance ("Women Dancers") presents a wedding dancer in a Russian peasant dress, accompanied by the instruments of a Jewish klezmer band. At her feet, a man stands upside down, stressing the carnival atmosphere. Outside the yellow ring and inside it are the words of the Hebrew wedding song: **KOL KHOSN, KOL KALE** (The voice of the groom, the voice of the bride). In the upper left triangle, a worker collects the folded-up *khupa* (wedding canopy).

Drama ("Wedding Jester") presents a *badkhn* (wedding jester), again immensely taller than the surrounding figures. His task is to amuse the audience by reciting improvised and topical rhymed couplets in Yiddish: satirical, humorous, and often bawdy. Behind him is the purple *khupa* (a canopy held up by four posts, only one of which is seen here) and, on both sides of it, the mother and father. The bride and the groom are pale, and the women on the right bemoan the loss of virginity. Yet the purple *khupa*, with the rabbi (or father) behind it, is waiting for the ceremony to be held. The painting is rich with ornaments and cubic shapes.

Literature ("Torah Scribe") shows a scribe pursuing his traditional profession, dedicated to the careful copying of Torah scrolls by hand on parchment, a task that must be executed without a single error or blemish. He wears a prayer shawl at his holy work; yet he is writing not a Hebrew sacred text but a Yiddish folk story: "Once upon a time" (**AMOL IZ** [**GEVEN**]). Yiddish literature takes over the role of religion and Hebrew. Above, behind the blue space, the same yearning animal as in *Music* moos the word **ƧHAGA⅃** in Yiddish, with the last two letters, "A" and "L," inverted to read the Russian way, left to right. And the chair carried by a boy in the back, as if behind the globe of this universe, has a sign: **DER T**[**EATR**] (The Th[eater]).

II **ESSAYS, PLAYS, MEMOIRS**

Abram Efros
The Artists of Granovsky's Theater (Excerpt) 1928, Russian[*]

I

The years of war and the years of revolution occurred in a period of crisis for the Russian theater. Its development in those fifteen years was not organic, but was indeed, at times, paradoxical; secondary elements played a greater role in it than basic ones. Its history is one of scenic accessories rather than of theatrical art, a history of the external formation of the stage; in many ways, it is just a history of stage designers.

This is not contradicted at all by the fact that the Russian theater has now achieved a world name. In some European centers, it has even had a transforming influence. But should we console ourselves with the fact that the situation there was even worse? Western criticism, having recovered from the earlier excitement, now claims in revenge that we were only an exotic episode. As proof, they add that we were succeeded by a fashion for Negroes. This would have sounded devastating had we pronounced the word "Negroes" with the same accent. But you don't have to live through the Russian Revolution to give such words their true significance. For that, it is enough to be a hero of His Highness Vulgarity. We, however, are prepared to say this: Russian and Negro art were a fresh wind for the West.

This does not change anything in the internal processes of our theater. I could have described the striking aspect of their appearance as the blush of the crisis. In the beginning, Russian theater was in a fever of decorationism, with the role of the artist made disproportionately large. I am not afraid to assert (as my professional memory reminds

[*]Originally published in *Iskusstvo* (Moscow), 4 (1928), books 1–2, pp. 63–74.

me) that the premieres of 1912–1917 were impressive mostly for the triumphs of their design rather than for their actors. Later, after the October upheaval, came the era of Futurism. This happened not because Russian Futurism was belated, as the innovations of Western culture were usually late in penetrating Russia. This time, Europe was hasty and we were very complacent. But in 1917, owing to one of the most brilliant paradoxes of the Revolution, the Futurists became the power in art. They were part of the new government, delegated to the domain of art. Incidentally, there was no equality in the use of time. The Futurists did not fill their five years of fame. The rage of their abstractions, shifts, and breaks evoked a reaction as early as 1920, which soon assumed the character of a violent outburst of simplification. The theater was, in Tolstoy's words, attracted to "gruel." Even the nihilism about decorations now saw its hour of triumph, only it appeared on the stage under another name—common in theatrical practice! Such is the "Constructivism" of Meyerhold and his group: the stage was shamelessly bare, with only cranes, ropes, traps, hatchways, back walls, workers. It was pretty cynical, and enough to become fashionable and infect the theaters with pandemonium. Though it was soon over, Russian theater emerged exhausted: its decorations are now withered and melancholy. There is an artist on stage, but in essence there isn't. He is hardly active and almost invisible. In the best case he imitates himself. He is a veteran member of the staff and not a leader of the theater as he was in that decade between 1910 and 1920. The artist has reverted to the status of nonentity, while the actor, the ensemble, the acting, again stand on the first plane. I would be willing to consider this a sign of healthy growth were I not afraid that today's indifference to the artist would deteriorate into apathy.

The artist, however, has his place in the scenic system of elements. It is not dominant, but it is not third-rate, and so our stage is still unbalanced. We now have much experience, but little tact. And in art, it seems that there is no greater sin. We have not recovered a sense of measure. The Russian stage of the period 1925–1930 is still sick with disharmony.

II

Granovsky began building his theater in the heat of the Revolution. This is natural, for there is no time more favorable for both creators and adventurers. The year 1919 was terrible. The period of Military Communism was at the zenith of its crisis. Lenin's strategic genius was already looking for a detour. The Revolution exploded all

PLATES

Marc Chagall, Introduction to the Jewish Theater, 1920. Tempera and gouache on canvas. 111⅞ × 308¾ inches.

*Marc Chagall, Music,
1920. Tempera and
gouache on canvas.
83⅝ × 40¾ inches.*

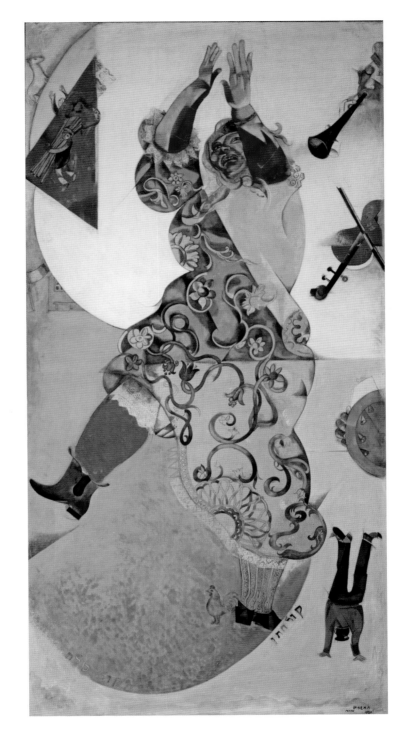

Marc Chagall, Dance,
1920. Tempera and
gouache on canvas.
84⅛ × 42½ inches.

Marc Chagall, Drama,
1920. Tempera and
gouache on canvas.
83 ¼ × 42 ¼ inches.

Marc Chagall,
Literature, 1920.
Tempera and gouache
on canvas. 85 × 32
inches.

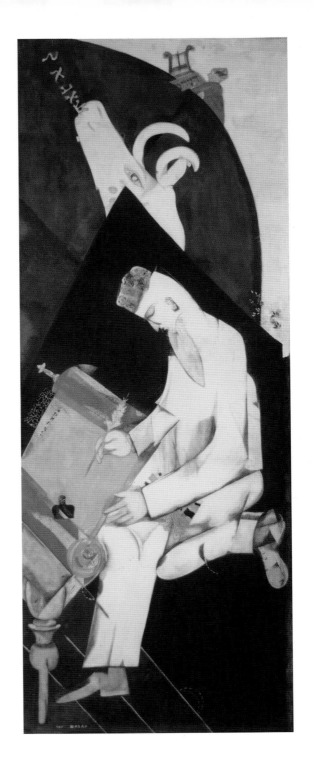

Costume design by Itshak Rabinovich for The God of Vengeance by Sholem Asch. Performed in 1921 at GOSEKT (State Yiddish Chamber Theater), Moscow. The edges burned in the fire set to the theater archives around 1950.

Costume designs by Itshak Rabinovich for The God of Vengeance.

Group costume design by Itshak Rabinovich for The Sorceress: An Eccentric Jewish Play, based on a play by Abraham Goldfaden. Performed in 1922 at GOSEKT in Moscow.

Costume designs by Itshak Rabichev for 200,000, *based on Sholem-Aleichem's* The Winning Ticket. *Performed in 1923 at GOSEKT in Moscow.*

Curtain design by Itshak Rabichev for The Three Jewish Minimal Dots [*or: Raisins*]:
An Evening of Parody *by Yikhezkel Dobrushin and Nokhem Oyslender. Performed in 1923 at GOSEKT in Moscow. Director: Aleksey Granovsky.*

Set design by Robert Falk for At Night in the Old Marketplace: A Tragic Carnival *by Y.-L. Peretz. Performed in* 1925 *at GOSET (State Yiddish Theater) in Moscow.*

Costume design by Robert Falk for At Night in the Old Marketplace.

Costume design by Robert Falk for At Night in the Old Marketplace.

Costume designs by Robert Falk for
At Night in the Old Marketplace.

Stage design by Natan Altman for The Tenth Commandment: A Pamphlet Operetta *by Yikhezkel Dobrushin based on a work by Abraham Goldfaden. Performed in 1926 at GOSET.*

Costume designs by Robert Falk for The Travels of Benjamin the Third: Epos in Three Acts, based on Mendele Moykher Sforim's novel and adapted by Yikhezkel Dobrushin. Performed in 1927 at GOSET.

possibilities. Russian culture swelled and burst in geysers of projects and schemes. In the theater, Meyerhold proclaimed his "October." Vakhtangov led the Third Studio [of Stanislavsky's Moscow Academic Art Theater, MkhAT] onto twisting rails. Granovsky founded the Yiddish theater.

To do so he couldn't simply put up minus signs and work with the method of negation, as did Meyerhold. Nor was Vakhtangov's complex stratagem available to him. Either solution presupposed the existence of a highly developed theatrical culture which had already exhausted its straight paths. Granovsky had to build on an empty space. He was his own ancestor. There was nothing behind his back. From time to time, itinerant theatrical groups of Jewish ne'er-do-wells, unfit for any other profession, had crisscrossed the Pale of Settlement. And in the 1910s, a sad shtetl symbolist, the Vilna Maeterlinckoid Perets Hirshbeyn, had pulled before the puzzled Jewish petite bourgeoisie his infinite nose, his meager possessions, and his loving, naïve, and unwitting parodies of the dramaturgy of European modernism.

True, along with Granovsky there was HaBima [a new theater, founded in 1917 with performances in the newly revived language Hebrew], which radiated well-being. All the good fairies of aid and publicity surrounded it. It was supported by an amazing amalgam of Zionists, the Rabbinate, parts of the Communist Party, and those liberal anti-Semites who considered the language of the Bible the only thing bearable about the Jews. One of the first proofs of Granovsky's real talent was that he circumvented HaBima, recognizing with some higher sense the parasitism of that phenomenon. HaBima lived with an alien mind, claiming for itself the wages of others. It cloaked the devices of Russian directors and the conventions of the Russian stage in a cover of the modernized ancient Hebrew speech. It was Stanislavsky's bastard child by an accidental Jewish mother. I remember one skit staged by HaBima in which one character addressed another character with the words *Adoni ha-student*—"Mr. Student!"* Then and there, at the premiere, I thought that the whole nature of an obedient little theater was reflected in this Esperanto. Not in vain did it fear Jewish artists, who were young and entailed risk. HaBima instead preferred either to have a nameless nobody or to invite the experienced conventionality of Eastern decorations by Yakulov and even Miganajan. Only when the pleiad of Jewish artists, roaring and shimmering, went through Granovsky's stage, did HaBima stretch out its hand to them. Had I written

---

*Efros mocks both the formal style and the Sefardi Hebrew, which sounds strange and artificial to Ashkenazi ears.

memoirs, I could have told about my meeting with Zemach, who tried to persuade me to influence [the stage artists] Chagall, Altman, and Rabinovich to work for HaBima. It became dangerous to ignore them, and they themselves did not show any desire to offer themselves. Incidentally, even for that step, an instruction from the side was necessary, which appeared in the person and authority of Vakhtangov, who came to HaBima to stage *The Dybbuk*.

Granovsky did not find his course from the start. Like a thoroughbred puppy beginning to walk, he at first stumbled comically in various corners. Now it is funny to read his pathetic declarations of 1919. The brochure proclaiming them has long since become a bibliographical rarity. For Granovsky, it is no longer dangerous. It contains many nouns written with capital letters and even more exclamation marks. In essence, the most important thing in it is the will to exist; the least significant are its theatrical dogmas. This was confirmed by the early productions, in which Granovsky stood shakily on his legs and often groped in a vacuum. *The Prologue* [by Mikhoels] worked with harlequins and columbines. *Amnon and Tamar* by Sholem Asch retailored the Bible for the nth time. *The Blind* by Maeterlinck came late by an immense decade. If that were to become the predominant direction, Granovsky's theater would merely have produced a more complicated variant of HaBima. But in fact the change of formal elements was significant, and it became the foundation of Granovsky's further work. Jewish folk speech supplanted the bookish Hebraism; German theatrical methods deformed the Russian stage tradition.

This, however, did not resolve the problem, did not yet create a Jewish theater. The essence was not here. These were only separate levers. An Archimedean point was needed.

III

Granovsky selected his first designer in a manner typical in other Russian theaters at the time, not foreseeing the role the artist would later play in realizing his projects. Furthermore, he apparently did not notice what was happening with artists on the Russian stage, where the exacerbated dialectics of their interrelationships took a tragic turn. In the decoration systems, entire historical layers were being shaken out in the open; yet Granovsky remained unconcerned. *The Prologue* was concocted with homemade means, which seemed simple as long as, for the protagonists—Harlequin, Pierrot, and Columbine—there were uniforms granted them once and for all; and, accordingly, the curtain was of course made like a chessboard—white and black squares. For *Amnon and Tamar*, he invited the assistant of a famous master, and for *The Blind*, simply the daughter of a famous father. Granovsky warmed his hands in the slanted rays of someone else's fame. When he decided finally to approach great people, he unexpectedly selected Dobuzhinsky.

What charms did he find in this master? Did he himself find him, or was he given him? I don't know; I think it was by accident. I don't believe Granovsky when he says that Dobuzhinsky understood him, because Granovsky didn't understand himself; more precisely, neither of them knew what Granovsky needed. It's not worth seeking lofty motives; in retrospect, all the reasons for historical events look very important; Stendhal and Tolstoy unmasked the writing of history. Be that as it may, Dobuzhinsky was accepted, and Granovsky was happy. But that meant handing over a matter requiring young inventiveness and fresh devices to a brittle second generation of the "World of Art." Thus, naïvely, on the way to his room, Granovsky stumbled into another. He regressed to the decoration experiments of the 1910s.

Of that pleiad, Dobuzhinsky was not the most interesting; and, besides, his best days were far behind him. In 1919, when Granovsky suddenly offered him the chance to speak Yiddish, he was already in deep obscurity. He didn't know what to do with himself, for his contemporaries didn't know what task to give him. He still wore the popularity he had once achieved through the productions of the Moscow Art Theater, but he was exhausted and couldn't always repeat himself faithfully. He tried only to preserve his clichés, but with worried jealousy, as one guards a hard-earned yet insufficiently large property. Here his nature as a follower, not a leader, was evident. The elders of the "World of Art," who raised and influenced him were different—they lasted longer and risked more.

Dobuzhinsky brought to Granovsky's stage his old-fashioned aestheticism, his love for the beauty of costumes, a subdued nostalgia for things and architectural forms, and the worn-out clichés of emblems and accessories—from the logo of the theater, with its stylized Hebrew letters and black-and-white contrasts of surfaces, to the stylized interiors and human figures used for Asch's *Winter*. His sketches have been preserved; you can see them at Granovsky's even now. But Dobuzhinsky didn't make any special effort, and the handwriting of an artist betrays him as much as does the handwriting of a writer. Dobuzhinsky didn't take pains; his hand was guided by condescension. From this work, he expected "neither loud fame, nor persecutions" [Pushkin]. It

Scene from The Sorceress: An Eccentric Jewish Play, *based on a play by Abraham Goldfaden, 1922. Adaptation: Yikhezkel Dobrushin. Director: Aleksey Granovsky. Set design: Itshak Rabinovich. Music: Yosef Akhron.*

was with only slight interest in Granovsky's project that he just as slightly helped his "young friend."

I met him casually in the auditorium of the Yiddish theater in Moscow, at the time of Granovsky's brilliant success. I think they were performing *The Sorceress*. He was agitated, distributed compliments, and occasionally, as if unwittingly, dropped phrases about how good it was to work on such young stages. He was clearly waiting for an invitation. Obviously, he assumed that he, the godfather of the theater, could expect this as a matter of course. We made believe we didn't understand. All roads to artists of his type were taboo. He departed, tense, officious, and angry. He didn't understand a thing about what took place in those years.

IV

The theater moved to Moscow in the spring of 1920, which became the date of its second birth. The real history of the Yiddish theater begins here. Feverish, raging, roiling Moscow, headquarters of the revolutionary state, potential capital of the world,

Scene from The Sorceress.

shaken daily, hourly, by the thrusts and explosions of events, the turns of the wheel, the breakdowns of the machinery, engulfed with typhus, covered with rumors, starving on rations, heating its ovens with fences and furniture—but constantly seething with a triumphant, historical effort of will, crystallizing the dim movements of the masses; emitting—"To everyone! Everyone! Everyone!"—protests, appeals, orders, slogans; thundering with the triumphant brass of hundreds of orchestras; in the weekdays of its new calendar, pouring the scarlet of its red banners over dense crowds marching through the streets; turning into reality the creative chimeras of dozens of directors, hundreds of artists, thousands of actors, bare-legged dancers, circus performers, dilettantes, and adventurers; generously giving them money (though devalued), buildings (though falling apart), materials (though disintegrating)—Soviet Moscow ignited in Granovsky a decisive spark. He became himself. He found the Archimedean point of the Yiddish theater.

I am slightly afraid of the term I would use to characterize it, a term brown with the clotted mud of centuries, which you won't find in any other language but Russian. But

Scene from The Sorceress.

it expresses what I need and I shall utter it. This word is—"Jewyness" [*Zhidovstvo*]. I am prepared to explain: Is it a metaphor? Yes and no. The Russian Revolution accustomed us to posing a question about the social meaning of every artistic phenomenon. The Revolution has the right to demand it, for under the conditions of a social cataclysm, there are no neutral forces; art becomes the same accomplice or enemy as anything else. My term means that Granovsky's theater, like a screen blown up by light, reflected the appearance of the awakened and agitated masses of the Jewish people on the stage of revolution. The upturned daily life of shtetls and cities, with all their people and smells, flooded onto the stage. This was both the strength and the weakness of the theater. The old world was broken down, and Granovsky showed it with an immense expressiveness; but the new had not yet been found, and Granovsky didn't know how to anticipate it and present it prematurely. His theater was passive. This is not a reproach. Show me if it was different anywhere else! All other theaters of Soviet Russia were like this.

But my word loses its metaphorical arbitrariness in the artistic-theatrical sense. Here it is literal. Granovsky accomplished an immense and positive revolution. Political radicalism is often combined with aesthetic reaction. The power of taste is protected

Scene from The Sorceress.

more securely than the power of classes. Granovsky was one of the few who not only dared but could perform the upheaval. This "Jewyness," which the anti-Semitism of the pogroms mocked and tormented, which the Russified Jewish intelligentsia hushed up in confusion, which the Europeanizing progressives of university chairs haughtily suggested eliminating, which offended the ear and stung the eye—in a word (here at last is a fitting case for a theological quotation!), "The stone which the builders refused is become the headstone of the corner" [Psalms 118:22].

People should have howled with indignation. They didn't dare, because, in the yard and at home, the Revolution performed. Visiting Granovsky, to the sacramental formula of petit bourgeois opposition of "What a country, what a government!" they added, "What licentiousness!" Afterward, they went to HaBima to view an aristocratic Jew, with biblical speech, pathetic gestures, and exotic costumes. Incidentally, some higher echelons of the Revolution preferred the same comeliness. Negatively, this was expressed in the fact that the people didn't go to Granovsky; positively, at the premieres of HaBima, you could see Moscow Chief Rabbi Mazeh next to Politburo member Kamenev, both nodding to each other in satisfaction.

v

Granovsky really unfurled the "Yid" on the stage. He threw his audience the forms, rhythms, sounds, colors of the phenomenon that bore this nickname. Had it only been by imitation of shtetl daily life, by a naturalistic counterfeit of the countenance and life of the everyday Jew, even with a light admixture of a Jewish anecdote, that traditional consolation of both the friendly and the hostile citizen—so be it! Ultimately, it would have been acceptable to everyone, and you could have pitied them: "Poor people . . . How good it is that history, nevertheless, moves!" But Granovsky demanded something entirely different of the auditorium. He wanted the filth he unfolded to be accepted as having immense, self-sufficient value. Granovsky deepened its theatrical and artistic features to the level of an all-encompassing imperative, a universal generalization. From dross he made gold. On an evening of self-parody at the theater, the young actor Zuskin masterfully portrayed "a series of magical transformations" of a dignified Jew who found himself at Granovsky's and, at first, couldn't believe his ears, then turned scarlet, and finally dashed out of the auditorium screaming, "Ay, ay—what an anti-Semite!" As a matter of fact, the long hems of the *kapotas* and fringed undergarments, the curls of beards and hair, the curves of noses and backs, hovered over the space of the stage in Granovsky's theater, if one can say so, as absolutes. The singsong, guttural speech, squeaking at the ends of sentences, entered the ear like a molded, finished, self-sufficient system. The scattered, hurried movements and gestures, interrupting one another, ran like a counterpoint of beads. Granovsky turned the features of small daily life into a theatrical *device* and a stage *form*. From this moment, the Yiddish theater came into being.

But the key to the problem was not with the director but with the artists. Granovsky had to borrow. He didn't hesitate, for he never suffered from stupidity. He caught the artist by the lapels and didn't let go of him until he attained his objective. The artist gave him the basic formulas for the images he sought, the first devices for their embodiment, and the initial stages of their development. And it was this that formed the contrast between the role of a designer on the general Russian stage and his later significance for the Yiddish stage. In the 1920s, when the masters of theater painting were allowed into the auditorium only condescendingly, as traditional guests at the premiere—and were, as much as possible, prevented from working on the stage as executors of the decorations—it was precisely then that the Jewish artist played a primary role in creating his national theater. This assertion will not surprise anyone; I mention the well-known phenomenon only in passing.

Among the components that went into the construction of the Yiddish theater, painting was the most mature in its development and the most specific in its manifestations. It did not get entangled in elementary searches for its own artistic form the way that the tongue of Yiddish writers tripped over itself and formulated more jargon than Yiddish. Neither did it have such quantities of raw ethnographic slang as did the works of Jewish composers, who were satisfied with copying folk songs and melodies that they peppered only lightly with modernism. Painting and graphics gave Granovsky a ready-made solution for conquering the auditorium. The entire group of Jewish painters worked dynamically and triumphantly, creating work that was saturated with personalities, rich in nuances, and unquestionably contemporary in its formal expressiveness. In every trend of European and Russian art, in every school, it had leading representatives.

True, this diapason was too broad. Danger was inherent in it. You had to select correctly. The story of Dobuzhinsky might have been repeated. There were all sorts of people and programs. Granovsky had to understand that in the artistic revolution, as in the social revolution, you always have to steer the most extreme course; the resultant force of intentions and possibilities will sort itself out. The Yiddish stage needed the most "Jewy," the most contemporary, the most unusual, the most difficult of all artists. And so I mentioned Chagall's name to Granovsky. Granovsky's always-sleepy eyes opened with a start and rounded like the eyes of an owl at the sight of meat. Next morning, Chagall was summoned and invited to work on Sholem-Aleichem's miniatures. This was the first production of the Moscow period. Chagall began a dynasty of artist-designers.

VI

He had just returned from Vitebsk, where he had been commissar of art but, fed up with power, had abdicated this lofty title. At least, that's his story. The truth was that he was deposed by the Suprematist Malevich, who took over Chagall's students and usurped the art school. He accused Chagall of being moderate, and of being just a neo-Realist, still entangled in depicting some objects and figures, when truly revolutionary art is objectless. The students believed in revolution and found artistic moderation insufferable. Chagall tried to make some speeches in his own defense, but they were confused and almost incoherent. Malevich answered with heavy, strong, and crushing words. Suprematism was pronounced the heresy of revolution. Chagall had to leave for (I almost wrote "flee to") Moscow. He didn't know what to do and spent the time telling stories about his experience as commissar in Vitebsk and about the intrigues of the Suprematists. He loved to recollect the time when, on revolutionary holidays, a banner waved above the school depicting a man on a green horse and the inscription "Chagall—to Vitebsk." The students still admired him and covered all fences and street signs that had survived the Revolution with Chagallian cows and pigs, legs turned down and legs turned up. Malevich, after all, was just a dishonorable intriguant, whereas he, Chagall, had been born in Vitebsk, and knew well what kind of art Vitebsk and the Russian Revolution needed.

Meanwhile, he quickly consoled himself with work in the Yiddish theater. He set us no conditions, but also stubbornly refused to accept any instructions. We abandoned ourselves to God's will. Chagall never left the small auditorium on Chernyshevsky Lane. He locked all doors; Granovsky and I were the only ones allowed in, after a carping and suspicious interrogation from inside as from the guard of a gunpowder cellar; in addition, at fixed hours he was served food through a crack in the half-open door. This was not simple intoxication with work; he was truly possessed. Joyfully and boundlessly, he bled paintings, images, and forms. Immediately he felt crowded on the few meters of our stage. He announced that, along with the decorations, he would paint a "Jewish panel" on the big wall of the auditorium; then he moved over to the small wall, then to the spaces between the windows, and finally to the ceiling. The whole hall was Chagallized. The audience came as much to be perplexed by this amazing cycle of Jewish frescoes as to see Sholem-Aleichem's skits. They were truly shaken. I often had to appear prior to the performance with some introductory remarks explaining what kind of thing it was and why it was needed.

I talked a lot about leftist art and Chagall, and little about the theater. That was natural. Today we can admit that Chagall forced us to buy the Jewish form of scenic imagery at a high price. He had no theatrical blood in him. He continued doing his own drawings and paintings, not drafts of decorations and costume designs. On the contrary, he turned the actors and the production into categories of plastic art. He did not do actual sets but simply panels, processing them with various textures, meticulously and in detail, as if the spectator would stand before them at a distance of several feet, as he stands in an exhibition, and appreciate, almost touching, the beauty and subtlety of this colorful field plowed up by Chagall. He did not want to hear about a third dimension, about the depth of the stage. Instead, he positioned all his decorations in parallel planes, along the apron, as he was accustomed to placing his paintings on walls or easels. The objects were painted with Chagallian foreshortening, with his own perspective, which did not consider any perspectives; painted objects were contrasted with real objects; Chagall hated real objects as illegitimate disturbers of his cosmos and furiously hurled them off the stage; with the same rage, he painted over—one might say plastered with color—that indispensable minimum of objects. With his own hands, he painted every costume, turning it into a complex combination of blots, stripes, dots, and scattering over them various muzzles, animals, and doodles. He obviously considered the spectator a fly, which would soar out of its chair, sit on Mikhoels's hat [in his role as Reb Alter], and observe with the thousand tiny crystals of its fly's eye what he, Chagall, had conjured up there. He did not look for types or images—he simply took them from his paintings.

Of course, under these conditions, the wholeness of the spectator's impression was complete. When the curtain rose, Chagall's wall panels and decorations and the actors on the stage simply mirrored one another. But the nature of this ensemble was so untheatrical that one might have asked, Why turn off the light in the auditorium, and why do these Chagallian beings move and speak on the stage rather than stand unmoving and silent as on his canvases?

Ultimately, *A Sholem-Aleichem Evening* was conducted, as it were, in the form of Chagall paintings come to life. The best places were those in which Granovsky executed his system of "dots" and the actors froze in mid-movement and mid-gesture, from one moment to the next. The narrative line was turned into an assembly of dots. One needed a marvelous finesse, with which Mikhoels was endowed, to unify in the role of Reb Alter Chagall's static costumes and images with the unfolding of speech and action. The spectacle was built on compromise and tottered from side to side. The thick, invincible Chagallian Jewishness conquered the stage, but the stage was enslaved and not engaged in participation.

We had to break through to the spectacle over Chagall's dead body, as it were. He was upset by everything that was done to make the theater a theater. He cried real, hot, childish tears when rows of chairs were placed in the hall with his frescoes. He claimed, "These heathen Jews will obstruct my art; they will rub their thick backs and greasy hair on it." To no avail did Granovsky and I, as friends, curse him as an idiot; he continued wailing and whining. He attacked workers who carried his handmade sets, claiming that they deliberately scratched them. On the day of the premiere, just before Mikhoels's entrance on the stage, he clutched the actor's shoulder and frenziedly thrust his brush at him as at a mannequin, daubing dots on his costume and painting tiny birds and pigs no opera glass could observe on his visored cap, despite repeated, anxious summonses to the stage and Mikhoels's curt pleas—and again Chagall cried and lamented when we ripped the actor out of his hands by force and shoved him onto the stage.

Poor, dear Chagall! He, of course, considered us tyrants and himself a martyr. He was so deeply convinced of it that, ever after, for eight years, he never touched the theater again. He never understood that he was the clear and indisputable victor and that, in the end, the young Yiddish theater had struggled because of this victory.

May 1928

Abram Efros

Marc Chagall
My Work in the Moscow Yiddish Theater   1921–1928, Yiddish*

"Here are the walls," said Efros. "Do what you want with them."

It was an apartment, rundown; its tenants had fled.

"See, here we will have benches for the audience, and over there, the stage."

To tell the truth, "over there" I didn't see anything but vestiges of a kitchen, and "here"?

I shouted: "Down with the old theater that smells of garlic and sweat! Long live . . ."

And I dashed to the walls.

On the ground lay sheets; workers and actors were crawling over them, through the renovated halls and corridors, among slivers, chisels, paints, sketches.

Torn tatters of the Civil War, ration cards, various "queue numbers" lay around. I too wallowed on the ground. At moments, I enjoyed lying like this. At home they lay the dead on the ground. Often, people lie at their heads and cry. I too love, finally, to lie on the ground, to whisper into it my sorrow, my prayer . . .

*Published in *Di yidishe velt: Monthly for Literature, Criticism, Art, and Culture*, no. 2 (Vilna, Poland: B. Kletskin Publishing House, 1928).

I recalled my great-grandfather, who painted the synagogue in Mohilev,* and I wept: Why didn't he take me a hundred years ago at least as an apprentice? Isn't it a pity for him to lie in the Mohilev earth and be an advocate for me [in the World to Come]? Let him tell with what miracles he daubed with his brush in the shtetl Lyozno. Blow into me, my bearded grandfather, a few drops of Jewish truth! . . .

To have a bite, I sent the janitor Ephraim for milk and bread. The milk is no milk, the bread is no bread. The milk has water and starch; the bread has oats and tobacco-colored straw. Maybe it is real milk, or maybe—fresh from a revolutionary cow. Maybe Ephraim poured water into the jar, the bastard; he mixed something in and served it to me. Maybe somebody's white blood . . . I ate, drank, came to life. Ephraim, the representative of the workers and peasants, inspired me. If not for him, what would have happened? His nose, his poverty, his stupidity; his lice crawled from him to me—and back. He stood like this, smiling feverishly. He didn't know what to observe first, me or the paintings. Both of us looked ridiculous. Ephraim, where are you? Who will ever remember you but me? Maybe you are no more than a janitor, but sometimes by chance you stood at the box office and checked the tickets. Often I thought: They should have put him on stage; didn't they take janitor Katz's wife? Her figure looked like a square yard of wet wood covered with snow. Carry the wood to the fifth floor and put it in your room. The water streams . . . She screamed, declaimed during rehearsals like a pregnant mare. I don't wish on my enemies a glance at her breasts. Scary!

Right behind the door—Granovsky's office. Before the theater is done, there is little work. The room is crowded. He lies in bed; under the bed, wood shavings: he planes his body. Those days he was sick. "How is your health, Aleksey Mikhaylovich?"

So he lies in bed and smiles or scowls or curses. Often acrid words, of the male or female gender,† fell on me or on the first comer. I don't know if Granovsky smiles now, but just like Ephraim's milk, his futile smiles console me. True, sometimes I felt like tickling him, but I never dared to ask: "Do you love me?"

I left Russia without it.

---

*The eighteenth-century synagogue in Mohilev Province was painted by Chaim Segal. The connection to Chagall is possible, for Lyozno was in Mohilev Province, and in some Jewish subdialects the letter "s" is pronounced like "sh," but the connection is not supported by any other evidence. On the other hand, "great-grandfather" (in Yiddish: *elter-zeyde*) may simply mean "forefather, ancestor," with no hereditary commitment.

†That is, Russian pornographic curses.

For a long time, I had dreamed of work in the theater. Back in 1911, Tugendhold wrote somewhere that my objects are alive. I could, he said, paint psychological sets. I thought about it. Indeed, in 1914, Tugendhold recommended to Tairov, the director of the Moscow Chamber Theater, that he invite me to paint Shakespeare's *Merry Wives of Windsor*. We met and parted in peace. The goblet was overflowing.* Sitting in Vitebsk, commissaring away, planting art all over the province, multiplying students-enemies†—I was overjoyed to get Granovsky's and Efros's invitation in 1918 to work in the newly opened Yiddish theater. Shall I introduce Efros to you? All of him legs. Neither noisy nor quiet, he is alive. Moving from right to left, up and down, always beaming, with his eyeglasses and his beard, he is here and he is there, Efros is everywhere. We are bosom buddies and we see each other once every five years. I heard about Granovsky for the first time in Petrograd during the war. From time to time, as a pupil of Reinhardt, he produced spectacles with mass scenes. After Reinhardt's visit with *Oedipus Rex* in Russia, those mass scenes created a certain impression. At the same time, Granovsky produced spectacles using Jews of all kinds of professions whom he assembled from everywhere. They were the ones who later created the studio of the Yiddish theater.

Once I saw those plays, performed in Stanislavsky's realistic style. As I came to Moscow, I was internally agitated. I felt that, at least in the beginning, the love affair between me and Granovsky would not settle down so fast. I am a person who doubts everything under the sun, whereas Granovsky is sure of himself, and a bit ironic. But the main thing is that, so far, he is absolutely no Chagall.

They suggested I do the wall paintings for the first production and the opening of the theater. Wow, I thought, here is an opportunity to turn the old Yiddish theater upside down, the Realism, Naturalism, Psychologism, and the pasted-on beards. I set to work. I hoped that at least a few of the actors of the Yiddish Chamber Theater and of HaBima [the Moscow Hebrew theater], where I was invited to do *The Dybbuk*, would absorb the new art and would abandon the old ways. I made a sketch. On one wall, I intended to give a general direction, introducing the audience to the new Yiddish People's Theater. The other walls and the ceiling represented klezmers, a wedding jester, women dancers, a Torah scribe, and a couple of lovers hovering over the scene,

---

*The goblet of tears and suffering is overflowing.

†Many students left Chagall for the more radical abstract painter Kazimir Malevich, who also had an original aesthetic theory. Specifically, Chagall alludes to El Lissitzky, who was a "pupil" of Chagall's in Yiddish book illustration and "reneged," accepting Malevich's Suprematism.

not far from various foods, bagels and fruit, set tables, all painted on friezes. Facing them—the stage with the actors. The work was hard; my contact with the work was settling down. Granovsky apparently lived slowly through a process of transformation from Reinhardt and Stanislavsky to something else. In my presence, Granovsky seemed to hover in other worlds. Sometimes it seemed to me that I was disturbing him. Was it true? I don't know why he did not confide in me. And I myself didn't dare to open serious discussions with him. The wall was breached by the actor Mikhoels, who was starving, just like me. He would often come to me with bulging eyes and forehead, hair standing on end, a pug nose and thick lips—entirely majestic.

He follows my thought, he warns me, and with the sharp edges of his hands and body he tries to grasp. It is hard to forget him. He watched my work, he begged me to let him take the sketches home, he wanted to get into them, to get used to them, to understand. Some time later, Mikhoels joyfully announced to me:

"You know, I studied your sketches, I understood. I changed my role entirely. Everybody looks at me and cannot understand what happened."

I smiled. He smiled. Other actors quietly and carefully snuck up to me, to my canvases, began observing, finding out what kind of thing this is. Couldn't they also change? There was little material for costumes and decorations. The last day before the opening of the theater, they collected heaps of truly old, worn-out clothes for me. In the pockets, I found cigarette butts, dry bread crumbs. I painted the costumes fast. I couldn't even get out into the hall that evening for the first performance. I was all smeared with paint. A few minutes before the curtain rose, I ran onto the stage to patch up the color of several costumes. For I couldn't stand the "Realism," and suddenly a clash: Granovsky hangs up a plain, real towel! I sigh and scream.

"A plain towel?!"

"Who is the Director here: you or I?" he answered.

Oh, my poor heart, oh, sweet father!

I was invited to do the stage for *The Dybbuk* at HaBima. I didn't know what to do. Those two theaters were at war with each other. But I couldn't go to HaBima, where the actors don't act but pray,* and, poor souls, still idolized Stanislavsky's theater.

If between me and Granovsky—as he himself put it—the love affair didn't work out, Vakhtangov (who had then directed only *The Cricket on the Hearth*) was a stranger to me. It

---

*From a Yiddishist position, the Hebrew language is a language of prayer, i.e., reactionary and clerical.

will be very hard, I thought, to find a common language for the two of us. To an open declaration of love, I respond with love; from hesitations or doubts, I walk away.

For example, in 1922, they invited me lovingly to Stanislavsky's second art theater to stage, together with the director Diky,* Synge's *Playboy of the Western World* ... I plunged into it body and soul, but the whole troupe declared a strike: "Incomprehensible." Then they invited somebody else and the play was a flop.

At the first rehearsal of *The Dybbuk* in HaBima, watching the troupe with Vakhtangov, I thought: "He is a Russian, a Georgian; we see each other for the first time.—Embarrassed, we observe one another. Perhaps he sees in my eyes the chaos and confusion of the Orient. A hasty people, its art is incomprehensible, strange ... Why do I get upset, blush, and pierce him with my eyes?"

I will pour into him a drop of poison, and later he will recall it with me or behind my back. Others will come after me, who will repeat my words and sighs in a more accessible, smoother, and clearer way.

At the end, I asked Vakhtangov how he intends to conceive of *The Dybbuk*. He answered slowly that the only correct line is Stanislavsky's. "I don't know," said I, "of such a direction for the reborn Jewish theater." Our ways parted.

And to Zemach:† "Even without me, you will stage it my way. There is no other way." I went out into the street.

Back home in the children's colony in Malakhovka, I remembered my last meeting with An-sky,‡ at a soirée in 1915, at Kalashnikov's Stock Market.§ He shook his gray head, kissed me, and said: "I have a play, *The Dybbuk*, and you're the only one who can carry it out. I thought about you." Baal-Makhshoves, who stood nearby, blazed agreement with his eyeglasses and nodded his head.

"So what shall I do? ... What shall I do?"

Anyway, I was told that a year later, Vakhtangov sat for many hours at my projects when he prepared *The Dybbuk*. And they invited someone else, as Zemach told

---

*Aleksey D. Diky (1889–1955)—Soviet theater director. In Chagall's time he worked in the First Studio of Stanislavsky's theater, MKhAT (Moscow Art Theater).

†Nakhum Zemach (1887–1939)—founder of the first modern Hebrew theater, HaBima, in Moscow in 1917. In 1926 he settled in the United States.

‡S. An-sky—pseudonym of Shloyme-Zanvl Rapoport (1863–1920), born in Vitebsk Province; scholar, folklorist, writer, author of *The Dybbuk*.

§A hall for public events in Moscow.

me, to make projects à la Chagall. And at Granovsky's, I hear, they over-Chagalled twentyfold.

Thank God for that.

Malakhovka 1921—Paris 1928

P.S. I just heard that the Muscovites are abroad.[*] Regards to them!

Marc Chagall
My First Meeting with Solomon Mikhoels   1944, Yiddish[†]

My destiny brought me here to America; and, suddenly, after so many years, I see here my old friend Shloyme Mikhoels. He arrived with my new friend, the poet Itsik Fefer, bringing regards from our homeland.[‡]

Since you have asked me to write something about Mikhoels, who is now celebrating his twenty-fifth year in the Yiddish theater, I remember with pleasure my first meeting with him.

Those years when I first started working in the Yiddish theater rise up in my memory. In my dreams . . . I transpose myself to my city. Thin young trees, bent, sighing as on a day of *Tashlikh*.[§]

In my youth, I walked like this through the streets, searching . . . For what?

Among my festive moments, once upon a time, there was one great one: Sholem-Aleichem came to read his writings in my city. I had no money for a ticket, but anyway I was angry at the small-town guys who read Sholem-Aleichem and laughed all the time just for the sake of laughing. I, on the contrary, didn't laugh so much and thought that Sholem-Aleichem was a "Modernist" in art. Someday, I would show them.

Some twelve years later (around 1919), a Yiddish theater studio from Petrograd, with an unknown director, arrived in our city. The director surely came to our city because his wife was from Vitebsk. The "studio" was a conglomeration of young and old amateurs. After the performance, I walked around glumly in the lobby of the city theater accompanied by my old teacher, the artist Yehuda Pen, who teased me with

---

[*]Allusion to the tour of the Moscow Yiddish State Theater in Western Europe in 1928.

[†]Published in *Yidishe kultur: Monthly of the Jewish World Culture Union* (New York), 6, no. 1 (1944).

[‡]During World War II, Mikhoels, director of the Jewish Anti-Fascist Committee in Moscow, and the Yiddish poet Itsik Fefer were sent to the United States to mobilize public opinion in favor of the Soviet war effort against Nazi Germany.

[§]The ceremony of casting unleavened bread into the water (a river).

his *misnaged* smile—you don't know why or wherefore . . . Finally I ran into the direc-tor himself.

Aleksey Granovsky—tall, supple, blond. He looked a bit like a Christian. He would rarely open his mouth—maybe because of his bad teeth. He could speak with his mouth shut. His eyes smiled from an incidental, unknown pleasure that would alight on him like a fly. And he would look both at you and at somebody else on the side . . .

"I really need you, Chagall!" he says suddenly. "You know, I have a play . . . just for you . . ."

For quite a while, I had thought it was time for me to get into Yiddish theater. Something had to "burst," to open up in me. But why wasn't I drawn to Granovsky as to somebody else? To whom? What for? Meanwhile, my friend Efros called me from Moscow to come paint the walls of the new Yiddish theater and design the sets for the first production of the theater to be founded there.

I came to Moscow and found the producer and director Granovsky in bed. He was coquettishly playing sick and indulging himself in bed. He conducted conversations from his bed. I showed him the finished sketches I had brought from Vitebsk. As we talked, Mikhoels entered the room. Delicately, carefully. He said something very respect-fully, listened attentively, and exited confidently, as the future theater soldier and general.

Granovsky would make short, smiling remarks, which would be snatched up by the actors all around like a treasure and later lapped up in the long corridors.

"You hear?"—Granovsky said—"You hear?—Granovsky laughs! Hush—Granovsky sleeps! A man sits in his room! He declares his love." . . .

But my "affair" with him—he said—somehow doesn't hold together? . . .

Why?

I really didn't have much luck with directors. Not with Vakhtangov, who at first empathized neither with my art nor with my sketches for *The Dybbuk* in HaBima, and yet later asked to make it à la Chagall without me; nor with [Aleksandr] Tairov, who was still sick with Constructivism; nor with the Second Studio of the Moscow Art Theater, which was still drowning in psychological realism . . . All of them, as well as others, asked me to make sketches and later got scared of them.

And here was Granovsky. Truly a seeker. He spoke only Russian in the Yiddish theater. He really did have talent, perhaps eclectic yet gracious; but he was straying on the paths of his German teacher, Max Reinhardt, with his theories of mass scenes, which were then in fashion. Granovsky searched gradually, not so much with the fervor of a Jewish soul, but as if through books. He wanted to liberate himself from the decorative

German path, and kept looking for new Jewish forms, which began appearing here and there in the Jewish plastic world.

It fell to me to be the first painter in the new Yiddish theater, but Granovsky didn't talk to me and got away with just a smile; I, with my "character," was also silent.

The rehearsals of Sholem-Aleichem pieces, which were to open the new theater, were conducted on one side, and I was steeped in my work on the other side.

But I harbored a very special hope for the magical Mikhoels. He didn't get underfoot like the others, who walked back and forth in the long corridors of the small theater, which had just been rebuilt from a private home (later it moved to a bigger house). Everywhere pieces of wood, old newspapers, boards, sticks, and other rags were lying around. One actor carried a ration of black bread and another carried a bottle of bluish milk mixed with water into his room. And I sat on the ladder, painting the murals. The janitor Ephraim, a young wild animal, would bring me my ration of bread and milk and meanwhile laugh his fill over my paintings. So I would sit like this on the ladder, painting the wall. I wanted to paint myself into it, you, my own cities and towns. My Bella would come to "console" me with the little angel—Idochka [Chagall's daughter, Ida]—hardly two feet high. She would wander around below and look at Papa above—it's too high for her. Meanwhile, Mama would go learn Yiddish performance from her teacher Mikhoels. From afar I would hear her voice, "Bells are ringing . . ." [a Yiddish song], and I would sit and think about the new art in the new theater, with no pasted-on beards scaring me like ghosts. I would think about those Purim-players, about that beggar with the green face and the sack on his back where he hides a *siddur* [prayer book], a herring, a piece of bread, and now I would see him at night, in the moonlight, with his beard swinging like a tree in the city park. I wanted to paint him and take him to the stage . . .

When I let myself "think" like that, I was liable to lose my balance and fall from the ladder on top of my Idochka below. Silently I begged my distant dead relative—who, once upon a time painted, to his good fortune, the walls of a synagogue—to help me. I felt that, nearby, a young Jew was sitting and walking around—he could help me if he wanted to approach me first, to open his mouth—perhaps he himself would become a different person . . .

That was young Mikhoels—strong though short, thin but sturdy, practical and dreamy; his logic merged with feeling, his Yiddish language sounded as if it came from Yiddish books. He could help, he would pull himself out and pull other actors along, even the director himself.

Right at my first meeting with Mikhoels, I was amazed by that rare though still vague artistic striving and force, which one day will stumble onto logic and form, which—if you find them—take on various sounds, rhythms, and colors, although it all may look both illogical and unreal. Those are forms that break old artistic conventions and promise something important in life . . .

I sat on the ladder in the auditorium for a long time surrounded by my murals and sketches for the Sholem-Aleichem pieces.

I locked the doors. Only rarely did Granovsky himself come in to discuss art and theater, and the forthcoming production. Once Mikhoels approached me with his mincing steps and said in measured, clearly veiled words, "Mark Zakharovich,[*] lend me your sketches. I want to study them. We cannot continue like this—you here and we there, everyone separate!"

But indeed, I could sit like this for a long time, do my work, gather up my bundles and disappear.

Mikhoels's open and friendly approach was symbolic of a new type of Jewish man and artist at the beginning of the great Revolution.

Therefore, I cannot forget how, a few months later, I heard Mikhoels's long call from his distant room in the corridor, "Chagall, I understood! . . . Where are you? I understood . . ."

And he came up to my ladder holding the sketches.

"See, Chagall!" With joy in his eyes, covered with a smile reaching to his feet, he stood and moved with Sholem-Aleichem's text beaming from his mouth. There was no doubt: Mikhoels had found something, found the true nuance and rhythm—that is, the form, the content, the new spirit, the new actor. It was a new world.

I was happy and continued my work, which had to be finished, for soon the theater was to be opened. Jokingly, Granovsky said they would take me off the ladder and call two doctors to pacify me when they hung my big canvases on the walls.

I was waiting—what would happen? The rehearsals of Sholem-Aleichem's pieces continued in the old style. The familiar psychological realism. I imagined that Mikhoels alone would stand out from the whole troupe, and the other actors along with Granovsky would be puzzled: What happened? they would ask themselves. How did Mikhoels suddenly break loose from the chain while we can't adapt to it? Once, I was sitting on my ladder, listening. I heard feet tramping on the other side of the wall . . .

[*]Chagall's Russian name and patronymic.

From left, the two star actors of the State Yiddish Theater (GOSET)—Solomon Mikhoels, chief actor and director, and Benjamin Zuskin—with the author, adapter, and playwright Yikhezkel Dobrushin, 1922.

Hands opened my door and all the actors suddenly entered the auditorium and said in chorus, "Chagall, Mikhoels has sent us to you. He has changed his role entirely. We asked him, 'What is this?' He says, 'I don't know, go to Chagall, he will explain.' So we came to you to tell us how and what to do, to be like Mikhoels." . . .

I listened to them and grew sad. I jokingly wanted to sic my painted animals on the walls on them; let the klezmers "scare" them with a sudden playing and let them go back. I was "ashamed" of myself—look, I had been hanging before their eyes for a long time; but when Mikhoels changed his art, they came to me. Isn't there a director?

I answered, "Mikhoels himself can explain a lot to you, much better than I can."

What kind of art is it—Mikhoels's art?

It is almost the same question that could have been asked in the past about the objectives and dreams of the new Jewish plastic art.

Goldfaden, Peretz, Sholem-Aleichem, and others are for the actor what "nature" is for the artist.

For the artist does not copy nature, but creates it facing it. Thus, both the artist and the actor create a new kind of nature. And only this means to have "respect" for the playwright as for nature. Otherwise, the artist creates mere photography, copy, illustration, and not art. And if, at a certain moment, the theater merged its soul with Jewish plastic art, it would come to life and show the world its soul. But if, however, the theater kept itself distant, it would remain "local," with its accidental actors' talents. I don't mean the accidental, "decorative" help of the invited artists. This is often a triviality.

It's not enough to speak about the history of Yiddish theater from the point of view of worn-out literary psychological plays for reading and roles confined to their time. Of course we had this and still do have a dozen fine and great Yiddish actors—born talents. Fortunately, I have seen some of them at different times. Just as the history of art has had several fine greater and lesser artists. Yet those who perceived and merged with the whole period in art have had a deeper significance. Just like, recently, the French trends in plastic art; and like, among us Jews, the classics of the new Yiddish literature that created style—so is the new Yiddish actor in the theater. In the same way, Mikhoels strove to create a new Yiddish actor in the new Yiddish theater and a new theater style. And when you discover inside yourself the important meaning of the technical material, you also see the whole human being inside you.

Thus Mikhoels opened the wide road on which he can deepen and broaden his theater art with his own power. Mikhoels is one of the rare happy people who arrived on such a road of art, understood it, and discovered himself.

Later I saw other actors of the Moscow Yiddish theater, especially Zuskin, with a melody on his thick lips, walk the same road.

Later I saw the director Vakhtangov sitting in the auditorium before my murals and, like one set ablaze, leading the troupe of HaBima with Rovina* and others in *The Dybbuk* on the same road, though earlier he had been opposed.

Studying art in such a way, Mikhoels grasped life. And, just as on the theater stage, so on the stage of life, he transferred an understanding and analysis of the problems of our life in that tragic and great time. For our time, too, is our material; we work and breathe with it in our art.

This shows the absurdity of the opinion that there is a "pure" art, art for art's sake. On the contrary, art that is ostensibly called "pure" is very often dirty.

---

*Chana Rovina—the lead actress of HaBima.

And if Mikhoels, as he said, once learned from me, perhaps I must now learn from him.

Then I myself wouldn't have been drowned in my doubt as in a pot of paint that paints the Jewish face and soul in a hue of mystery and sadness.

Yosef Schein
Mikhoels and Chagall
1964, Yiddish*

Mikhoels's success in the role of Menakhem-Mendel Yakenhoz was greatly due to the painter Marc Chagall. Mikhoels used to tell of this collaboration with a wise, good-natured smile. "On the day of the premiere, Chagall walked into my dressing room. After preparing his colors, he set to work. He divided my face into two parts. One he painted green, the other yellow (as they say, 'He is green and yellow' [downcast, defeated]). Chagall lifted my right eyebrow two centimeters higher than the left. The wrinkles around my nose and lips spread all over my face. These wrinkle lines highlighted Menakhem-Mendel's tragic lot.

"I looked in the mirror and was convinced that the makeup created the dynamism and expressivity of the character. The artist continued working diligently. Suddenly his fingers remained hanging over my face with a question mark. Something bothered him. He put a finger to my eye, took it back, and, taking several steps back, observed me and added regretfully, 'Oh, Solomon, Solomon, if you didn't have your right eye, I could have done so much.'"

Mikhoels laughed but soon became pensive and serious.

"My living eye, my Mikhoels eye, hindered Chagall from bringing Menakhem-Mendel's eye, which he saw and sensed so vividly. The reason apparently was in me."

Marc Chagall
Letter to the Management of GOSEKT
1921, Russian

When I finished my work, I assumed, as was promised, that it would be exhibited publicly, like many of my most recent works. The management will agree that, as an artist, I cannot rest until the "masses" see it, etc.

---

* *Arum moskver yidishn teater* (Paris: Les éditions polyglottes, 1964).

Instead, the works appear to have been placed in a cage and can be seen by at most a hundred crowded (though happily so) Jews. I love Jews very much (there is plenty of evidence for this), but I also love Russians and various other peoples and am used to painting serious work for many nationalities.

Hence, my demand and appeal to the theater are natural and legitimate; I am asking you to put at my disposal twenty-eight hours in the course of two weeks—two hours a day—for the organization of an exhibition and survey of my works for all interested parties. The expenses for the organization of the exhibition, such as posters, etc., will be borne by IZO NKP [Section for Graphic Arts, People's Commissariat of Enlightenment] or by me. I cannot give up this demand.

Expecting an official answer,

Marc Chagall

February 12, 1921

Invitation to the Exhibition   1921, Russian[*]

June 1921

XXIII EXHIBITION OF THE CENTRAL SECTION OF IZO OF NARKOMPROS[†]

Murals of the artist

MARC CHAGALL

1. Introduction to the Yiddish Theater	5. Literature
2. Music	6. The Wedding Table
3. Dance	7. Love on the Stage
4. Drama	8. Decorated Ceiling

In the auditorium of the Yiddish State Chamber theater (B. Chernyshevsky, 12)

Open for viewing from 3:00 to 5:00

Entrance Free

Cultural-educational organizations, factory committees, and educational institutions are invited to organize excursions.

Information by telephone 2-16-04 and 3-45-67

---

[*] Included in Chagall's triumphant collage titled *Tsedek* (in Hebrew: "Justice").
[†] Section for Graphic Arts in the People's Commissariat of Enlightenment.

CHAPTER FOUR

The Program of the Yiddish Chamber Theater
on Its Opening in July 1919

1919, Yiddish[*]

Lev Levidov

The Jewish Theater Society and the Chamber Theater

"Let there be light"—and the Yiddish Chamber Theater appeared in the white world
. . . Dreams came true, all our wishes were fulfilled.

I remember it was on November 9, 1916, that the Jewish Theater Society was inaugu-
rated. A joyful, festive day. The auditorium was packed, excited faces, solemn speeches,
an enormous elation of the soul. A new society was born and it called aloud: "Come
work for a Jewish, national, artistic theater!" . . . The congratulations, the speeches,
the telegrams flowed together, as in a chorus . . .

Isn't it strange, frightening? Jews, who have contributed the best artists, who have
given the most splendid flowers to the universal altar of art, don't have their own
theater to speak Yiddish with them? . . . No! Such a theater must be. This is demanded
by the honor and dignity of the Jewish people, this is demanded by our national culture . . . The new Yiddish Theater Society promised to create such a theater, a theater
for us. They swore to devote all their strength to carry out that assignment. And with
excitement, with love, they set to work.

It was a hard time. The old regime lay dying, and as always, as it died, bloodthirsty
and merciless, it persecuted the exhausted Jewish people.

A Yiddish theater . . . What had borne such a name in the Jewish street was not a
theater: the Yiddish actors had no right of sojourn, no place to rest; the Yiddish language
was persecuted and derided; the surrogate theater that existed was not cultural and was
benighted. The whole being of Yiddish theater was like a stupid, invented tale . . .

---

[*]*Dos idishe kamer teatr* (Petrograd: Jewish Theater Society, 1919). The whole brochure, printed by Togblat
printers, is translated here as Chapter 4.

Meetings of the new society began—raging, passionate, long. No one knew what they should begin to do. What to do first, how to build the new building? . . . Hadn't all previous attempts come to nothing? . . . There was no clay, no bricks for the building . . . At the first meetings, the word was spoken for the first time: "a Yiddish studio," a Yiddish theater school. And that word was soon accepted, found a warm resonance in all hearts. Yes, we really should have one, we really should begin here. Three long meetings were devoted to the single question of whether to create a school-studio or a studio-school . . . How many arguments were poured out, how much excitement . . . They discussed programs, they prepared a repertoire, they listed the teachers and actors by name, they wrote estimates . . . and then . . . the Revolution blazed up, and the light of our work disappeared in the glow of the Revolutionary sun. A series of meetings and assemblies began, political arguments took over. The issue of the theater was left by the wayside. In vain did some try to go back to work—no one thought about theater any longer. The convention of Yiddish actors in Moscow did no more than force some to think again about beginning the halted work. That was hard to do. The political sea was too flamboyant, the world order had moved too much for people calmly to be able to begin again to build the national cultural life. But it seems that culture is stronger than the transient phenomena of life. New times came, new songs, new faces. And among the new, also old and good friends. Why not? . . . Welcome . . . Let us now begin our work for the community again. The thought has again appeared that excited us and made us all happy. Out of the chaos, our idea is born again, the idea of the studio. The studio is our own child, our only child, the holy dream that was dreamed by the Yiddish Theater Society. And now the dream is realized. The studio began to live, not only in words but in action. And it lives, and works, and gets out into the wide world. The Yiddish Chamber Theater is yet a second step from our studio. And the current performances of the Yiddish Chamber Theater are the beginning of a new period, of a new life in the Yiddish theater. What kind of spectacles these will be we shall see later—we shall see what they will give the Jewish people. But, on the other hand, we see here young, capable people, who love with body and soul their theater, their language, the idea of our own national theater, and they work hard, very hard. And that says everything.

The new word has already been said, the new word has been turned into new action . . . New Theater, you have our best wishes. The Jewish Theater Society sends you its blessing.

Lev Levidov
Chairman of the Jewish Theater Society

Aleksey Granovsky
Our Goals and Objectives

A hundred and fifty days ago, we opened the doors of our studio and beckoned to those who wanted to work and lend a hand to build the Yiddish theater.

A hundred and fifty days—in such a short time, one normally cannot speak of achievements and realization.

And if, today, we raise the curtain, we won't and can't say: See, this is what we have accomplished. No, we just want to say: Look, this is the path we want to take.

Do not be concerned about the technical roughness of our first performances. We are still young: we have been alive for only five months . . . We invited no professional artists, no experienced stage workers; not only did we not invite them, we didn't let them in, because more than anything we hate in art the artisan smugness of the "professionals," their artisan approach to "play" and "performance," their inability to abandon themselves to the joy of creation.

On our path we took along no artisans; but we ourselves, obviously, had no time in 150 days to become masters. And what we show you, raising our theater curtain for the first time, is just a vague hint of the path we tread.

Yiddish theater . . . It never existed, and the mess that dominated the Yiddish stage was an eternal reminder to build the Yiddish theater! And our task, our goal, is to create something we never had and always strove for—the Yiddish theater.

We do not agree with those who assume that Yiddish theater has its own special laws, must feed on a specific repertoire, and must not depart from daily life, or, what is called in Russian, *byt*.

We say: Yiddish theater is first of all a theater in general, a temple of shining art and joyous creation—a temple where the prayer is chanted in the Yiddish language. We say: The tasks of world theater serve us as the tasks of our theater, and only language distinguishes us from others.

How and what will our theater be? What gods will it serve?

We cannot answer these questions. We don't know our gods . . . We seek them . . .

Seeking—this is the word we put at the head of our program . . . We shall seek roads for the actors, as for the director, the painter, and the playwright.

We shall not stand still for a moment. And, perhaps, in seeking a path, we will have to stray, perhaps we will make gods for ourselves whom we will later topple from their thrones . . .

Perhaps . . . But one thing will serve as our justification—our will to find the right path to the true gods.

I have the great honor to be a leader of the first Yiddish theater. And today, with a serious feeling of the responsibility I assumed, opening the doors of the theater to the general audience for the first time, I beg everyone who has come to our little lights to transfer the whole weight of criticism and carping to us, the leaders, and not to touch the studio workers—because none of them thinks he is ripe enough to appear before your observing and serious eyes, for each of them treats reverently the task he has set himself—to become an actor of the Yiddish theater. And if, today, they stand face to face with you, it is only because they fulfill the disciplinary requirements of their leaders.

We found it necessary to open our doors so early to the general audience in order to proclaim to everyone, to all who cherish Jewish art, Jewish culture, Jewish theater; to all who are willing to take pains, seek, struggle, and achieve: "Come to us!"

In using the kind proposal of the Yiddish Theater Society to write a few lines for the opening of the Yiddish theater, I cannot refrain from expressing my profound gratitude to all my colleagues in our work for finding a way to devote themselves entirely to the work, for their extraordinary attitude toward the goals and objectives of our studio, for their ability to forget personal interests in the name and for the sake of the common work.

Aleksey Granovsky
Artistic Director of the Yiddish Chamber Theater

M. Rivesman
The Past and the Future of Yiddish Theater

The sad, almost hopeless situation of Yiddish theater is known to everyone who was ever more or less interested in it. We can say that in no area of Jewish art have the Jewish people been so frozen as in the area of theater art. Before our eyes lies a desert with no hint of an oasis. In that desert, no Moses ever appeared, no Pillar of Fire ever arose to eject even for a moment the darkness, the chaos of Yiddish theater. And saddest of all is that those who strayed in the gloomy and broad desert, the Yiddish actors, could not say, "We want to return to Egypt to the fleshpots." . . . No! The Yiddish actor never had a good, satiated day; never has his pharaoh, his bitter lot, shown him a ray of happiness.

If we want to find out why it happened, if we want to ascertain the reasons for the harsh, almost fatal illness, to investigate the source of this poverty and, let us say it openly, this shameful weakness of Jewish theater art, we have to admit that the whole responsibility falls on the cultural elements of the Jewish people.

Until the 1870s, no one even knew or talked about a Yiddish theater. The *Haskala* people with their conspicuous tendency to quote the "Holy Tongue," on the one hand, and the assimilationist elements of the Jewish people, on the other, both were hostile to the "jargon" [Yiddish] and contemptuously put a black seal on the "mother tongue," called it "maidservant." And only such true friends of the Jew as Sh. Abramovich [Mendele Moykher Sforim] had the boldness and courage to write in Yiddish.

If the Yiddish language was a maidservant, the Yiddish theater was her brother. Forty years passed, and throughout that long period the Yiddish language triumphantly showed that it was not a maidservant at all, although it does faithfully and honestly serve the Jewish people. Mendele Moykher Sforim, Sholem-Aleichem, Peretz, Sholem Asch, Frug, Morris Rosenfeld, Yehoash—such names can adorn the finest European literature, and they have indeed crowned the "jargon" with an enduring crown studded with the most precious diamonds. And still the Yiddish stage remained poor, neglected, and debased, morally and artistically downtrodden, almost as it was forty years ago.

The Jewish intelligentsia, the Jewish art patrons, showed no sign of attention to Yiddish theater. A sickly weakling, it was born in southern Russia forty years ago and has remained anemic and weak to this day. The pioneer of Yiddish theater, Abraham Goldfaden, may have been cultural and talented to a certain extent; but he had absolutely no idea of theater art in the European sense of the word. With no plan, no view toward the future of the Yiddish theater art, he laid the first feeble stone for the Yiddish theater building, and the material, the bricks he took for this building, were so weak, the building was shaky from the first day. Its architecture was far from an aesthetic taste, from what is called art. The first Yiddish actors were ignorant artisans, often people who left their workshops looking for an easier piece of bread, mostly promiscuous young people for whom acting on the stage was the same as a "Purim-shpil." With no literary taste, no sign of intellectual development, they played, sang, and danced, and were happy when the rich contractors in Romania burst out laughing at their "Purim-shpil" barbs. Today a lover, the next day a "Kuni-Lemel" [shlemiel], tomorrow a witch, the Yiddish actors, as it were, did not feel their shame and "thundered"—as they put it—in the same manner wherever the police allowed them to. The Jewish cultural elements stood at a distance, criticized, mocked, but did not dip a finger in cold water to remove all ugliness and clumsiness from the Yiddish theater. Chaos reigned: you will find no art, no direction, on the Yiddish stage. And if you recall such talented Yiddish actors as, for example, Kaminskaya, Edelman, Zhelyazo, Libert, and others, you must admit with deep grief and despair that those talented actors, too, were content with the heavy atmosphere prevailing on the Yiddish stage; that they, too, never protested the contemptuous order, never strove to progress; and for that very reason, they regressed. Their god was Gordin; to him they bowed and knelt and brought offerings. But those offerings had no sweet smell of art either, for the altar, the Yiddish stage, remained dirty, desecrated by ignorance and frivolity.

Yes, there were moments when rays seemed to appear, which were supposed to illuminate the darkness of Yiddish theater art, the mundane dusk in which it was covered like a mourner. The immortal Peretz wanted to be Samson and rip the chain binding Yiddish theater art. He traveled through cities and towns, screamed "Save us!" rattled an alms box inscribed with the terrible words "Charity saves from death." But it didn't help. Kuni-Lemel and the Witch Yakhne screamed louder, the Jewish intelligentsia didn't respond, the portly Jewish patron carefully hid his wallet, and the Yiddish stage remained a dirty, promiscuous maidservant, laughing wildly, dancing, making ugly grimaces, here, in Russia, and overseas—in America. The same lot fell to the poor, sickly, and talented Perets Hirshbeyn, who tried to start a new page in the Book of Lamentations of the Yiddish theater. Neglected, rejected, despairing, filled with grief and rage, he had to fall like a scorned Don Quixote and buried all his hopes. Swindlers, speculators, dead souls, good-for-nothings, ignoramuses governed the Yiddish stage, and *Holy Sabbath* gave way to the play *To Be a Jew; The Jewish Core* irritated along with *The Soul of My People* and other trash.

And only a year ago a mournful shout was heard: "How long?" Till when will the immortal "Kuni-Lemel" and the screaming "Witch Yakhne" dominate? The shout was issued by the newborn Yiddish Theater Society.

Of course, from shouting to doing is a long way. We must, however, admit that the shout resonated among a small group of people, and the "dry bones" of the Yiddish theater art caught the attention of several social activists. The positive result was that, for the first time, not a dilettante but a professional, A. M. Azarkh [Granovsky], became interested in the Yiddish theater. He gave a lecture to the Drama Section, where he developed a plan to create a theater studio, modeled on European theater studios. With courageous energy, he strove to realize his plan, and—let there be light—the doors of the Yiddish theater were opened.

The first Yiddish theater studio set serious objectives for itself. It encountered great difficulties on its path. It experienced grave doubts, moments of groping and of despair. But it has come to life—it demands existence. It wants to produce the kernel from which a normal Yiddish theater, Yiddish theater art in a European sense, will develop. It wants the future Yiddish actor to be first of all a true professional, to respect the art he wants to serve. It wants the Yiddish stage to become a "Holy Place," the Yiddish actor to feel responsibility for his work; though a son of his people, he will, at the same time, be a faithful son of art in the highest and finest sense of the word. It wants the most talented Yiddish writers to create for the Yiddish stage, aware that their work will not be profaned, that the Yiddish actor and the Yiddish audience will respect the place that holds up a mirror to Jewish life. It wants to refresh the dirty, moldy Yiddish repertoire and illuminate it with masterful translations and truly literary, original dramatic works. In short—it strives, and the striving is, in itself, a great achievement. The will to create something better and more serious will be its advocate; the call, the waking, must attract the attention of the best Jewish cultural forces.

We believe we are standing on the threshold of a new Yiddish theatrical age. We believe the revolution that wants to destroy the old, sick building of the former Yiddish theater will bring good fruits. We believe the activity of the young Yiddish "Chamber Theater" will be treated not with disparaging criticism, a suspicious smile, a shrug—but with empathy, with seriousness of word and deed. We believe those who will criticize will honestly admit that every beginning is hard, that only he who does nothing makes no mistakes.

The situation of Yiddish theater today is harsh and bitter. But even harsher are the conditions, the hostile atmosphere in which one has to work, which can be defined as "plenty of critics and few doers." . . .

So come, writers, experienced professionals, musicians, painters! Answer our call

Solomon Mikhoels as King Lear, *in* King Lear *by William Shakespeare, 1935. Translated into Yiddish by Shmuel Halkin. Directors: Sergey Radlov and Solomon Mikhoels. Set design: Aleksandr Tyshler. Music: Lev Pulver.*

and courageously help build a beautiful, strong, and truly Yiddish-European theater building! Don't stand aside, bring bricks and clay—and let the language of the builders not be confounded. Let us understand and empathize with one another. Let us strive for the sun with the tower we are building, and let us remember that only in unity, in a united striving and will, lies the future of the new Yiddish theater.

M. Rivesman
Literary Director of the Yiddish Chamber Theater

Sh. Mikhoels
In Our Studio

. . . Outside, the revolutionary wave raged. Human eyes and too-human thoughts, scared and scattered, were blinking in the chaos of destruction and the chaos of becoming . . .

Mikhoels as King Lear.

. . . At a time when worlds sank, cracked, and changed into new worlds, a miracle occurred, perhaps still small, but very big and meaningful for us Jews—the Yiddish theater was born.

And like every miracle, it came suddenly and unexpectedly.

We studio pupils were sitting dispersed and scattered, each in his own corner. The cold of Diaspora scrunched us up . . . we could only dream of what has now become a reality . . . each of us felt the great need for a Jewish theater-temple. Some of us had already experienced hard tests in their life, but . . . the tests ended the way any creative initiative in the Jewish world ends. We serious seekers were tripped up in our progress by the story of Shtif,* which smothered every spark of hope with an atrocious force . . . And we were falling under the lashes of the heavy whip of fate . . . But now: "A heavy hammer splinters glass and also forges the arms for battle." The same story of

---

* Nokhem Shtif (1879–1933) was a Yiddish linguist, political activist, and academic. The story referred to here is not clear.

Benjamin Zuskin as the Fool in King Lear.

Shtif, which bent us and dropped us to our knees, at the same time raised the one we needed, the man who said the first needed word.

He came to us armed with European education, theatrical know-how, and great organizational forces . . . he called us and became our leader . . .

Two feelings struggled in our hearts: the great will to create on the stage in the Jewish world and the internal doubt in our own strength . . . Indeed, who were we?— lonely dreamers with fuzzy strivings; what did we bring with us—except for oppressed and tense limbs and internal constriction, complete ignorance and helplessness in stage work and stage technique?—nothing . . . Yet one thing each of us had—an ardent will and readiness for sacrifice . . . And our leader told us it was enough . . .

Our leader . . . I cannot talk here about talent or artistic trends.

For us, he is the highest authority and the last word in this respect.

But we studio pupils see what is still concealed from everybody . . . We see the labor filled with sacrifice, the love of art and the people, and the rich content filled with ideas, which breathes in his work!

Scene from King Lear.

. . . It was in January . . . We all assembled for the first time . . . We came as strangers from distant places, each one with his own dreams and steeped in his own thoughts . . . The scale of ages here had many rungs: young, very young, medium, older; from different levels of society and with different social situations. Some of our colleagues had had a harsh life. Some of our colleagues are not only mothers but even grandmothers. Apparently, the love of the nation and of creation is deep and great; apparently, the voices of our calling spoke loud when they could not be stifled by the dark of our Diaspora destiny . . .

. . . We strayed in the big, many, barely furnished rooms of our studio . . . And it was hard to believe that, in a flash, we would all be united into one family, breathing one desire, and that the cold rooms would be transformed into a temple . . .

This we felt by the second day.

This was influenced by the magical power of our leader.

Our first steps . . . they were helpless and childishly insecure.

Evening. The light of the chandelier illuminates the fervent faces of the studio workers . . . "First and foremost is the imagination. Only what becomes real to you through
the force of your imagination also becomes real for your audience. With the sharpness
of your imagination, you must *see* snow-white, sky-high mountains, green fields, blue
infinite distances, for your audience really to forget the cardboard and other decorative conditions of the stage set . . ." . . . This is a lecture devoted to stagecraft, those are
the words of our leader . . . He calls a colleague to him. We are all very curious: what
role will be assigned him . . . Silence—you can hear only breathing. "You're the head
of a great army . . . you're anxiously watching the development of the bloody struggle
between millions of soldiers . . . With one gesture, you hurl the last reserves into the
breach . . . You are waiting: 'Victor or slave?' asks your face . . ."

. . . The colleague sits down and this time, our attentive ear did not perceive the
"Thanks" with which our teacher evokes a smile of satisfaction on the student's face.
"Yeah," everyone thinks, "it's hard for the Diaspora Jew to transform himself into a Napoleon . . ." All studio pupils go through this exercise . . . And as we left the teaching hall,
several faces glowed with satisfaction . . . A Napoleon was found, and not just one . . .

"Not you, not any person, not any feeling, not any movement, now only the idea
lives on the stage." . . . "An idea sweeps over the stage, an Idea with a capital 'I' . . .
and . . . you are only its attribute." . . . That is how he explains one moment of a play
in rehearsal . . . And it becomes clear: to create means first of all to think . . . first of
all to know . . .

We are working . . . no one notices time passing. Often you go home unhappy that
the working day went by so fast . . . We are consoled by the expectation of the next day
. . . We are working . . . Our work is a prayer; we kneel to the gods and all we know of
them is that they are great and beaming and accept a serious prayer . . .

"The most important thing is the emotional side of creation . . . You must tap the
secret well of your soul. I seek the key of your internal creativity . . . and when you
cry—tears must flow from your eyes, and when you laugh, you must illuminate the
faces of your audience with a radiant smile." This is what our leader demands.

And we, even those who had become hard and cold to the rapping of destiny, who
had forgotten about tears even when the venom of death choked off the air around
them, even they dropped heavy, hot, big tears . . . Some who picked up the rumor of
such exercises called it "vivisection." . . . Our leader has a different opinion . . . So do
we . . . The tears gave birth to a feeling of great happiness in our hearts . . .

"Stagecraft consists of four elements: light, sets, music, and Man . . . You must give the stage Man . . ."

We could only give ourselves, the Jew; . . . to give the stage *Man* with a capital "M," man in general—this became our goal . . .

The voice might be transformed from Jacob's into a universal human voice, but the hands were still Jacob's hands . . . Our feet trod insecure, our hands were tied—a Jew can only walk like a Jew, and when he speaks, he must call for help with his hands, with their wild gestures—this is how many thought.

The stage needs first of all Man in general . . . this was one of our leader's lines . . . and his great truth is clear to us . . .

And when we got the list of our repertoire, which did not contain any genre play or mores play, it was unexpected and unintelligible to only a few of us . . .

This is not a Jewish theater—they complained. Not a single play from Jewish life.

"If you're going to put on plays of mores—you will show only yourself . . . The realistic repertoire is what lies on top of a mountain we climb!" . . .

To our temple came the Jewish souls who are happy with the creative sacrifice . . . And in the first row are our teachers, who lead our work . . .

The famous writer M. S. Rivesman . . . is also a prominent figure in our group . . . And if our main leader conducts the abstract work in our art workshop, M.S. is the one who injects the Jewish cultural stream into our creation . . . But we see not just what he creates, but how he creates . . . Day and night, in our literary editing meetings, in the classes on the Yiddish language, his eye gleams with excitement, and his word glows with the enthusiasm of hope . . .

I remember . . . a rehearsal goes on under the artistic direction of R. A. Unger[-Shternberg] . . . M.S. assists as literary director . . . One of the colleagues who acts in the piece tries and cannot yet find the required tone . . . Suddenly a voice is heard: "Permit me, R.A., I shall explain to him in Yiddish what you require." And M.S. stands up and fills the role of our colleague . . . Only this way could he curb his enthusiasm.

. . . The leaders of the musical part in the studio . . .

. . . Z. Rosovsky, Z. Kisselgoff, Joseph Tomars . . . Those who already devoted a lot of effort to Jewish music.

How much fanatical belief in the task you need to convey the hope that our voices will be able to form a harmonious choir in such a short time. But their task is the Jewish national aspect of music . . . In the long winter evenings, I remember, they would come in toward the last hours of our work with pale faces, dull and weary after a long, heavy, prosaic day . . . But they were soon steeped in the holiness of our studio atmosphere . . . and songs would mix with folktales, and studies of melodies with whole lectures about Hasidic music . . .

We learned "to think as we create," we learned to seek not just the feeling but also the idea of the melody . . .

This was the principle of our leader and of our most talented music teachers . . .

"Creative excitement knows no national borders . . . Creativity is felt and excites with a universal force . . . We must learn from the nations that know more and better than us . . . We must take from them everything that can strengthen us in our work." . . . Our leader also invited Christian artists as teachers.

And the serious attitude from the hearts of our beloved Christian teachers toward our new theatrical edifice, their complete devotion to the work, is the best illustration of what we said above . . . The new work enveloped them completely . . . The mime class and some stagings are conducted by R. A. Unger-Shternberg . . .

He's so interested in our language that he asks us to help him study Yiddish . . . One of our studio pupils gave him an alphabet as a gift and made the director so happy. R.A. often scolds the pupils for their lack of knowledge of the Yiddish language . . .

One of his many rehearsals is under way . . . he's immersed in the work . . . his gaze is strict and demanding . . . with an appropriate tension, he observes the faces of the rehearsing studio pupils . . . and suddenly—a bright smile smoothed the tense lines on his forehead: we know the joyous cause—in the foreign language, he heard some familiar words . . .

He already knows quite a few . . . even Hebrew words . . .

"The Word is the greatest weapon of stage creation. Its value lies not only in speech but in silence . . . The normal state is silence . . . The Word is a whole event, a supernormal state of Man . . . The intervals of silence between the phrases and moods in human utterances are the background from which the great, meaningful Word emerges . . ."

This is how our leader defined the value of the word in his early explanations, which he, as director, presented to us when he started the work on Maeterlinck's play *The Blind*.

The word class is conducted by the actress K. A. Aleneva.

The voice—the word—is Man's most intimate aspect. And the uneasy timidity with which each of us demonstrated to our teacher his potential of voice—and word—can be understood . . . "I myself am seeking—let us seek together"—with the open Russian simplicity, she told us . . . And she evoked the best feelings in our studio . . .

The teaching is conducted in Russian . . . the study of Yiddish diction is still a task for the future which our studio activity has to reach . . .

The weaker colleagues attract the greatest and wonderfully patient attention of our teacher . . . and she extracts gold and silver notes, copper and steel voices . . .

She is our close friend . . .

"The movement in the scene has a difficult task . . . It must overcome the distance from the actor to the audience . . . Therefore it must be meaningful and whole . . . A movement must be logically articulated into its basic elements as a complex algebraic formula is broken down into its simple multipliers.

The normal state [of Man] is static . . . The movement is an event, a supernormal state . . . Every move must start from the static state, which is the main background from which the meaningful movement emerges . . ."

This was one of our leader's favorite themes . . . He devoted a great deal of effort and substantive exercises to that side of our artistic education . . .

As I said above, movement, arms and legs, was our weakest point . . . and for our movement education, he invited the famous ballet master of the imperial theater, B. A. Romanov, who conducted the class of rhythmical movement, plastics, and dance . . . I cannot forget the impact and enthusiasm evoked in us by his first exercise class . . . Every movement B.A. demonstrated was so refined, so logical and meaningful, that after he left, we stood enchanted for a long time and lamented our movement limbs, still dead and tiny and insignificant. He taught us the economy of movement. Every movement is the result of experience; it accompanies the word . . . Movement is an expression of the idea . . . The same principle . . . The system of our leader . . .

"I see the ensemble performance, the stage action, as a choral action . . ." Our leader shared with us his views on art . . . "Every type, everybody's movement, everybody's acting, painting, every role of individuality in the play, is only a part of the architectonic whole . . . Our artistic goal is the play as a whole . . . And the value and significance of the smallest role is great in its relation to the whole dramatic construct . . . One false performance of a word, or a move, not just of the central figure in a play but of the smallest and most overshadowed, can corrupt and cheapen the whole artistic image . . ."

. . . Now we know it . . . We know how great is the work of the theater artist . . .

With a holy feeling and modesty, we approach our work . . . And everyone feels: the architectonic whole is actually even broader and greater . . . This is the spiritual edifice of the Yiddish theater, and we . . . we play in it the small role of the first experimental materials . . . And many of us say: Our task is only to be at the guard post until central figures come to us, and prominent great individual talents . . . But as for the future totality . . . and the joy that fills our hearts . . . we dream of the future wholeness of the Yiddish theater.

Mikhoels
Actor of the Yiddish Chamber Theater

CHAPTER FIVE

The Reception of the Moscow Yiddish Theater
in the West

Contemporary Responses to the Moscow Yiddish Theater (Excerpts)

Huntley Carter   1926, Russian[*]

By a happy coincidence, the first productions I managed to see were the performances of the Moscow State Yiddish Theater. The new productions of the theater reinforced in me the deep conviction that the work of GOSET has no equal in Europe. What is so impressive is how they employ all the theatrical means in the service of the plot, the outstanding economy and simplicity of the structures—the absence of any foreign elements. The interaction of all movements, sounds, and decorations achieves a stunning effect. The subordination of all elements of the performance to the basic idea of the production embodies something utterly new. Compared to Granovsky's theater—the significance of the contemporary English theaters is negligible.

Society for Cultural Relations with the USSR   1925, Russian[†]

Of all the immense achievements of the Moscow theaters we saw, we were most strongly impressed by the productions of the State Yiddish Theater (*At Night in the Old Marketplace, The Sorceress*, 200,000). The delegation, composed of scientists, writers, artists, journalists of Czecho-Slovakia, especially values the creative work of the towering

---

[*]Interview with the English theater critic Huntley Carter, who was on a visit to Russia; the interview was published in *Leningradskaya krasnaya gazeta*, August 30, 1926. Carter wrote several books on the Russian theater of his time.

[†]A Czecho-Slovakian delegation of the Society for Cultural Relations with the USSR, including Professor Mathesius, who later became president of the Prague Linguistic Circle (the scientific forum of Czech Structuralism), and the architect Karel Taige, theoretician of the avant-garde.

Scene from 200,000—A Musical Comedy, *based on Sholem-Aleichem's* The Winning Ticket.

director Granovsky, who, in a wasteland, from absolutely "nothing" (that was the Jewish stage art before him)—could create a theater of immense cultural importance.

Moscow, November 3, 1925

Alfons Goldschmidt   1925, German[*]

Once, in the evening, I found myself in the Moscow State Yiddish Theater. It is a theatrical vision we have never seen. Here we see a truly new spirit . . .

The art of the Moscow State Yiddish Theater—is reality. It has nothing in common with that "realism" which is no more than a "true" leaf covering naked problematics and decay. Similarly, the masques of the Yiddish theater—are reality itself, and to such an extent that not only is each one clear separately, and apparently full of vitality, but all together appear connected in their life and lifeblood. Precisely because theater here

---

[*]A German theater critic.

has become life itself, i.e., life in the deepest sense of life development, the masques, too, have become alive in their interrelations. In other words, a truly collective kernel has emerged here, capable of entering the vital blossoming future.

Alfons Goldschmidt, Berlin, 1925

Niko Rost   1924, Russian[*]

Here I saw what I did not see in the State theaters: the fruitful and profound influence of the Revolution. In this theater, for the first time, stage art is shown as the art of the collective. This assumption, asserted by all the ideologues of Soviet theater and verbally defended by the leaders of the State theaters, is realized here, only in this theater. The performances are dominated by the grotesque, a stunning or deadly irony. This is evident, it is the breeze of the Revolution hovering above the actors, the theater, the production; the Revolution the theater absorbed in itself. There can be no talk of tenderness—the whole performance is a ringing, living truth.

Niko Rost, Amsterdam, 1924

Alfred Kerr   1928, German[†]

They act in Yiddish, sing and dance. Everything in a marvelous rhythm. They present an outstanding mixture of precision and fantasy.

The evening has no dead point.

K...r [Kerr]

Nakhmen Mayzel   1928, Yiddish[‡]

Speaking of Granovsky's theater, the name Tairov was always used. [...] But in essence, the Yiddish theater is very different from [Tairov's] Russian Chamber Theater. Play of colors, rhythm of movement, word and gesture, become ends in themselves, the

---

[*]A Dutch critic.

[†]"The Moscow Yiddish Academic Theater in Theater des Westens," *Berliner Tageblatt*, April 12, 1928—a review by a major Berlin theater critic of the first performance by GOSET in the Theater des Westens.

[‡]"The Great Stage Miracle," *Literarishe bleter* (Warsaw), 5, no. 17 (April 27, 1928). Mayzel was a Yiddish literary critic.

Scene from 200,000.

beginning and end of theater life. There it is not departure or dawn, curse or blessing for a dying life, and a rising up, imagined, dreamed of. Careless theater performance, which is a value in itself. While, in the Yiddish theater—burden of generations, the hump of a hunchbacked mundane lifestyle you want to throw off, tear out, and it is so hard, and often—as it happens with true artists and poets—they come to curse and find themselves blessing . . .

The Yiddish theater began to reveal all the valuable things the preceding generation, or generations, created—both positive and negative—in literature, music, lifestyle. To reveal—not in a photographic-faithful, ethnographic-precise manner, but in a grotesque, theatrical way. Not a direct continuation of literature (like the Moscow Stanislavsky theater), nor as an antipode, a denial of literature (like Tairov's theater). Creating on the stage not classical types with all their literary, psychological, and lifestyle excrescence and thicket, but pointed stage characters, with sharp edges, all the movements, gestures, grimaces, tones, and motifs that Jewish life of the past and Yiddish classical literature have created.

Scene from 200,000.

Aleksander Granach   1928, Yiddish*

"You Comedians!" This is what your sorcerer Granovsky likes to call you; and because he uses this word, it becomes noble, and with the word—the whole class of
Comedians.

The comedians of the whole world should pay homage to Granovsky with a wreath of
trembling clown-hearts and a barrel of clown's tears, for his art, his essence, his world
is built on feelings covered with makeup and tears muted with thunder. Mikhoels, his
chief clown, is the clown of God. Mikhoels is no longer a character, a type; no, he is
the embodiment of many generations of this race—which cries no longer—in the sigh,
you no longer hear the pain, but the strength that can bear the pain and conquer it.

---

*"Granovsky, Mikhoels, and Zuskin—Congratulations!" Literarishe bleter (Warsaw), no. 20 (1928), p. 390.
Granach was a Yiddish and German actor-director.

Solomon Mikhoels as Shimele Soroker in Sholem-Aleichem's The Winning Ticket, *1923.*

Alfred Kerr
The Moscow Yiddish Theater   1928, German[*]

I

This is great art. Great art.

External image and soul-shaking. The sound of words, the sound of blood, the sound of color, the sound of images. There are calls, voices, questions, shouts, choruses. It is enjoyment and horror . . . and in the end, human communion.

That is, of course, pantomime with movement into eternity. Something wonderful. (Great art.)

[*]Published in Hugo Fetting, ed., *Mit Schleuder und Harfe: Theaterkritiken aus drei Jahrzehnten* (Berlin: Henschelverlag, 1981).

II

Yet it is only half pantomime. Mortals differing in occupation, age, beliefs, sex, and class, whirl around, calling, talking, singing, complaining, lamenting, shouting, snickering, praying, and bawling all night in the Old Market of a time-covered, world-forsaken nest somewhere in Podolye . . . or anywhere else.

Walls, gray dusk, angularity, age rust, mouse holes—and grave holes . . . And grave holes.

(A profound Yiddish summit path.)

III

Lowlands, bastions, bridges, heights, corners, stairs.

There: the synagogue (say *Shul*, with the preserved German word). Up above, the church.

Light in the synagogue. Steps to the church . . . Popular rabbis (*Rabbonim*) shoo away, pace, wander over the marketplace. Deacons sing up above.

IV

The people go home. Lantern lighters. Night watchmen. Streetwalkers—with naked bellybuttons. Lingerers. Strollers. Staggerers. Night brutalities. Scamps. Vulgarity. Children in the dark. Warning voices. Shadows. Latecomers. Musicians. Noises. Vital admonitions.

Everything shoos, whirls, leaps, creeps, stalks, slinks, reels, climbs, flits, roams, dwindles, twinkles, sinks.

Something wonderful.

V

How strong the director Granovsky is in all that. What I present here in words, he has created palpably and visibly.

The little Mikhoels, a great actor, flies, hovers, darts, does gymnastics, crowns, sparkles, flies and sings: like a Puck on the Hebrew Day of Atonement, Yom Kippur, the most dreadful and introverted of all human holidays. Like an angel of death who makes himself into a buffoon.

A second fool, or *badkhn*, the actor Zuskin, always near him, against him. Like the hurricane.

VI

Both laugh, tickle, play tricks, fly—and squeak to heaven:

> Got, Got
> Iz bankrot[*]

One of the jesters roars on the edge of the well . . . Soul twilight breaks open. The dead are called out of the grave. (The explanation says: "The Hour has rung.")

VII

In the second part of this unprecedented mournful buffoonery, the dead really do clamber out of the grave. (Underlying is a work of the deceased Yiddish poet Y.-L. Peretz: *At Night in the Old Marketplace*. It is a fantasy of the Hasidic sect.)

Lemurs' farce and Temple seriousness. Distant singing. Mouldering faces. Coffin monkeys. Brides and grooms. The *Khosn* and the *Kale* [bridegroom and bride]—both dead. Waving to one another. Has been . . . says Liliencron. (And noble songs composed by Johannes Brahms.) Is a life even conceivable? Possible to hope for? They would all like to come back to the world . . . "when I was still prince of Arcady . . ."

VIII

This is immortal. Something hardly known on stage before. The dead are even still waiting for the Messiah . . . (Pronounced here "Moshiach.") The dead say their prayers . . .

Everything profound in every human literature grows here into magnificent enormity. Incomparable.

IX

Those slaughtered by the pogroms march by; show their sword wounds. Holiness shines over all the dancing and all the chatter and all the leaping and all the sparkling

---

[*]"God, God / Is bankrupt."—Toward the end of *At Night in the Old Marketplace* by Y.-L. Peretz, performed in Granovsky's theater.

and all the shadows . . . on the nocturnal market of a world-shaken nest in Podolye . . . or wherever else.

Finally, one seems to recite the Prayer for the Dead, or the Kaddish (but for the stage, one more round is made, which is too much).

X

Every name remains to be mentioned. All. With a quarter of a hundred, this is certainly impossible. So only: Aleksandr Krein—music. R. Falk—color designs.

Of the actors . . . merely according to the charm of the sound of the names (for there are thirty): Finkelkraut; Lurie; Silberblatt; Rottbaum; Ingster; Ashkenazi.

XI

Great art. Great art.

October 10, 1928

David Ben-Gurion
Diary (Excerpt)

1923, Hebrew[*]

Moscow, 14 Kislev, 11/22/23

This evening, I attended the State Yiddish Chamber Theater. They presented Sholem-Aleichem's *Two Hundred Thousand*. As in all other theaters, here too there was a Jewish audience, although Russian was the only language heard in the auditorium. And there were no laborers among the audience here either. The words written mockingly by *Emes*[†] about HaBima also applied to this theater. "It doesn't exist for the Jewish working masses either. In Moscow, there are a lot of theaters for the NEP audience,[‡] and among them there is also—the '[Yiddish] Chamber Theater.'"

Most of the audience were NEP people and their fat wives, embellished with gold earrings and bracelets, décolleté, and viewing through opera glasses.

The acting is "leftist." They sit on roofs, ledges, and stairs, don't walk but hop, don't

---

[*]Itzhak Norman, ed. *Be-reyshit Ha-Bima* (Jerusalem: The Jewish Agency, 1966), pp. 241–242.

[†]*Der emes* (The Truth)—Yiddish Communist Party newspaper, parallel to the Russian *Pravda*.

[‡]NEP is Lenin's New Economic Policy, allowing some private business and commerce. NEPmen were the nouveaux riches.

go up but clamber, don't come down but tumble and leap—Sholem-Aleichem is unrecognizable. The characters are caricatures. Only the end of the fourth act is wonderful!
Marvelous acting movements, slightly reminiscent of the dance in *The Dybbuk*. Indeed,
there is no connection between that scene and the play as a whole. But the hushed
singing, the rhythm of the movements of Shimele and the two actresses on either side
of him, the soft and sad tune, the silence of all the huddled actors and their subtle,
rhythmic movements—all is steeped in harmony and beauty.

1928, German*

Ernst Toller

A Salute to the Yiddish National Theater

One day, Radek asked me: "Have you been to the Yiddish State Theater yet? Go there soon; it is one of the best theaters we have in Russia."

I went once, and I went back again—I saw all the plays in the repertoire. The director of the Yiddish State Theater is named Granovsky, one of the strongest directing talents I have encountered.

You don't find any false romanticism in this theater, whose collective unity stands out even in the life of the Russian stage.

The stage figures: Jews, who want to live like their fathers and forefathers, between the Talmud and haggling, are gripped by the pace, the mechanical compulsion of the time, defend themselves, yet must obey it.

Granovsky's opponents say he makes fun of Jewish ghetto life, doesn't distinguish between appearance and reality. That is wrong. With agitated bodies and gestures, Granovsky makes the tragedy of these people turn somersaults, as it were; they are scared and smile at the comedy they drag into the framework of everyday life.

"The old God is bankrupt," a voice says in *At Night in the Old Marketplace*.

It is wonderful to see how reality and vision, word and gesture, light and music, are bound into a theatrical unity; how the movement of one actor is taken up by the chorus of others, as when an orchestra rechannels, and accompanies the isolated individual voice.

---

*Ernst Toller, Joseph Roth, and Alfons Goldschmidt, *Das Moskauer Jüdische Akademische Theater* (Berlin: Verlag Die Schmiede, 1928); binding and logo by Georg Salter. Reproduced here as Chapter 6 is the whole text of the book published in Berlin on the occasion of the theater's visit to Germany. The book was illustrated with photographs from actual performances, some of which are reproduced here. On the publisher, see Hermann and Schmitz, *Der Verlag Die Schmiede*.

Scene from The Travels of Benjamin the Third: Epos in Three Acts, *based on a novel by Mendele Moykher Sforim alluding to* Don Quixote. *Adaptation: Yikhezkel Dobrushin, 1927. Director: Aleksey Granovsky. Set design: Robert Falk. Music: Lev Pulver.*

The performances of *The Sorceress* and *At Night in the Old Marketplace* were unforgettable evenings.

Granovsky will find a ready audience both in Europe and in America.

Joseph Roth
The Moscow Yiddish Theater

It has been fifteen years since I attended a Yiddish theater for the first time. It [the famous traveling Vilna Troupe] came from Vilna to Leopoldstadt [the Jewish immigrants' quarter in Vienna]. I still remember the posters clearly. They were distinguished from the announcements of other theaters by a very definite simplicity, a so-called makeshift roughness, a primitive coarseness; they were theater programs with no tradition, probably produced with a handpress. Made of cheap and loud yellow paper, without margins, stuck haphazardly on walls and not on the official poster boards, put up in nasty smelly corners, they attracted attention and had a stronger effect than refined

The scene "Benjamin's Dream" from The Travels of Benjamin the Third.

advertisements. They were composed in a language you could often hear in the little coffeehouses of the Jewish quarter, but which seemed to consist only as sound, never in written form. On these posters, Yiddish was written in Latin letters. It was like a grotesque German. Coarse and delicate at the same time. Many words were German with Slavic diminutive endings. If you spelled them out slowly, they sounded ridiculous. If you spoke them fast, they sounded affectionate.

In the evening, on the stage, they were spoken fast. An operetta was performed. One of those operettas from the infancy of the Yiddish theater, called *Tragedies with Song and Dance.* I have never found these words ridiculous. They never seemed to me to contain a contradiction, except that I never thought of ancient tragedy. It was enough to think of everyday Jewish life, which is a kind of tragedy with song and dance. I saw several of the operettas; they were kitschy, whiny, and yet true. Their problematic—for these operettas contained problems—was clumsy, their action was accidental, their characters were extremely typical, their situations seemed to exist only for the songs that characterized them. But these songs really formed the artistic significance of the Yiddish

Solomon Mikhoels (right) as Benjamin (Don Quixote) and Benjamin Zuskin as Senderl di Yidene ("Senderl the Woman," Sancho Panza) in The Travels of Benjamin the Third.

theater. These songs (mostly folk songs, Oriental and Slavic melodies, performed by untrained voices, but sung with the heart rather than the throat, and repeated at the end by everyone), these songs justified the Yiddish theater. Their ballad-like texts dramatically summed up the proceedings that had just been played out with awkward dilettantism. Behind the content, not next to it, the melody sounded. The words and events were in it. Therefore, you imagined far behind the melodies the great fate they were a small part of. Therefore, far behind them, dense and foggy, stretched a world you knew would be the tragedy which sent only singing and dancing onto the stage and hadn't yet revealed itself. What was behind the primitive Yiddish stage was high, tragic art and the justification for the stage.

Mikhoels as Benjamin and Zuskin as Senderl in The Travels of Benjamin
the Third.

Later, over the years, I have seen three or four other Yiddish acting troupes in various
Western cities. I regretted the European development that threatened to take over the
Yiddish theater. I was sorry it fell victim to the strict European distinctions between
the so-called dramatic categories. That it wanted to produce "pure tragedies" and had
decided to follow the Western theater—without Western traditions. That Shalom Asch
could be played on the German stage almost without change or concession seemed
to me a proof of the decline of the Yiddish theater, not its rise, as was proclaimed. I

Mikhoels as Benjamin and Zuskin as Senderl in The Travels of Benjamin the Third.

have never stopped thinking of Sholem Asch as a Yiddish brother of Sudermann. That a Western, civilized, shallow, watered-down layer of emigrant Jewry saw their European ambitions satisfied by the sight of a "modern" Jewish play, constructed along Western dramatic rules, seemed to me just as foolish as the childish joy of naïve Zionists about the good hits of Palestinian marksmen and all the fighting mischief called the "rebirth of the Jewish nation."

I didn't understand this ambition that called itself "national," but was only an ambition for civilization. Why not "Tragedy with Song and Dance?" Why not rough, yellow theater programs, produced with a handpress, poor but conspicuous? Why not an unpunctual beginning, why not dressing rooms and infants in the auditorium, why not an endlessly long intermission? Why all of a sudden this solid, European reliability, this closing time, this prohibition to wear your hat, smoke, and eat oranges in the auditorium?

Only once—in Paris—have I again seen such an unruly Eastern theater in the Jewish quarter. There were only a few performances. It was a poor itinerant theater. They sang songs there I had heard fifteen years earlier in Leopoldstadt. "Tragedies with Song and Dance" were presented; the audience interrupted the actors in the middle of the text; an actor entered, shoved the gesticulating people aside, and gave his little speech, then the play went on; the seats weren't numbered; children's prams stood in the dressing rooms; infants cried in the auditorium.

A few weeks later HaBima came to Paris. I have never seen this Hebrew theater. Of the fourteen million Jews barely three million understand Hebrew, and these three million out of the fourteen million scattered over the whole world are also scattered, so I can't understand the existence of a Hebrew theater. Many experts were thrilled with HaBima. I understand that one is thrilled by a luxury item. It may have artistic value. But the artistic is only the essential.

In the winter of 1926, I attended the Yiddish Theater in Moscow. After the first act, Mr. Granovsky invited me to tea. (Fortunately, the intermissions in Russian theaters are so long you can drink tea.) I was then incapable of formulating an impression. If custom had allowed me to be sincere and not demanded compliments, I would have said the following:

I am shaken and frightened. The harsh glow of the colors has blinded me, the noise deafened me, the vitality of the movement confused me. This theater is no longer an intensified world: it is another world. These actors are no longer bearers of roles, but bewitched bearers of a curse. They speak with voices I have never heard in any theater in the world, they sing with the ardor of despair; when they dance, they remind me of bacchantes, and of Hasidim; their talk is like the prayers of Jews in a *talis* on Yom Kippur and like the loud blasphemies of the Korahites; their movements are like a ritual and a lunacy; the scenes are not set or painted, but dreamed. I need a whole evening to let my ears grow accustomed to this loudness, my eyes to this harshness. I do not yet distinguish between intentional exaggeration and natural (or supernatural) ecstasy. All criteria I bring from the West fail in this theater. That makes me happy, but it doesn't help me.

I need time to get used to the Yiddish theater, its tension, which cannot endure any more intensity, which was there right from the first word of the first entrance to the last word of the play, which was even in the lobby, in its pictures, in the staircases and on the walls. It seems to me that this Jewry portrayed here was a more Oriental one than we usually encounter, a hotter and older one, from other zones. Every idea of the proverbial vitality of Jewish people you may have brought to this theater, was outdone by the vehement gesticulation of the actors. They were Jews of a higher temperature, more Jewish Jews. Their passion was a few degrees more passionate, even their melancholy had the aspect of savagery, their grief was fanatic, their joy a dizziness. It was a kind of Dionysian Jew.

Not until I determined this and tried to imagine myself in the higher climate of the theater could I begin to enjoy the performances critically.

It seemed to me that in the Moscow Yiddish Theater, that world appeared which I had imagined backstage fifteen years earlier in Leopoldstadt, watching a Tragedy with Song and Dance. It seemed to me that the old operettas had finally received their meaning, and the justification of their existence no longer had to be derived from the songs. They had been "transformed," the old songs had gotten new texts (not all new texts are better than the old ones anyway), the tragedies and the comedies were actualized—and it was perhaps not even the intention of the innovators and the transformers to make the Yiddish plays "more authentic," to transform what were pretexts for a play, which they had been, into the purpose of the play. No, I have the impression that the transformation of the accidental into the design of destiny happened unconsciously, and that it was the act of a new Jewish generation, realized by a few of their representatives (Granovsky, the painter Altman, and the extraordinary actor Mikhoels). I deliberately refrain from connecting this Jewish generation with the Russian Revolution to explain the former by the latter. But I have absolutely no doubt that, without the great Russian Revolution, the Moscow Yiddish Theater would have been impossible.

This theater transformed the tradition of the old Yiddish stage so cleverly that it almost looks like a protest against the tradition. But it should not have gone further.

Ultimately, every novelty in art looks like a protest against tradition and yet is its continuation. But the Moscow Yiddish Theater sometimes violates the law, allowing offspring to be an opposition but not to make an opposition. Where Yiddish Theater deliberately goes beyond a formed protest to a rhetorical one, its freedom begins to deteriorate into that quality correctly called "chutzpah."

I could note this chutzpah, but I tried to explain it. It is certainly to be ascribed to the influence of that revolutionary by-product, which I may call "infantile iconoclasm."

It is the expression of a naïve and insecure rationalism, which, instead of negating silently, blasphemes noisily. It accompanied every revolution, and it dishonored every natural and thus holy urge of oppressed people for a free altercation with unknown, for all I know, metaphysical forces. This ridiculous rationalism, which even Darwin discovered in Russia, also exercises its influence on the Yiddish Theater—which otherwise confronts the ridiculous by-products of the Russian Revolution not uncritically. On the contrary: the Yiddish Theater in Moscow is the only place where Yiddish irony triumphs over the censored and even prescribed "revolutionary" passion with a healthy joke. In the Yiddish Theater, that critical gift prevails which is so urgently needed in the official educational institutions of the Soviets and would be sought in vain. But an irony that is still effective against the Narkompros [People's Commissariat of Enlightenment] can only be ridiculously ineffective when presented against the Talmud. A trace of the futile aspiration of the Soviets to make the Jews a "national minority" without religion, like the Kalmyks, is also felt in the Yiddish Theater. Not as if it were its spirit! But it seems to have influenced the worldview of the actors—which is not possible otherwise. For you don't have to be a convinced anti-Semite to know that the Jews gave the world its saints and its blasphemers. Some of them incline to death on the cross. Others to the demolition of crosses. It would be insane to speak of the influence of the Jewish gift for blasphemy on modern Russian rationalism. But we may assume that it is agreeable to many intellectual Russian Jews.

That is the childhood disease of the Yiddish Theater, as of the Russian Revolution, as of every revolution. The theater remains Jewish even when it attacks Jewish traditions. For to attack traditions is an old Jewish tradition. I was also shaken when they were mocked. They caricature—but they caricature in a Jewish way; they are authentic, as authentic as the Children of Israel were when Moses smashed the Ten Commandments.

Alfons Goldschmidt
The Yiddish Theater in Moscow

Authentic theater always plays from below. Authentic theater is nothing but the portrayal of community feelings, community aspirations. It is the playful expression of life itself. It is nothing but the concentration of life on the stage. People are pushed against and toward one another, not like puppets and not as chimeras, but vividly.

Without this direct creation through the medium of the community itself or of one of the community-feeling poets, the theater is no theater. Theater directors and producers who want to strike the taste of the audience from above may be directors and producers, but not presenters of those lively community forces which should be expressed in acting.

I have seen community theater of the Indians in Latin America, direct living theater, which was nothing more than movement and expression of the Indian body and soul, thus theater of interest or theater of intention in the noblest sense. No speculation can be made about such theater, for the authentic theater audience demands the acting of its life and won't be deceived. It certainly wants the performance of the actor, but not a star performance, the fame of one individual, one talent, one beauty, or some quality—it must be absorbed in the collective play if it is to make a truly communal impact; it may not rise ambitiously above the collective on the stage and thus above the totality. Theater from above is artistic theater or theater for the presentation of a few artists with an appendix that no longer belongs organically to them. A genius actor can powerfully unite in himself a mass of actors, or the collective play, express the collective will and the collective yearning in his acting; but those are rare occasions and are not the same as the collective expression on the stage insofar as they [the other actors] inspire and excite, but do not perform as equal to equal but as figures separate from the mass. Consequently, we cannot blend them with the mass, as the collectivity on the stage, which is nothing but the common will itself. When stage and spectator are not one, we cannot talk of an organic theater. It is a basic instinct of humans to want to see themselves; and the entire theatrical art of our time, aside from a few exceptions, does not satisfy this instinct. It is not educational in the highest sense, it is only entertainment. It can be tragic or comic, but it remains separate and, at most, in search of genuine contact.

The second time I was in Moscow, in winter 1925, I was invited to the Yiddish State Theater, directed by Granovsky. I was skeptical because, five years earlier, I had seen individual theater performances in Moscow. But I was told: "Just go; on this stage, you will find a direct acting impression, and not only of the Jewish mass." I thought: If the Soviet Russian state is the firm of a theater, after the Soviet Union has existed for eight years as a community expression, I will certainly find Soviet things on the stage. And in fact it was so. The Soviet Union is the direct representation of and the direct reverberation in the represented masses. This is also how the theater must be if it wants to be a community theater of the newly transformed urge for community. In fact, I found acting that was absolutely connected, not only with me but with all the spectators. It was indeed a Yiddish play, *At Night in the Old Marketplace,* by Peretz; but this particularity was universal. It was only a play. Now and then the movement, the comings and goings, were reinforced by a shout or a grunt. This was not a usual kind of pantomime, but rather the very lively and silent portrayal of a whole epoch in decline. A grandiose history lesson without hero worship.

Nothing was shown on the stage but a funny and weak decadence, the decline of the medieval Jewish epoch with all its peculiar additions, with the tradition of thousands of years that has become distorted, with a rigid God and rigid temple rites, with a dismantled culture in its death throes. These characters leaped, danced, chirped, and swung as living and dead people. A small life, which was not satisfied with itself, but rather officious, underestimating its limits, rotting with the sense of eternity. It was medieval, but so is our time, only with a more intense life and more connections; but the arrogant rottenness is not different from then. To be born or to die in the day, life or death, everything is a dying.

This simple fact of Jewish junk, a period of crisis with universal validity, was portrayed so that I was overcome by a dread of my own fate. It was the play of a genuine community, with the awareness both of events on the stage and the reality in our world. The masks, comic and dreadful, mummies' masks in life and death, were unspeakably urgent. Every bandage, every shroud, every ram's horn, all the trash in the light and in the grave played a part, was part of these bodies, which pressed around each other, through each other, against each other and toward each other, without one star rising presumptuously. The smallest achievement, the middling achievement, the great effort, it was an organic whole. The strongest realism in costume I have ever seen on the stage seemed to me to be genuine theater. Genuine didactic theater, genuine performing theater, genuine connection theater. I sat there, fearful, wishing I could recognize the death of our epoch and stay far away from it by managing to look beyond this grave and preach. I felt a kind of catharsis and I asked myself: What have you done to accelerate the dread so that people, out of the false, sophisticated community, which is really only separation, can become connected?

When I sat in Granovsky's office after the play and told him how moved I was and how happy to have seen this direct expression of a need, the actors came in and there was a real community. There was no higher or lower; you saw friendly discipline, a collectivity of excitement and awareness of the task. They were all friends, comrades for a higher concern than their own lives. Precisely because of that, they gave their own lives to the community and lived them more authentically than before. Granovsky told me that, and I saw the artistic satisfaction, which had nothing more to do with individualistic pride in appearances. Now I hear that this theater is coming to Germany. It should go through the whole world. It is not a Jewish theater in the vulgar sense. It is a real world theater, for the great phases of the development of the world were revealed to me from this stage. The decline was portrayed, the rise must follow. If we understand our horrible epoch, how should we not have the wish to change it by overcoming it?

Y. [Osip] Mandelshtam
The Moscow State Yiddish Theater
1926, Russian[*]

On the wooden walkways of an unsightly Byelorussian shtetl—a big village with a brick factory, a beer hall, front yards, and cranes—shuffled a strange figure with long hems, made entirely of different dough from the whole landscape. Through the window of a train, I watched that solitary pedestrian move like a black cockroach between the little houses, among the splashing mud, with splayed arms; and golden yellow glimmered the black hems of his coat. In his movements, there was such an estrangement from the whole situation and, at the same time, such knowledge of the road, as if he had to run to and fro, like a windup toy.

Sure, big deal, never seen: a Jew with long hems on a village street. However, I remember well the figure of the running Rebbe because, without him, that whole modest landscape lacked justification. The coincidence which that very moment pushed into the street this crazy, charmingly absurd, endlessly refined, porcelain pedestrian helped me understand the impression of the State Jewish Theater, [a performance of] which I recently saw for the first time.

Yes, a short while before that, on a Kiev street, I was ready to approach a similar respectable bearded man and ask him, "Didn't Altman do your costume?" I would have asked just like that, with no mockery, quite sincerely: in my head, the realms grew confused . . .

How fortunate is Granovsky! It's enough for him to assemble two or three synagogue

[*]Originally published in *Vechernaya krasnaya gazeta* (Leningrad), August 10, 1926, this review was included in Mandelshtam's posthumously published collected works with the title "Mikhoels (1926)": G. P. Struve and B. A. Filipoff, eds., *Sobraniye sochineny v trekh tomakh*, vol. 3 (New York: Inter-Language Associates, 1969), p. 106.

beadles with a cantor, summon a matchmaker-*shadkhan*, catch in the street an elderly salesman, and a spectacle is ready and, in essence, even Altman is superfluous.

This paradoxical theater, which, according to some critics as profound as Dobro-lyubov,[*] declared war on the Jewish petite bourgeoisie and which exists only to eradicate prejudices and superstitions, loses its head, gets drunk like a woman when it sees a Jew, and immediately pulls him into its workshop, to the porcelain factory, scalds and tempers him into a marvelous biscuit, a painted statuette, a green *shadkhan*-grasshopper, brown musicians of Rabichev's[†] Jewish wedding, bankers with shaved, layered pates, dancing like virtuous girls, holding hands, in a circle.

The plastic fame and force of the Jews consist of having worked out and borne through the centuries a sense of form and movement, which has all the traits of a fashion immutable for millennia. I am speaking not of the cut of their clothes, which changes, and which we need not value (it doesn't even occur to me to justify the ghetto or the shtetl style aesthetically); I'm talking of the internal plasticity of the ghetto, of that immense artistic force which outlives its destruction and will finally flourish only when the ghetto is destroyed.

Violins accompany the wedding dance. Mikhoels approaches the footlights and, stealthily, with the careful movements of a fawn, listens to the music in a minor key. This is a fawn who has found himself at a Jewish wedding, hesitant, not yet drunk, but already stimulated by the cat-music of a Jewish minuet. This moment of hesitation is perhaps more expressive than the whole subsequent dance. Intoxication comes, tapped on the spot, a light intoxication from two or three drinks of grape wine, but this is enough to turn the head of a Jew: the Jewish Dionysius is undemanding and immediately produces joy.

During the dance, Mikhoels's face assumes an expression of wise weariness and sad exaltation, as if the mask of the Jewish people, approaching antiquity, is almost identical with it.

Here the dancing Jew is like the leader of an ancient chorus. The whole force of Judaism, the rhythm of the abstract, dancing thought, the whole dignity of the dance, whose only impetus is ultimately empathy with the earth—all this is absorbed in the trembling hands, the vibration of his thinking fingers, inspired like articulated speech.

---

[*]Dobrolyubov was an extreme social critic of Russian literature in the nineteenth century.

[†]Itshak Rabichev was one of the artists of the Yiddish theater.

Mikhoels is the epitome of national Jewish dandyism—the dancing Mikhoels, the tailor Soroker, a forty-year-old child, a blessed *shlimazel*, a wise and gentle tailor. And yesterday, on the same stage, Anglicized jockey ragamuffins, on tall girl-dancers, patriarchs drinking tea in the clouds, like elders on a porch in Homel [Byelorussia].

Viktor Shklovsky
Jewish Luck   1925, Russian[*]

What does a Jew do? He spins around.—This is from *Jewish Luck*. It was very hard for Jews to spin around. Small towns, filled with houses and children. Huts with dilapidated roofs. Their own soil only in the cemetery. And that's where they grazed their goats. They lived on air, and that wasn't fresh either. Jews, separated from productive work, from land and factories, a whole nation living in the cracks and interstices of life. Petty buying and selling, shaving, mending dresses. The lowest wages in the world. So crowded that new buildings weren't constructed because there was nowhere to go during the construction. On the old house they patched up a new one, a wall on top of a wall, a roof above a roof.—Mice have such a disease when their tails grow into each other in the cellar. Thus houses and people grow into each other in Jewish shtetls. Stifling, closed everyday life, and on the Sabbath, wires encircle the whole town. All around, alien fields and alien, hostile people. People in a prison create their own language. The downtrodden are sharp-witted. The best Jewish anecdotes are created by Jews about themselves. One of those anecdotes is Sholem-Aleichem's story about a man of air, a destitute pauper, a failing and indefatigable tradesman, insurance agent, and—finally—matchmaker. Jews say of such people, "He doesn't walk by himself—his guts carry him."—For us, *Jewish Luck* is almost a historical film. Such Jewish life no longer exists. The Civil War hit them hard. Pogroms rolled through the shtetl. The very places where the pasted-together huts stood were plowed up. Hunger came in the wake of the pogroms. In Kherson, orthodox Jews, fearing they would die in the general devastation and not be buried by the rules, came to the cemetery and lined

---

[*]This review of the 1925 film *Jewish Luck* (with Menakhem-Mendel), directed by A. Granovsky, with text by Isaac Babel, photography by Ed. Tisse, and sets and actors of the Yiddish theater, was published in a brochure for the film, *Evreyskoe schastye* [Jewish Luck] (Moscow: Kino-petshat' [Kino-Izdatelstvo RSFSR], 1925). In Yiddish, "Jewish luck" in the plural is uttered ironically and means the exact opposite, describing the failure of a hopeful situation.

Benjamin Zuskin as Soloveichik in Airman [200,000 (?)], Berlin, 1928. An "airman" is the typical Jew of Yiddish literature, hovering in the air and living on air.

up for death. The Revolution was a hulling mill for the Jews. The old closed world was shattered. Everyday life was finished. Small trade, middleman trade, was crushed under the pressure of state capitalism and cooperatives. In the new tight life there was no room to spin around. But the Revolution removed all limitations from the Jews and destroyed the most essential trait of the Jews—the Pale of Settlement. The plants and factories were opened for Jewish workers. The proletarian supplanted the artisan. And instead of the right to graze a goat in a cemetery, Jews got the right to the land. Now, in Byelorussia and at the Azov Sea, an immense effort to grant land to the Jews is proceeding. Kolkhozes emerge, the soil is irrigated. Now it is clear that Zionism, a Jewish state in Palestine, will produce only a southern resort for rich Jews. A patriotic resort with oranges. The Jewish colonies at the Azov Sea get 1,620,000 acres. In the

Soviet state, a new autonomous district will be added, perhaps a new republic.—No need to pity the torn umbrella of Menakhem-Mendel, no need to look for romanticism in the past, in the grown-together tails of a mouse cellar. But we need to know the old daily life. Director Granovsky has succeeded in reconstructing much of the past in his film. The film is theatrical. Granovsky doesn't want to sell his "theatrical sword." But in film, you don't need swords, you need to know the technique. Therefore, the film has a new handwriting for the cinema. There is real everyday life. The artist Natan Altman has treated his task very carefully. Natan Altman is a person with a great national culture, a person with his own facts. But the film, as I said, is a historical work; in it "thus it was" is more important than "thus I want it to be." Altman constructed the Jewish rooms well; he did not overburden them with details; he hid his work in the film as the illuminator hides his work. Light in a film should shed light and not appear as a separate item in the program. The titles in the film are made by Isaac Babel. They exploit the material of the film well and are closely connected to the actors. They are not titles but conversations. They are speech. They endow the film with the charm of the human voice.

Abram Efros
The Historical Path of the Yiddish Theater   1922, Russian*

[. . .] I sat in the empty hall at night, not used to being a stranger, watching Granovsky knock on the banister, interrupting the rehearsal and changing the complex pattern of movement for the hundredth time; the mass body of the troupe, when stopped, scatters immediately, softens, rearranges itself on the stage, only to reassemble obediently, fuse, freeze, and dart ahead—pattering, leaping, and somersaulting—over the surfaces, roofs, ladders of a fantastic Jewish shtetl, invented and populated by the generous talent of [the artist Itshak] Rabinovich. Sensing in myself a growing joy in this unfolding "Jewish game," in these sayings, songs, purely national intonations that suddenly became theatrical, in the beautiful subtlety with which Mikhoels serves them up, in the freshness of young Zuskin's talent (an undoubted discovery of the theater),

---

*"Before the Opening Curtain: The New Season at the Jewish Theater," *Teatr i muzyka* (Moscow), no. 9 (November 1922), pp. 110–111. After leaving the theater for several months, Efros wrote this article apropos of the dress rehearsals for Granovsky's staging of Goldfaden's *The Sorceress*. The first part of the article is omitted.

I felt clearly one thing which I had never felt before and which suddenly explained to me why—in spite of all our disagreements and distancing, in spite of my skepticism and negation, the failures, clumsiness, artificiality, unjustified elements in the performances—I nevertheless am drawn, I would say hypnotically, to the stream of GOSEKT, as to the riverbed of the imperative, unavoidable, historically unique path of the Yiddish theater.

Oh, that Yiddish theater!—Without a foundation or a roof, without borders to its domain or any blueprint! A theater that is its own grandfather, father, and son. A theater that has not yet any past, present, or future, and that must create for itself a past, a present, and a future. A theater that has to live simultaneously in three dimensions of time. A theater with no tradition, but which has to invent for itself a historical line; a theater without a present, but which has to be at the cutting edge of contemporary theater art; a theater without perspective, but which has to mold the form of what is to come. That is why we have no choice here. Here we cannot prefer one thing to another. Here talk about trends is more negligible than anywhere else. Here you can either be in the center of the Jewish "stage"—or be entirely outside it. Coexistence is impossible here; there is room here for only one way of thinking, and one yardstick: What stands before us? A theater of all dimensions of time? "A theater of three times," creating of its "now" both a forward and a backward? Speaking simultaneously with the triple voice of history, reality, and future? If so, then *no matter what it is* in its composition, quality, magnitude, it is the center, the regulator, the lawgiver; it is history, no matter how little the tribal philistine recognizes it, no matter what fashionable or approachable admirers it has gained for itself on the side, and no matter where it may be drawn by alien pointing fingers.

In its national sphere, the Yiddish Chamber Theater is such a historical center, dominating the situation, directing the evolution [of theater], although alongside it there is the very good HaBima and the very bad Brandesco or Zhitomirsky (I have little orientation in using those pseudonyms, for which I apologize). And though in HaBima, my dear fellow tribalists are so enthusiastic they come down with hiccups, and in Brandesco-Zhitomirsky they fill the auditorium till they faint, nevertheless, in spite of it all, both HaBima and Brandesco and many other things around are a mere mirage, fiction, while the chamber theater is a historical reality.

In this sense, its role is like Chagall's role in plastic art, in spite of the absolute

Scene from Trouhadec: An Eccentric Operetta by Jules Romains, 1926—the first non-Jewish play produced by GOSET *in Moscow. Director: Aleksey Granovsky. Set design: Natan Altman. Music: Lev Pulver.*

polarity of artistic temperaments. Chagall the ecstatic and Granovsky the intellectual. And so not in vain did Chagall enter the stage for the first time in the Yiddish theater, not in vain did he spread his theatrical forms precisely from this stage. These forms, like everything else in his art, became kinds of obligatory models essentially influencing the formation of characters in *The Sorceress* of Rabinovich, who created brilliant "variations on Chagallian themes" in his costumes.

Looking back, we may say that Chagall is "an artist of three times," as GOSEKT is "a theater of three times." Chagall, too, has absorbed in his art the traditions of the national past, the modernism of today, and the buds of the future. He drew threads back, in depth, to the past—close to the rooted, authentic, living faces of old Jewish life—and brought them to his paintings with all their living and dead inventory, with all their long coattails and long beards, canonicity and peculiarity, everydayness and fantasy, as GOSEKT brought them onto the theatrical boards in *The Sorceress*. But in the language of his paintings, Chagall is so contemporary that he marches in the front row

Scene from Trouhadec.

of the European masters of leftist art, while his relation to the future is determined by the stamp he has placed on a huge contingent of young artists, including many who are now eager to dissociate themselves from him.

Chagall's so-called Vitebsk period was in this sense crucial for the work of the young generation of Jewish artists. For the first time on the Yiddish stage, Granovsky's *Sorceress* succeeded in finding adequate theatrical solutions for the same age-old life in the forms of contemporary leftist art, and, with that precision that sets landmarks for the future, for the work to come. The solutions of *The Sorceress* constitute the first step of a "Vitebsk period" in the emergence of the Yiddish Chamber Theater as an important and influential force.

Scene from Trouhadec.

Aleksey Granovsky

Our Theater

1928, Yiddish[*]

In 1919, I was given the task of creating a Yiddish theater school; the school was opened the same year in Leningrad and then numbered thirty-some students. In 1920, the first graduation and simultaneously the first theater performance took place. Since we felt it necessary, considering our teaching methods, to produce a unified whole, we doubted if we should accept students from other dramatic schools or actors from different theaters. All the human material of our theater came to us as "raw material," and only after they had been processed in our workshops were they to appear on our stage. For us, the foundation of artistic education was that the actor himself must be in control of his own emotional apparatus; he then trains his own capabilities, his body and all his feelings to be subordinate to his will, his controlling reason, and that precise rhythm on which we build all our productions. In other words, the basis

[*]*Literarishe bleter* (Warsaw), 5, no. 17 (Apr. 27, 1928).

Scene from Trouhadec.

of artistic education is to train the actor's capability to become a part of the organic whole of the performance.

I consider stage art an independent and sovereign domain. Therefore, all elements constituting a finished performance—the man, the script, the music, the sets, and the lighting—must be subordinate to a single steadfast thought and the completed score of the production. I don't mean that I want to bind the actor and deprive him of the possibility of being creative—on the contrary, he is given the greatest opportunity to express himself. But since he is educated in the sharp consciousness of our task and feels that he is a responsible part of a monolithic whole, he is capable of subordinating himself to the primary task and of being creative within its framework.

For us, dramatic literature is also only one element of a harmonious whole and does not retain any independent meaning. We calculate precisely (or strive to) the rule-governed mutual relationships of all elements and subordinate them to the main thought that is our sole task and sole purpose. When I approach the production of a

Scene from Trouhadec.

work, my major task is to show the spectator how we perceive and understand this work, the whole atmosphere and the whole world in which our heroes live. Therefore, it is fully justified, when the author does not show his milieu (as for example, in Jules Romains's *Trouhadec*), that I create the milieu; that is, I create variations on Romains's theme. I do it because I believe that a work for the stage that does not show the "air" in which the acting figures live is superfluous and does not exist at all for the theater.

For the performances I select all kinds of dramatic means of expression (drama, comedy, operetta) according to what each stage moment foregrounds. Practically, we carry out this task in the following manner: When we agree on a specific play, I propose the script on the basis of which I create, together with my dramaturgical assistants, the text for the actor. Then I make a sketch of the actor's score, and everyone who participates in the staging—the composer, the painter, the technician—gets his precisely drawn task. As for the rehearsals, the work is conducted in the following manner: first of all, the actor has to master the text and the melodies, he must perceive the main rhythm of the performance, and only then is he set in motion. On average, every play is rehearsed 150 times, but never more than 250. That depends on how complicated the task is and how fast the actors master the total image and the relations between all the parts.

Such are the principles according to which we work and on which the theater has been built for the past ten years; and with this theater, we are launching a lengthy worldwide tour.

Berlin

CHAPTER EIGHT

Theater and Revolution

Y. *Lyubomirsky*
The Revolutionary Theater (Excerpts) 1926, Yiddish[*]

I

The Russian Theater on the Eve of October

For some years now, complaints have been raised about the theater in the Soviet Union: Why does it pretend not to know there was a social revolution in our country? And if it sometimes does show signs of a political intelligence, it is merely tricks, forced love, just to get rid of it, as they say. And with those complaints they keep nudging both the old aristocrats—the so-called academic theaters—as well as the leftist and youngest theaters that boast red foulards and a whole packet of Revolutionary props.

We shall try to analyze here to what extent these complaints are justified.

What was the state of the theater on the eve of the October Revolution?

The Theater of Atmosphere—At the Top

As we know, the years 1907–1917 were years of repentance for many of our Russian intelligentsia, who beat their breasts for their previous revolutionary sins. And those feelings of impotence, passivity, decadence, repentance, found their strongest and deepest resonance in the repertoire of the Moscow Art Theater, or, as it was nick-named, "Chekhov's Theater," because the most conspicuous aspect of the repertoire of the Moscow Art Theater was indeed Chekhov's plays, which contained masterful descriptions of the flaccid, passive Russian intelligentsia. This was the true mirror of the Russian intelligentsia; here they would cry their fill over the troubles of the Three

---

[*] *Der revolutsyonerer teatr* (Moscow: Shul un bukh, 1926).

Sisters or Uncle Vanya, who couldn't find a proper place or activity in the world, and of his niece, Sonya, who consoled him with the otherworld.

Theater of the Tragic Pose and Pure Fantasy

For those who wanted nothing to do with the surrounding reality and strove to get as far from it as possible, the best place was the Moscow Russian Chamber Theater—a theater of the fondled, adorned gesture, artificial pose, and declamatory word—the so-called stylized theater, with its outlandish tricks, lulling the viewer like a sweet sleeping potion, with absolutely no relation to the surrounding life.

The other theaters, both in the capitals and in the provinces, had mostly loyal pupils and followers of the Moscow Art Theater; i.e., they put on either atmosphere pieces (Chekhov, Andreev, Surguchev, etc.) or plays reflecting the old lifestyle (Ostrovsky, Gogol); from time to time Schiller's or Shakespeare's dramas would shimmer.

Emphasis on Deep Psychologism

How did they perform? Usually, the main thing was not so much describing what some protagonist did, but [presenting] his desires, intentions, experiences. Therefore, an enormous place on the stage was taken by the pause, silence, which led to seeing the word as the main thing on the stage. Movement became dispersed, slow. Since the focus was primarily on individualistic moods, the man as individual, detached from the surrounding world, pondering in his own isolation, the actor's gesture had to become diffuse and indefinite. Dreamy people walked around on the stage, out of this world.

Stanislavsky's "System of Experiences"

The main principle of acting was to take off your own "self" and merge with the soul of the protagonist, or, more precisely, to transform yourself entirely into the soul of the protagonist, share his sorrow and his suffering with your whole being. For the whole time of the performance, to swim in the stream of the protagonist's experiences; that is, the action on stage would occur as in a state of deep hypnosis. I repeat: the main thing was not to develop the actor into a flexible, accomplished man-motor, but [to develop] the ability to hypnotize oneself, to fall into a dream state.

If only the actor would contract the protagonist's moods, argued the adherents of this system, the external movements, gestures, and actions of the protagonist would grow by themselves, as a natural result of a certain state of the soul. This system of acting, where the main thing was "elation of the soul," delving into the "holy of holies" of the individual's experiences, the deep intention—is, in short, the famous system of Stanislavsky, the director, actor, and creator of the Moscow Art Theater, the so-called system of experiences.

A Theater Not for the "Crowd" but for the Spiritual Aristocracy

Naturally, if the theater delved into the depths of psychology, the philosophy of human life (in the Art Theater), or fantastic, outlandish, distant worlds—as in the Russian Chamber Theater (technically expressed in the select gesture and chiseled word)—there could be no talk of hearing a coarse word on stage or seeing clumsy movements. Adapted to its major spectator—the aristocratic or bourgeois intelligentsia—the theater cultivated subtle movements, noble words, and did all it could to avoid vulgar movements and speech—in short, adapted everything to exquisite taste and aristocratic aesthetics.

Decoration

The same was true for the decorative principle: colorful landscapes, painted by the best artists, so the eye could feast on colors and tones (incidentally, not always adapted to the *moods* of the hero) and thus achieve the proper passive aesthetic emotions.

They filled the stage box with various and sundry things—furniture, pictures, statuettes—in short, all sorts of paraphernalia surrounding the individual and the family.

The Method of Educating the Actor

For the beginner, the denizen of the actor's studio, the path to such scenic "work" lay: (1) through the immersion in mystical literature—Maeterlinck, Przybyszewski, and others were supposed to drench him in mysticism; (2) through narcotics (wine, ether, cocaine)—an exalted mood would lead him to ecstasy. The result of such an education for many actors of that school was neurasthenia and hallucinations. For many years, you had to lift your eyes to God and permeate yourself with mystical intentions to become an actor in that system.

The Spectator of the Theater

Who was the spectator of the theater? Mostly the upper middle class, the rich petite bourgeoisie, the intelligentsia: its suffering and joys were depicted in this theater. The worker or the simple spectator who came there observed in amazement a strange world appealing to dreams and yesteryears that don't want to know of today's evil.

How Distant Was the Theater from Life

No bullet touched the academic theaters. Even the Great Imperialist War [the Soviet name for World War I] found no echo in the most respectable theaters, unless we count the production of such flag-waving aborted fetuses as Andreev's *King, Law and Freedom* and a few other such plays.

II

Beginning of a Theatrical Revolt

But at the same time, when the Moscow theater world was entirely lulled in moods (Chekhov's theater), in idylls and fantasies (First Studio of the Moscow Art Theater and the Russian Chamber Theater), in the thick but already passé old manners (Ostrovsky)—in Petersburg, a storm was brewing: Meyerhold and Evreinov (in Moscow —Vakhtangov) had long been dissatisfied with the "overrefined" theater, where decadent moods flourished, where theater was transformed into a celibate from life, and into some kind of interpretation of literature and exhibition of painting; where the actor began to freeze; where they tried to wrench the actor's soul, his playfulness, with a kiss, to stifle in him the clownish qualities and transform him into an Indian or shaman.

Excursion into Theater History

The Petersburg innovators began to pave new theatrical paths. Unhappy with the theatrical present, they began with gusto to leaf through and partially restore the history of the Greek, Roman, Medieval, Oriental, and especially the Italian improvisational theater of the sixteenth and seventeenth centuries.

To understand thoroughly the methods and principles underlying the performance of the contemporary actor of the leftist theater—Meyerhold's, the Moscow

Yiddish State, Vakhtangov's, Kurbas's—I must discuss the properties of the Italian improvisational theater of the sixteenth and seventeenth centuries.[*] Here lies the true key to the curious things we see on the stage of the leftist theater.

The Actor of the Italian Masque Comedy

The actor of that theater was a different kind of actor, a real jack-of-all-trades. He knew lots of things: he himself would be the author of the scenario, the actor, the director, and was agile at various theater arts: singing, dancing, fencing, acrobatic tricks. And he was a *technically accomplished* master of all these arts. Indeed, that theater was called *commedia dell'arte*, an artistic comedy, for its high technique.

The principle of his acting was: not to be transformed into the character he was supposed to embody on the stage, that is, not to "experience" but to "*disguise himself*"—as a lover, a servant, a doctor—thus sharply underlining both the absurdities and virtues of the created character. Here everything was deliberately *exaggerated*. The twist, the make-believe, movement in general, was not a copy of normal life; on the contrary—it was supernatural, clumsy. Therefore, the theater was called Masque Comedy, for it did not strive to present copies of life as our naturalistic theaters do, but *masques*, human types transformed into poetry and painted with thick colors. Here they mocked men, just as you see today in *The Sorceress* in the Moscow Yiddish State Theater.

Are you worried when you see in *The Sorceress* the little commissar arresting Reb Avremtsia, and both of them hopping off the stage like marionettes? On the contrary—you take pleasure. Because the actor who acts Reb Avremtsia doesn't experience it either—*he disguises himself* as a comical father. And this is the main intention of the whole show: to poke fun!

Such was the actor of the Italian Masque Theater. What the hero he portrays experiences doesn't interest him. Just now he acted a tragic episode—and all of a sudden he stuck his tongue out at you—so you wouldn't forget it was only a play.

He did not derive his vitality from sharing the joys and suffering of the type he portrays (as in our atmosphere theaters). No! He delighted in controlling his own body and senses with such mastery, in being so agile and dynamic, in coming up with such happy, purely theatrical inventions. Not in vain was he an excellent acrobat.

---

[*] It was called "improvisational" because the scenario was outlined briefly and schematically. The real text was created during the play, as an improvisation. It was also called "the Masque Theater" and "Commedia dell'Arte," that is, professional comedy, art comedy. [Lyubomirsky's footnote.]

Meyerhold, who restored the comedy of the Italian Masque Theater, characterizes this kind of acting in the comedy *Harlequin the Matchmaker*:

> This is a deliberately coarse buffoonery with all the pranks favored by the theater at that time: kicking your adversary in the face with the toe of your shoe; disguising yourself as a magician with such simple circus tricks as wearing a traditional dunce cap and tying on a beard (made of a piece of towel); snatching up your partner on your back and exiting the stage with him; hitting one another with a stick; cutting off the glued-on nose with a wooden sword; various kinds of wrestling; leaping into the auditorium; harlequins somersaulting; thumbing their noses in the wings; screaming and screeching before leaving the stage.

Such disguises were calculated to rouse, refresh, and please the spectator, thus involving him in the art.[*]

With that legacy of the Italian and of the old theater in general, innovative directors like Meyerhold, Vakhtangov, and others trained the future actor of the leftist theater. Especially interesting experiments were made in Meyerhold's Petersburg studio, where the cornerstone was laid for Meyerhold's Biomechanics, which we shall discuss later.

With No Broad Social Base

But the social base of the theatrical rebels in the first years of the rebellion, 1908–1917, was too narrow. The revolutionary avant-garde of the working class, which prepared day and night the necessary premises for rebuilding all of life, including culture, on new foundations—when the foremost task was to dig a pit for the old tsarist system—had neither time nor opportunity to pay attention to the practical struggle for a materialistic approach to art. And there was no necessity for it then: the working masses and the peasants were rare guests in the theater, as they didn't participate much in building culture. The theater innovators themselves did perhaps feel that the new theater they were striving for had to throw out the schmaltzy spirit, specific to the intelligentsia, which predominated in the theater, and turn it into a place for healthy, seminal, mass joy and mass play, or into an arena where giant dramatic clashes of hostile classes are reflected.

But from a purely aesthetic standpoint, their intentions were initially simply a

[*]A precise and concrete conception of the Italian Masque Theater is *Princess Turandot*, staged by Vakhtangov in the Moscow Studio in his name: here you have all the major masques of Commedia dell'Arte. [Lyubomirsky's footnote]

reaction against the psychological-literary and perfumed-elegant salon theater. Evidence of this: Meyerhold, Evreinov, and others in the Petersburg of that time were busy restoring old theaters—mostly medieval—and even the classical theater of the period of the French king Louis XIV.

Moreover, during those searches, such rebels as Meyerhold and others plunged for a while into the depths of stylized theater, where the main thing was the painterly and musical aspects of the show, while the actor was secondary, and was here even more fettered than in the atmosphere theaters.

The shows of the stylized theater did not succeed with the general public because, with their unusual, overintellectualized form, they were incomprehensible even to many of the qualified spectators. For example, Meyerhold's classical stylized staging —Blok's *Balaganchik*—evoked only great amazement in the general public and failed. For quite a while Meyerhold was persecuted for his sharp tendency toward stylized theater. And though, on the whole, the stylized theater of that period was permeated with nebulous symbolism and mysticism, nevertheless, the cornerstones and premises of Meyerhold's theater today, and of the leftist theater in general, stem in form from that stylized theater. The Russian Chamber Theater* is also considered an heir of the stylized theater.

The theater rebels acquired a broad base only under Soviet rule.

Theater and Art Are Pushed to Serve the Revolution

The builders of the new system clearly understood that expropriating the land, the factories, the guns, the cannons, and the tanks from the landlords or the bourgeoisie was not enough—you also had to control the spiritual weapons, among which art played more than a minor role. With the same impetus with which the masses embraced political action they began to embrace art as well. And, naturally, the seekers of new paths in art could not be satisfied when such theaters as the Moscow Art Theater or the Russian Chamber Theater began ostensibly to "tilt to the left"; that is, they made an effort to go out and stage their old repertoire in the workers' neighborhoods of the city, when thousands of professional actors, like a broad stream, flooded into the barracks of the Red Army and into workers' clubs to plant drama circles; when hundreds of actors, forced by the labor mobilization (and perhaps for the rations) participated temporarily in mass carnivals, in the gigantic revolutionary mass performances staged in the early period, in the time of Military Communism.

---

*In Moscow, directed by Tairov.

Scene from The Family Ovadia *["Workers"] by the Yiddish Soviet poet Perets Markish on the twentieth anniversary of the Revolution, 1937. Director: Solomon Mikhoels. Setting: Aleksandr Tyshler. Music: Lev Pulver. Note Stalin's portrait in the center and the gaps between the old and the new generations.*

III

Don't Be a Follower, Walk Hand in Hand

The theater rebels wanted to turn the theater inside out, onto the left. In this sense they were brothers of the revolution. The revolutionary fervor, rage, and protest against the old forms, the passionate thrust to topple the rotten, worn-out, and dead world, infected them too.

The essence of the arguments presented to the theater art was more or less like this:

At a time when the country experienced and experiences such horrible catastrophes, when tens of thousands perish of hunger, die of typhus, freeze in unheated apartments, when thousands of Red Army soldiers, barefoot, starving, are hurled every day into the enormous fire engulfing free Russia—at such a time you are crying about the trouble of a ruined landlord's "cherry orchard" in the Moscow Art Theater, enjoying delicate subtleties in the Russian Chamber Theater, and emerging roiled up by the love story depicted for you in a drama of manners.

There cannot and must not be a place on the contemporary stage for such individualistic "experiencings," when such giant clashes of two worlds are raging outside. The stage must convey the same spirit that is blowing in the people's squares, in the streets.

You must not stand on the sidelines of the great struggle. There are no priests of pure art. Art was always a function of the surrounding life, and the immense struggle on the battlefield must find an echo on your stage. You must turn your stage into a tribune for agitation.

This was a kind of platform of the theater innovators who sniffed the mass spectator and understood that art must be adapted to his needs.

Thus a "Left Front" Emerged

Time worked in their favor. They were no longer isolated. They forged a "Left Front" of art activists. The Futurist poets, the leftist painters, the theater innovators, united and wrote on their banner: "Agitation through new revolutionary content and innovative revolutionary form." And not just wrote, but actually did: colossal Futurist banners screamed at the top of their voices from all walls and fences of the big cities; Futurist poets like Mayakovsky wrote thundering poems and plays (*Mystery Bouffe*) on themes of the Revolution.

Many think that the LEF (Left Front)* was born because of the *form seeking* of the left artists. But this is not quite correct. The Left Front was one of the first to demand that the theater be a *means for mass organization*—one of the principles of the October Revolution. We must admit that the form innovations in art were a result of that demand.

It is worth pointing out some of the most important stages of theatrical October: in 1919, the slogan "Proletarian Theater" was finally formulated. P. Kerzhentsev emerged as the ideologue of Proletcult [Proletarian Culture]; V. Tikhonovich, as ideologue of the workers' and peasants' amateur theater; the first journal appears to reflect the movement of thought in the revolutionary theater—*Vestnik Teatra* [The Theater Herald]. At the end of 1919, the first conference of activists of the workers' and peasants' theater was convened. Even then the extreme leftist group, headed by A. Gan, formulated its present position: struggle or "mass work" against a "professional" theater. And right after the conference a section for mass performances was created in the theater department of the People's Commissariat of Education. This section prepared a scenario for mass performances for May 1.

*LEF—Levy Front Iskusstv (Left Front in the Arts).

Where Are the First Strikes of the Left Front Directed?

Against the "apron," the stage box, against the theatrical apartment where the spectator usually remained passive. Attempts at mass performances in open spaces were made: on the third anniversary of the October Revolution, N. Evreinov directed *Victory over the Winter Palace*—a grandiose performance with a cast of ten thousand, with trucks, machine guns, artillery, and the battleship *Aurora*.

All those experiments received quite a new impetus when V. Meyerhold became the leader of the theatrical rebellion against the old theater. From 1920 on, when he was invited to become director of TEO (the theater division of the People's Commissariat of Education), he led a ruthless fight against academic theaters, both through his separate theater politics and his interesting stage experiments in *The First R.S.F.S.R. Theater*, which he founded.

Dawn and Bouffe

Meyerhold's *Dawn* (adapted from Verhaeren's *Revolt*) evoked especially great agitation. And there was plenty to be surprised about—Meyerhold demonstrated considerable theatrical innovations: first of all, he took Verhaeren's text and revised it in his manner for the purposes which he, Meyerhold, set for himself, adapting the work to the moment Soviet Russia was then experiencing. For example, to link the play with the present, he introduced in the middle of the performance Conrad Smilga's announcement about the [Red Army's] victory over [White Army General] Vrangel in Perekop.* He cancelled the apron—that part of the stage which creates a boundary between the spectator and the stage. On the stage, instead of painted decorations, there were various combinations of cubes, cylinders, triangles, and bows—to create an impression of scattered building material (an allusion to the scattered, not yet organized raw material of the liberated people's energy). The actors played their roles through exclamations and declamations.

In [Mayakovsky's] *Mystery Bouffe*—a sharp buffoonery, mocking the old world, which is hostile to Soviet rule—he scattered some of the actors in the auditorium, and the action leaped from the stage to the auditorium and back.

---

*Perekop—the narrow bottleneck leading from Ukraine to the Crimean Peninsula. Vrangel's defeat effectively concluded the Civil War in European Russia.

It Was Hard to Digest "Leftist" Art

The truth must be told that the demonstration of "leftist" art at first evoked strange and quite diverse feelings: least of all ecstasy, a lot of admiration, most of all—annoyance.

The colorful, often *plotless* posters, the structure of the songs, most of which were like handfuls of colorful but useless pebbles, the objectless cubes and cylinders on the stage intended to evoke dynamic emotions in the spectator, to reinforce his will to ruin the old world—[these] remained hard enigmas, esoterica for the general public it appealed to. True, those were interesting laboratory experiments with color, composition, sound, activation of the spectators. Those were the necessary premises for the so-called system of "Productional" Art. Nevertheless, it was too abstract, too dry, too sophisticated, if not worse—artificial. The true point of the Revolution, its idea—to rend the idealistic veil in the art world, too, and build a new art on healthy materialistic foundations—had to be brought to the general public *in a more concrete and utilitarian way.*

IV

Constructivism

Then in the "Leftist" art, the direction emerged that is known as Constructivism, meaning purposefully organized material production. In simple language it meant that, instead of busying themselves with art, which normally likes to soar in the skies of religion and idealistic philosophy, the artists have to become artisans creating and forming simply *useful things of daily life,* justified and functional, both economically and technically. That meant that the painters had to give up painting only paintings to hang in museums for the sake of beauty, for pallid aesthetic enjoyment, and must artistically work out advertisements, illustrate printed texts (books, book covers), clothing of the textile industry; in architecture—to build railroad stations, workers' palaces, in the style and spirit of the latest technical achievements. In short, Constructivism sharply posed the problem of the object in art.

The theater borrowed this idea of Constructivism—to permeate the whole surrounding lifestyle with purposeful artistic-technical utilitarianism—from the adherents of Productional Art. "The performance," says V. Pertsov, one of the theoreticians of LEF, "must be seen not as a means for agitation intending to organize the consciousness of the spectator, but as a unique exhibition of models for the new lifestyle, a concrete allusion."

And if everything on the stage must be purposeful, then the old painted decoration, which served only as background and often had nothing to do with the acting, just won't do. Now on the stage we need a construction, a kind of constructed workshop, as indispensable for the actor as the machine is for the worker. What relationship do we see between workers and machine? The working processes of the worker are rigorously adapted to the given workshop or tool and require a certain system of movements. In the same way, the acting of the actor must be precisely adapted to the given theatrical construction; of course, the creator of the latter, along with the director, must foresee all necessary movements, all mise-en-scènes for the actors. All those ladders, diagonal and horizontal surfaces, are means to maximize the use of the stage box—in the length, the width, the height; and to dynamize the production as strongly as possible, so it will have a profound impact on the spectator. Moreover, the construction has the advantage of being much cheaper than the old painted decorations. (Naturally, such extreme examples as Vesnin's construction for the play *The Man Who Was Thursday* are, in this sense, exceptions.)

Constructivism and the Proletarization of the Theater

But constructions alone are not enough. Constructions on the stage are only part of the means for proletarization of the theater, according to the Constructivists.

In his article "Theater as Means of Production," B. Arvatov, a theoretician of LEF, thus answers the question of what proletarianization consists of:

> First, one must turn the director into a master of ceremonies of work and lifestyle, that is, into an organizer of technically perfect work and a new lifestyle. Secondly, one must turn the actor, the current expert of aesthetic tricks, simply into a qualified man, that is, into a harmonious type of socially active personality.
>
> Simply put, the theater must become a factory for a well-rounded, and, first of all, physically developed, man.

Special Institutions of Theatrical Physical Exercise

As soon as the theater was assigned such a new role, the necessary conclusions had to be drawn. Therefore, the theater sections of the Central Political Enlightenment and the Central Directorate of Vsevobuch (Universal Literacy) together created a committee headed by Meyerhold, to be devoted especially to the theatricality of physical exercise. That means: (1) to organize the masses artistically for various festive demonstrations; (2) to educate the workers' movement on a theatrical-gymnastic basis.*

In addition, the higher school for the Art of Theater Direction was established under Meyerhold's leadership, as well as an institute for rhythmics where the education of the new actor was conducted according to Meyerhold's biomechanical system.

Meyerhold's Biomechanics

What, actually, is this biomechanical system?

While studying the movement techniques of the Italian actor of the sixteenth and seventeenth centuries—the actor of the Masque Theater—Meyerhold found that the actor of that time could and should serve as a model of scenic dynamics for the contemporary actor. The contemporary actor, who was paralyzed and fettered by the psychologism and mysticism that has dominated the stage in recent times, must learn again to command his body freely. But since there are no more such living actor-models (the Italians have been rotting for a long time), he created a whole system of original gymnastic exercises based on the research he conducted on the human organism (a part of those exercises is demonstrated in the spectacle *D.E.* [*Davay Evropu*—"Give Us Europe!" meaning: "Let us take Europe!"], in the physical exercise episode). The main principle of the exercises is that the actor *feels and controls the center of gravity of his body.* As soon as he fully controls the center of gravity of his body, he will be able nimbly and precisely to execute all kinds of stage movements that may be demanded by the stage; that is, he will be a perfect motor. And this, argued Meyerhold, is indispensable not just for the actor, but for every man of our time, especially the city dweller surrounded by *mechanical* culture. And even if a student learning biomechanics does not become an actor, he will still be a nimble artisan because his body will be maximally organized and flexible.

The Magnanimous Cuckold

All these new theater principles—Constructivism and Biomechanics—received their sharpest expression in early 1922 in Meyerhold's production of *The Magnanimous Cuckold.*†
Instead of the usual decorations, you saw on the stage a machine or, as it is called,

---

*To a certain degree, these principles were inherited by the Central Work Institute (TsIT). [Lyubomirsky's footnote.]

†Comedy by Fernand Crommelynck.

a Construction—something like a model of a windmill whose roof and walls have been torn off by the wind: a system of ladders, horizontal and diagonal surfaces, with wheels on the side, moving doors revolving on their axis. Everything was made here for the sake of the actor—to emphasize and help his acting to the utmost; the action on several levels should fill the whole space of the stage box with movement. Due to this Construction, the actor could demonstrate the plastic agility he acquired from Meyerhold's system. Moreover, you had here a whole series of features of the market-fair show booth and circus: naïve "disguises," slaps, spankings (an extraordinary profanation of the holy aesthetics), and various eccentric pranks. Even more remarkable was the fact that the actors acted *without makeup* and all wore blue *workers' clothing*. The stage *had no curtain* throughout the production.

We have intentionally dwelled longer on this production because it was a true sign of the times, the first loud shot of form-revolution on the stage. Because the ideological meaning of this spectacle *in the sense of plot* was negligible in comparison with its formal innovations. Who, in the theater of the Communist Meyerhold in 1922, outside of fat NEPmen,* could be interested in a story about a jealous husband who tormented his beautiful young wife with constant doubts for so long that a row of young men lined up at the entrance *to her bedroom*—in order to put an end to his doubts?

How Was the Production Interpreted?

The true intention of this production was a fiery slap in the face of the academic theaters: a production with a negligible plot, no makeup, no specific theatrical costumes, no decoration, no curtain, and still—so filled with life, with ardent dynamics. A production that shocks like a bomb, like a thunderbolt out of the blue (though malicious tongues claimed that *The Magnanimous Cuckold* was a kosher child of NEP).

The general theatrical world understood Meyerhold's production in its own way: that in the theater one must *emphasize* not agitation for reconstructing life on new principles, but agitation for *new art forms* in the theater.

---

*NEPmen are the nouveaux riches who made money during the New Economic Policy period of economic liberalization.

V

Race for Formal Sophistication

Meyerhold in this production poured full glasses of elements of the circus and the show booth of Russian fairs, while one of his most talented adherents, S. Eisenstein, the director of the First Workers' Theater of Moscow Proletcult, in his production of *The Wise Men,* splashed so many barrelsful of circus elements that the kernel of the production, the political satire, drowned in hundreds of circus pranks. And no trace was left of the "meaning"; apparently the tricks and pranks became an end in themselves.

Other leftist theaters, like Foregger's*Theater of Revolutionary Satire, plunged into pure machinism. Instead of sharp satirical sketches, Foregger created machine dances in which living actors copied the movements of machines.

The Russian Chamber Theater, which so brilliantly exploited Constructivism in its settings—*A Man Who Was Thursday* and the operetta *Giroflé-Girofla*—in terms of content, gave in *Giroflé* no more than an ornamented candy box; and in Chesterton's *The Man Who Was Thursday,* a staged (detective) novel of events, ostensibly with a revolutionary allusion (the struggle of anarchists with police agents on their trail). Urbanism, the spirit of the metropolis—London, New York—wafts from the construction, from the tempo of the production, but it also exudes ideological emptiness. Meyerhold himself, drunk on his successful *Cuckold,* took the misleading road of showing the audience formal "miracles." He turned such excellent dramatic material as *Tarelkin's Death* by Sukhovo-Kobylin into a crazy buffoonery filled with all kinds of curious tricks inherited from the Italian Masque Theater, where stools were shooting, seats of chairs danced up, tables fell to the floor and got up by themselves; where people flogged each other not with whips but with pig bladders. Only very few understood clearly the production, and very few were satisfied.

Naïve Playing with Objects

True, from his own point of view, Meyerhold was consistent. If the truly theatrical aspect of a production consists, on top of the conflict between people, of the *conflict of the actor with real objects* on the stage, of fighting against all the ladders, doors, tables, benches—then the acting of the actor becomes even stronger, more dynamic, when the objects themselves begin to act. When you fall on a table and it helps you fall and

---

*He too became a film director. [Lyubomirsky's footnote.]

stands up right away with you; when you dash to the door and the door seems to hit your forehead (*The Cuckold*) and revolves so much on its axis that you remain standing before it like a fool and the door seems to be teasing you. Thus, your comical situation is even more foregrounded.

Still, perhaps there was justice in the arguments against Meyerhold that he exaggerated the purely show-booth tricks he so generously sprinkled in *Tarelkin's Death*, and thus veiled it in a show-booth cloak, which contradicts the very essence of the play.

This race and eagerness for formal sophistication derailed almost all theaters of the "Leftist" front and gave them a specific aftertaste that was worst of all for them—an aftertaste of "art for art's sake."

The Profound Synthesis in the Moscow State Yiddish Theater

Only one theater maintained the balance between revolutionary content and revolutionary form. This is the State Yiddish Theater. If you compare its productions *The Sorceress* and 200,000, which were born almost at the same time as Meyerhold's *Tarelkin's Death* and Eisenstein's Proletcultish *The Wise Man*, you see the enormous difference between those two camps in terms of the relationship between content and form. While in the other theaters of the Left Front, a struggle between content and form is raging, and form achieves a complete victory—that is, the plot, the true essence of the play, is entirely diluted in the rich and sophisticated form—in the Moscow Yiddish Theater, a perfect harmony between plot and form prevails. Such a naïve, almost childish plot as *The Sorceress* is intertwined from beginning to end with motifs of political satire, antireligious propaganda, and, above all, with *klezmers* accompanying the old Yiddish theater to the pillory, and all of this—playfully, as if marginally—all the while exploiting the deepest sources of folk theatricality in terms of sound, movement, and musical motif. Not to mention 200,000, where the richness of classical form of A. Granovsky's successful composition aims at underlining the antithesis: puffed-up, depressive, boorish notables and—merrymaking paupers, dynamic masses; and yet it is so natural, so artistic, and the tendentiousness doesn't poke you in the eye. Furthermore, in spite of the authentic national form of the productions, each of them attains great international significance.

In his book *Five Years of the State Yiddish Chamber Theater*, M. Litvakov says:

The Yiddish Chamber Theater found the secret of Jewish gesture, Jewish movement, Jewish plastics and dynamics, and, peeling the skin of Jewishy "wheeling and dealing" off it, the theater discovered the boundary where the national is transformed into the international. The theater created such a Jewish theater style, which can justly claim to be one of the styles that will in their ensemble construct the new style of the future international freedom-theater.

And he goes on:

The theater was the first in the Jewish milieu to give classical stage embodiments of poetic characters (Menakhem-Mendel, Reb Alter, Hotsmakh, Shimele Soroker in Mikhoels's characterization; the sorceress—Zuskin; Sore-Khantsie—Rotboym) which can justly take their place in the gallery of personages of the world theater.

Therefore, there is absolutely some truth in M. Litvakov's conclusion: "No theater in Moscow in these years created so many types bound to endure in the history of theater culture."

M. Litvakov
Five Years of the State Yiddish Chamber Theater (Excerpts) 1924, Yiddish[*]

1.

In quiet epochs, all arts, including art of the theater, lead a quiet life. They digest and transform the achievements of the past epoch of *Sturm und Drang* into facts of daily life. They express the tempos and rhythms of the inertia that has set in. But revolutionary epochs, toppling all previous foundations of life, also shake up the arts. And what art is as sensitive to social upheavals as the art of the theater? For theater is the most social of all arts; theater lives only in an audience, and not only does the actor infect the auditorium, but the auditorium also has a powerful impact on the actor and on the spectacle as a whole.

Why is it that, in Moscow, this center of world revolution, we feel such an indescribable theatrical chaos, a real world-confusion, a noisy brouhaha? The continuous destruction of old theater foundations and the painful search for new ones, the feverish toppling of old gods and the wild pursuit of new idols? Where does it come from?

If it had remained in the hands of the famous caste of art-priests, everything would have stayed as it was, with no changes. Because there is no more moldy, organically

[*]*Finf yor melukhisher yidisher kamer-teatr: 1919–1924* (Moscow: Shul un bukh, 1924).

conservative social stratum than this stratum of narcissistic Dalai Lamas. But the spectator has changed. The spectator, the audience—with no distinction of class or social group—that emerged from the mangle of the great imperialist war and that, to this day, lives under the pressure of the workers' revolution—in short, the public of the epoch of the October Revolution and the Comintern—conceals in its soul, consciously or not, powder kegs of storm-alarms and dynamic unrest. Bourgeois idylls à la *The Cricket on the Hearth* don't get into their heads, and the boring sighs of the pre-Revolutionary petite bourgeoisie in various "cherry orchards" cannot calm their firestorm yearning.

But a completely unexpected bankruptcy occurred, not only with respect to the content of the theatrical spectacle, but also with respect to form. This creeping realistic description of daily life we are sick of, this antiquated loyalty to forgotten details—all this smacks of a museum of antiquities and not of the burgeoning art of throbbing contemporaneity. Naturally, to the extent that, in such a theater, we feel vigorous mastery, even of the old style, we may watch the spectacle with some enjoyment: dear past. And those social groups who look in various ways for such sanctuaries where the thunder of the impetuous revolution cannot reach would give such theaters top priority.

But here art absolutely ceases being a moving force of the cultural development of the masses; it is transformed into a store of "sublime swindle" (Pushkin), which is dearer to some than a "wealth of mundane truths."

Other theaters, the theaters of today, which strive to keep pace with the Revolution and consider themselves only a segment of its immense front, strive to expose this "wealth of mundane truths." They aim at exploding the hidden powder kegs of unrest in the soul of the spectator, they lift him forcibly on the waves of dynamic tempos, leaping rhythms, dazzling colors, and dizzying movements.

One of the most conspicuous theaters of this type—and such theaters are scarce even in the Soviet Union—is the State Yiddish Chamber Theater.

2. THEATER AND COMEDIANS OF REVOLUTIONARY JOY

For many years, pious intellectuals and anxious caretakers of the spirit have been preparing to build a "serious" Yiddish theater. What did they mean by "serious" theater? Lengthy explications of literature on the stage through exhaustive emoting by the actors. In the old Yiddish theater, they denied not only its latter-day popular smut but also what remained intact: the mobility, the popular trumpeting, the harlequinade, the ecstasy of the whole body. The ideal was at least some reflection of the Moscow

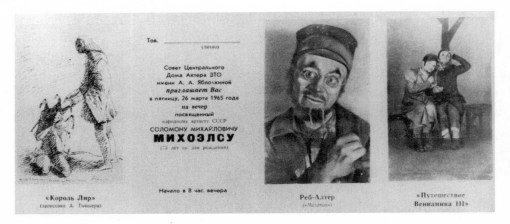

Solomon Mikhoels's rehabilitation: Invitation to a Celebration of His Seventy-fifth Birthday (he was murdered at age fifty-eight). From left: Mikhoels as King Lear (drawing by Aleksandr Tyshler); invitation; Mikhoels as Reb Alter in Mazl-Tov; Mikhoels as Benjamin in The Travels of Benjamin the Third. *The Invitation obverse is on p. 151.*

Art Theater, where the twisted soul of the Russian intelligentsia would be transformed into the Jewish piety of a small-town grandson of the Besht*—in short, a kind of Yiddishist HaBima.

But instead they got the State Yiddish Chamber Theater!

And revolution, according to the petit bourgeois caretakers of the spirit, is just asceticism, a kind of monkish withdrawal from the world. Poverty with no light or color, nakedness of body, and emptiness of soul.

But it turns out that the masses who make the revolution are much richer in life, light, colors, movement, and joy than the peripheral people-providers, for, precisely because they possess all that, they can go to revolution and triumph!

And the State Yiddish Theater came precisely as one expression of that mass ecstasy. It is the embodiment of "serving with joy"—serving art with joy, with impetus. And the ecstasy does not lie hidden in the soul, but gushes from every limb of the body.

A treasure of light, a wealth of colors, a chasm of movement, a richness of rhythms—this is what the Yiddish Chamber Theater has discovered for the Jewish working masses. A liberated body which is the organic collaborator of the liberated spirit. Both serve the red virgin soil of revolution and are hostile to all vestiges of Jewishy junk. The Jewish

---

*Besht—acronym of Baal Shem Tov, the founder of eastern European Hasidism.

Obverse of Invitation on p. 150. From left: Mikhoels as Tevye the Dairyman; Mikhoels as King Lear; back of invitation; Solomon Mikhaylovich Mikhoels.

grimace, which they tried for generations to transform into an idly Jewish feature, the Jewish gesture, which was supposed to remain forever godly pious—here they have become new, free, sharp gestures of an epoch of "iron and concrete."

The ecstasy in the Yiddish Chamber theater is not arbitrary, not spontaneous, but regulated, planned. For we live in an epoch when the spontaneous thrust of the masses is regulated by the genius of collective rationality—through the avant-garde of the working class, the Communist Party, planned economy, rationalized working processes. And as in political-economic life in general, so in the life of art is ecstasy not weakened by the progressive consciousness and calculation, but rather is strengthened and attains its greatest triumphs. An expression of that is the State Yiddish Chamber Theater.

In *A Sholem-Aleichem Evening*, we see the mathematical fantastic. The generally known and almost banal Menakhem-Mendel is elevated by the artist Mikhoels to the level of an unforgettable art symbol; for the first time, an artistic, scenic embodiment is found for the popular Yiddish Don Quixote, Reb Alter.

In *Uriel Acosta*, the unrest of Uriel's free thought merges wonderfully with the unrest of Altman's decorations; the enraged narrowness of the representatives of religious fanaticism is amazingly framed in Altman's ornate mannequins. An artistic-rational approach to the tragedy of the tottering free thought of the late Middle Ages was found here.

Not to mention *The Sorceress!* Such a plethora of colors, a treasure of movements, a wealth of sounds—Jewish art has never before provided such a dizzying rush of folk masses, liberated from their Jewishy Diaspora essence.

Here an immense and joyous theatrical explosion was brought together, aiming its full blade against the social and the spiritual, and especially against artistic junk.

Mathematical conspicuousness of gesture, precisely calculated movements, with a rapid tempo, laying bare the skeleton of the theatrical narrative in the resonating interplay of sets and music (where the necessity of music is dictated by the organic logic of the scenic intention), white-hot rhythm, dazzling collaborations of light, provocative expressiveness of color, multifunctionality and vividness in every inch of the stage boards—such are the principal features of any spectacle of the Yiddish Chamber Theater. And it is all dominated by the liberated body and the firm and elastic spirit of the actor.

What is primary in the Chamber Theater—the whole ensemble or the individual comedian? It is hard to tell. One thing is clear—the Yiddish Chamber Theater created the new, free, joyous, agile Jewish comedian, the comedian of the liberated proletariat. It has also created a joyous ensemble—a new *kapelye* [orchestra], and "a *kapelye* is more than a minyan"—according to one of Peretz's characters.

3. THEATER OF ORGANIZED RATIONALITY

Therefore, the State Yiddish Chamber Theater has many foes and even more friends. Each new production provokes, on the one hand, excited recognition and, on the other hand, wild rage. But soon, many of the most "outraged" begin to attend the loathsome spectacle, declaring in embarrassment that "you have to get used to it."

This in itself shows that the Yiddish Chamber Theater is not just a theater where "the actor does an act, and the spectator casts a glance," but one of the institutions that does battle in the domain of art in Moscow and, indeed, in the entire Soviet Union.

The success and triumph of the State Yiddish Chamber Theater was determined by its artistic essence.

First, this is the first and so far the only Yiddish theater with mastery of a European theater style. Before the State Yiddish Chamber Theater, Jewishy "culture-providers" only dreamed of a "real" Yiddish theater; small-town Talmudists, however, took great pains to realize this dream, through hairsplitting arguments about the theories and methods of an art theater. And here in the Chamber Theater true theatrical mastery came and declared, "I am!" And, though unexpected, it came full of joie de vivre, young, confident, like all the creations of October.

A new director and a new comedian arrived for whom "Jewishness"—that is, nationalistic smugness and folkloristic shmaltz—was totally alien. The key to the theatrical re-creation of Jewish folklore was found for the first time by the State Yiddish Chamber Theater—first in its performance of Sholem-Aleichem's miniatures and then in other works, especially in *The Sorceress.*

But the chief property of the Yiddish Chamber Theater, which attracts more attention than any other, I would say, is its "planned creation," or the rationalist methods of its artistic work.

The Yiddish Chamber Theater completely rejects the method of "experiencing," the cult of emotionality. Above the "kingdom of necessity"—above the spontaneous force of unregulated feelings—it puts the "kingdom of freedom"—the organized and determining understanding. Hence, in the productions of the Yiddish Chamber Theater, mathematical formulas were transformed into intuitive revelations, which, after the fact, when the habituated spectator begins to grasp them, appear as intuitive revelations, distinguished by the surprising obviousness of mathematical formulas.

This explains the interesting and "sensational" gestures of the Yiddish Chamber Theater, its groupings and pauses, which seem outlandish at first glance. The Sholem-Aleichem spectacle initially provoked embarrassment, anger, even rage, and now it is already a canonized spectacle; many of the former protesters even tend to think that the theater condescended to them and "softened" its gestures. The same holds for *Uriel Acosta,* perhaps the best work of the Yiddish Chamber Theater: in *Uriel,* theatrical mastery, based on rationalist ecstasy or ecstatic rationalism, achieves a high level and tension.

And even in *The Sorceress,* in this most dynamic spectacle, filled with light, dance, brouhaha, notwithstanding the external emotionality of the staging and acting, there is a rigorous calculation and mathematical forging: precisely because of that, the emotional saturation is achieved, and not vice versa.

The same is true for Sholem-Aleichem's *Winning Ticket* and other productions, from the most monumental to the smallest comedian skits, such as *Three Dots* and even *Warsaw Thieves* and *Comedians' Carnival.*

And not only is this theater inspired by the artists, but it also inspires them, mobilizing each of them for a specific work in the style and spirit of the given artist, yet still within the rigorous plan of the given piece. For Sholem-Aleichem's sleepwalking characters, who see raging dreams in a quite calculated "reality," the theater found Chagall, who, for his part, found the Yiddish Chamber Theater. Such an ideal merger of a theater and an artist is rarely achieved. Sholem-Aleichem's characters, embodied by the artists on the stage of the Yiddish Chamber Theater, in the costumes and framework of Chagall's designs, which, despite their fantastic mood, are structured rationally and calculated mathematically—this is a beautiful theatrical spectacle, which gives the Jewish spectator a new *literary* Sholem-Aleichem. The same wonderful accord between the creative intention of the theater and its decorative realization by an artist is achieved in *Uriel Acosta*. In his design, the artist Altman expresses almost with genius the unrest of the struggling free thought in the context of religious fanaticism, indicated through a world of pompous mannequins. Altman's rationalist thinginess best matches Granovsky's methods.

And in *The Sorceress*, the bright, vivacious, Chagallized realism of I. Rabinovich proved itself a real revelation for the tasks of the Yiddish Chamber Theater.

And then comes the ideological revolutionary aspect of the theater: the merciless revelation of the Jewish lifestyle and the constant exposure of the flaccidity of the past, the theater's biting, life-loving mockery of the elements of the religious-nationalistic milieu, its striving toward October.

All this makes the State Yiddish Chamber Theater one of the first-rate contemporary European theaters, beloved and dear to the Jewish worker . . .

4. THEATER AND YIDDISH MASS CULTURE

[Before October,] literature held the hegemony in our cultural creativity. It led, stimulated, organized, and clustered the forces in all other areas of art. And its creativity itself proceeded in the spirit of that epoch—in the spirit of internal Jewish narrowness. In a certain sense, Yiddish literature did not completely withstand the pressure of October, and now it struggles consciously to overcome the crisis stemming from the previous, unfinished epoch.

Our theater did not have the rich, though often difficult, traditions of literature—therefore, it was easier for the theater to absorb the thrust of October. So the Yiddish Chamber Theater was created.

The Chamber Theater did indeed emerge from the soil of massive accumulated creative energy, yet its impulse still came from outside. Dimensions never before seen in the Jewish milieu, rhythms, and tempos never before heard or felt, achievements

Costume design by Robert Falk for The Travels of Benjamin the Third.

Costume design by Robert Falk for The Travels of Benjamin the Third.

Costume design by Robert Falk for The Travels of Benjamin the Third.

Costume design by Robert Falk for The Travels of Benjamin the Third.

Costume design by Aleksandr Tyshler for King Lear by William Shakespeare. Performed in 1935 at GOSET.

Costume design by Aleksandr Tyshler for King Lear.

Costume designs by
Aleksandr Tyshler for
King Lear.

Costume design by *Aleksandr Tyshler* for King Lear.

Mise-en-scène design by Aleksandr Tyshler for Freylekhs (Joy) *by Z. Shneer. Performed in 1945 at GOSET.*

Costume design by Itshak Rabinovich for
A Feast in Kasrilevke, based on a work
by Sholem-Aleichem. Performed in 1926 at
the Belorussian State Yiddish Theater, Minsk.

Costume designs by Yisoschor Rybak
for On the Chain of Repentance
by H. Leyvik, an American Yiddish poet.
Performed in 1925 at the Belorussian
State Yiddish Theater, Minsk.

*Costume design
by Aleksandr Tyshler
for* The Deaf One
*by Dovid Bergelson.
Performed in 1928 at
the Belorussian State
Yiddish Theater, Minsk.*

*Costume design by Aleksandr
Tyshler for* The Recruit.
*Performed in 1933 at the
Belorussian State Yiddish
Theater, Minsk.*

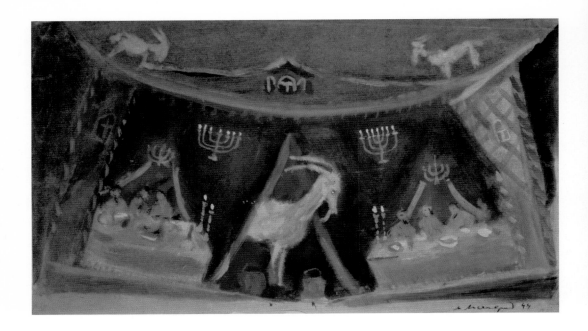

Curtain design by Meir *Akselrod* for The
Enchanted Tailor, *based on a work by*
Sholem-Aleichem. *Performed in* 1944 *at
the Ukrainian State Yiddish Theater, Kharkiv.*

Costume design by Itshak Rabichev for
Zagmuk by A. Glebov. Performed in 1933
at the Birobidjan State Yiddish Theater.

Costume design by Eugene Nivinsky for The Golem by H. Leyvik. Performed in 1925 at HaBima, Moscow.

"The Gypsy" costume design by Eugene Nivinsky for The Golem.

Costume design by Eugene Nivinsky for The Golem.

Costume design by Eugene
Nivinsky for The Golem.
The letters in Hebrew suggest
pseudo-Kabbalistic names.

Stage design by Eugene
Nivinsky for The Golem.

never before experienced, were the triumphs of this theater. For the first time in the history of Yiddish culture in general and of our mass culture in particular, there was a cultural creation that measured itself by—and was aligned with—the front line of European culture. For the Chamber Theater is indeed a Jewish theater, but it has attained its value outside the framework of purely Jewish art culture. In this very respect, it is the first and thus far the only October achievement of Yiddish mass culture.

But not only in this respect.

Usually, people imagine that October art is art that speaks directly about barricade battles, red banners, the hammer and sickle, shears and iron, bloodsucking capitalists, and oppressed proletarians. This is, of course, an oversimplified, vulgar position. If that were so, we should, for example, have renounced any proletarian or revolutionary music. For music speaks with tones and not with generally accessible words or paintings. Yet there is revolutionary music, and proletarian music is possible insofar as proletarian art in general is possible.

Revolutionary art in general, and October art in particular, is revolutionary not just in terms of its concrete themes and motifs, but in terms of its spirit, the moods it evokes, its play of colors, its rhythms, its tempos, the enchanted world into which it transposes us, the ideological thrust that dominates it. For art has methods of influence different from those of journalism. It remains art only when it leads to political conclusions, through its own ways and methods. If, however, it lacks agitational conclusions, it is socially dead even when it has purely formal achievements. And the Chamber Theater is the only theater here, and one of the few theaters in the whole Soviet Union, where a synthesis has been found between formal achievements and the ideological sediment of the October period.

5. IN THE RHYTHM OF OCTOBER

The Yiddish Chamber Theater is not a proletarian theater and does not claim to be. The Yiddish Chamber Theater, however, is the only theater that is *acceptable* for the proletariat.

Why?

The Yiddish Chamber Theater rejects the methods of internal emotings which are *explicated in a literary manner* on the stage; it provides *theatrical actions* that attain a colossal value even for purely literary works. The method of emoting cripples even collective actions and degrades them to the level of individualistic brooding, whereas the method of theatrical action elevates even the internal experiences of the individual to the level of a moment in the collective being.

This is because the Yiddish Chamber Theater bases its creation not on *emotion*, but on *rationality*; that is, not on the spontaneous force of unregulated feeling, but on the calculation of an organized understanding. It evokes feelings through the mathematical emphasis of rationality, through creation rather than spontaneous outbursts, which is entirely in the spirit of our October epoch.

Meyerhold in Moscow and Kurbas* in Kiev follow the same path, but they turn the *material apparatus* of the theater into a *machine*, while Granovsky *rationalizes the living material* of the theater. Of course, we cannot feel the present epoch without revealing its industrialism, without technical constructions, and therefore Meyerhold's and Kurbas's work are a great achievement for the future theater of the proletariat. But through such a method, we may eventually be able to feel the technical milieu of the worker—though not the worker himself, and not his living nature. Therefore, in Meyerhold's and Kurbas's theaters we remember only technical construction, while in the Yiddish Chamber Theater we remember living figures and excited masses. Therefore, those theaters may be revolutionary only when they perform concrete revolutionary plays that speak for themselves, while the Yiddish Chamber Theater is always revolutionary, regardless of its repertoire, because technique alone can also serve, did serve, and still serves the bourgeoisie, but living flesh and blood serves only itself.

6. A SHOLEM-ALEICHEM EVENING

The Yiddish Chamber Theater was a true revelation in our cultural creation, and this revelation came from the wintry north, from Petersburg.

We had old centers of our mass cultural creation: Warsaw, Vilna, later Kiev. In the course of generations, our mass life was created there; there our literature emerged and developed, there too the first dreams took shape of a real, artistic Yiddish theater. They dreamed—but nothing came of it. Then active agitation was conducted for a "true" theater. The first who began to suffer and torment himself was Perets Hirshbeyn; then A. Vayter began working toward this goal, and eventually Perets himself took over the task.

Under the impact of this heroic company, the unhappiness with the "old Yiddish

---

*Les Kurbas was director of the avant-garde Ukrainian theater.

From left, Aleksey Granovsky, director; Natan Altman, designer; Norvid, director. 1922.

theater," indeed, grew deeper—some signs of a new theater culture even appeared, but no new theater came out of it.

Meanwhile, a kind of cultural-history entanglement arose. For a long time, literature was the only element of our new culture. In time, literature also became the central organizational focus for all other domains of our artistic culture. Indeed, literature was the first to suffer in its isolation because of the actual lack of those other areas. Thus, after literature led an active campaign to bring them to life, a damaging illusion emerged in literature itself, an illusion that it was destined always to be the ruler, lawgiver, and tone giver in those areas of art, both during their emergence and after they had emerged. Writers became convinced that all other areas of art—painting, music, and especially theater—would and must be only appendixes to literature and would have to follow its directives. And if literature was creative in its own domain, in its relation to those other areas, especially the theater, it became a pure culture-bearer, didactic, and Jewishly dilettantish.

And suddenly—Petersburg!

Petersburg?

The city of the "Disseminators of Enlightenment" [a cultural organization to promote enlightenment and education among the Jews], of the Baron Ginzburg family, of *Voskhod* [a Russian journal for Jewish studies], of Slyozberg and Gruzenberg [famous lawyers], of Vinaver and "Deputy Friedman" [politicians], of Bramson and Pereferkovich [scholars]—in a word, the city of Jewish plutocratic junk—how is it related to the cultural creation of the Jewish masses?

Hence everyone was skeptical about the Yiddish Chamber Theater made in Petersburg. We know the "Societies for the Encouragement of Jewish Art" that used to emerge in Petersburg, with doctors, lawyers, and often led by State Councilors.

All of a sudden the Yiddish Chamber Theater moved to Moscow and gave its first performance: *A Sholem-Aleichem Evening.* It was an incredible sensation.

It was profanation enough that the theater was born without the midwifery of literature, but it also dared to manifest its independence in a Sholem-Aleichem performance! Isn't Sholem-Aleichem all "ours"? Don't we all know how he must be "interpreted" on the stage, what movements, gestures, and grimaces the performers must make, what decorative *illustrations* there must be—and here is everything topsy-turvy!

There was a hue and cry. Literature didn't recognize its dream image and began blocking the theater . . .

Several years of literary-dilettantish siege passed, supported by the Jewishy petit bourgeois small-mindedness of "everyday" Jews; and the Chamber Theater triumphed on the whole front. Now the Yiddish Chamber Theater celebrates its fifth anniversary, crowned with general and full recognition. At its celebration, it will have completed three hundred performances of the same, initially sensational, now canonized *Sholem-Aleichem Evening* . . .

Three hundred performances in four years! Not a small production program . . .

Permit me to quote myself. I once wrote about Sholem-Aleichem:

The major traits of Sholem-Aleichem's writings are daydreaming and skepticism; their unique combination creates lyrical irony, the lyric-Jewish humor. The daydreaming endows the skepticism with a hopeful character: it leaves the door open for the eternal "perhaps yes." The skepticism brings "a fair in the sky" (castle in the air) down to earth and transforms the tangible itself into a dream, into a question mark. This daydreaming that gives wings of hope to doubt, this doubt that is willing meanwhile to deny the dreams, give in their coupling the deep simplicity, the elementary force that often becomes the work of a genius. They undress the soul, taking off all the inherited sociocultural layers, and show it in its original form at the "time of Creation."

Sholem-Aleichem's lyricism, his lyrical humor, reveals the elementary force in the Jewish psyche. True, it is the psyche of certain Jewish strata in a specific historical epoch, but he succeeded in getting to the root, discovering our psychic skeleton. The unique coupling of daydreaming and skepticism in his lyrical work creates the world of chaos in which his enchanted figures spin around like primitive marionettes. They say words that are so elementary and obvious, that are really on the tip of one's tongue, that we are amazed that we didn't predict ourselves, and yet they are always new, as an artistic discovery. Their movements and grimaces are the eternally old-new—and it often seems to us that we didn't see it first in Sholem-Aleichem but that he copies it readymade from us. (*In Umru* [Kiev, 1918], pp. 93–94.)

Daydreaming and skepticism, dream and doubt—those are the two basic areas of the human psyche: the areas of emotionalism and rationalism, spontaneity of feeling and the kingdom of rationality. We shall not enter into an argument about what causes what. I think that moving from the "kingdom of necessity" to the "kingdom of freedom" means that our future life will be regulated by rationality and not by spontaneous feeling, on the condition that rationality itself will by then have the clairvoyance of feeling.

But the Yiddish Chamber Theater evokes in us clear-cut conceptions about Sholem-Aleichem's figures and their chaotic world through methods of rationalistic creation. Menakhem-Mendel Yakenhoz (Mikhoels) reaches us, after all, as living and feeling flesh and blood. But we can see tangibly that this is achieved through an iron band of mathematical movements and gestures. Only this is his "psychic skeleton" revealed to us, from which, covered with skin and flesh, endless variations of Menakhem-Mendel can blossom. Or take Reb Alter in *Mazl-Tov*. Here we see through the "bare mathematics," the "elementary simplicity that often becomes a work of genius." Dressed in Chagall's costumes and surrounded by Chagall's designs, which, with all their fantasy, are rigorously calculated, mathematically concrete, they become those "enchanted figures" that remind us of "almost primitive marionettes" that can give rise to a plethora of new types.

Or take the episode *It's a Lie!* Through the impulsive speech of two skeptical, daydreaming figures in Sholem-Aleichem's Jewish world of chaos, confined in the iron

grating of calculated movements and gestures and caged in Chagallized Altman-
ish frames, we feel and palpably perceive, newly discovered, two Jewish *luftmentsh*[*]
figures.

Because of a misunderstanding, our literature initially negated *A Sholem-Aleichem
Evening*. But, in fact, it was and remained a powerful impetus for literature itself, for it
created an entirely new key to understanding and comprehending one of the founders
of our modern literature. For the first time, Sholem-Aleichem received the classical,
truly artistic embodiment of his figures. In the Chamber Theater, Sholem-Aleichem
was just a beginning and a herald—*The Sorceress* proved what the new Yiddish Theater
can make even of Goldfaden . . .

It is good that the twin sisters in our art culture finally recognized each other and
learned to live together. This is one of the best laurel wreaths for the Yiddish Chamber
Theater on its fifth anniversary . . .

The Yiddish Chamber Theater has found the secret of Jewish gesture. Jewish movement, Jewish plastics and dynamics, and, peeling the skin of Jewishy "wheeling and
dealing" off it, the theater discovered the boundary where the national is transformed
into the international. The theater created such a Jewish theater style, which can justly
claim to be one of the styles that will in their ensemble construct the new style of the
future international freedom-theater.

By the force of an immense sociocultural leap, of which the theater is capable, it
filled the gap in Jewish theater culture—the absence of artistic traditions. At one and
the same time, the theater creates artistic traditions that bear the value of generations
of culture, and also overcomes them, transforming them into only elements of an
artistic tradition. The theater found the magic key to the treasures of Jewish folklore,
which it poetically reshapes into works of art of a new mass culture.

---

[*]"People of the air"—Self-image of the Jews in Jewish literature: people who live in the air and on
air, with no roots in the ground.

CHAPTER NINE

Sholem-Aleichem—Two Short Pieces

Agents: A Joke in One Act

1905, Yiddish*

Yakenhoz: a mnemonic device to remember the order of the blessings said at the Kiddush on a holiday that falls at the end of the Sabbath. In Yiddish, Yakenhoz is a funny name, and may suggest a kind of rabbit. In the introduction to the comedy *Yakenhoz, or The Great Stock Market Game,* Sholem-Aleichem wrote, "Y, K, N, H, Z [Yakenhoz] has five letters, the initials of five words: Yayin, Kiddush, Ner, Havdoleh, Zman [wine, blessing, candle, separation (of weekdays and Sabbath), time]—the five signs of a Jewish holiday. The word itself has no meaning. It is something, yet nothing; nothing to hold on to. He who knows the trade of stocks, papers, rates, etc., on the stock market will understand at once the taste of Yakenhoz; and he who is far from that business will digest it only after reading the whole work to the end.

	Cast
Menakhem-Mendel Yakenhoz	A young man from a small town, dressed in a new outfit fresh from the needle, with a new fedora (which doesn't sit well on his head) and with a collar that squeezes his eyes out of his forehead. In his lap he holds a large briefcase, also new.
Mark Moyseyevich Lanternshooter	A young dandy. Also with a large briefcase.

* *Ale verk fun Sholem Aleykhem,* vol. 4 (New York, 1944).

Agents was one of three plays performed at *A Sholem-Aleichem Evening,* the first production by the State Yiddish Chamber Theater. In this translation from the Yiddish, those phrases that were originally to be spoken in Russian are rendered in French. The text is preceded by the author's note.

Akim Isaakovich Bakingfish	A stout character who values eating. Also with a large briefcase.
Lazar Konstantinovich Turtledove	A character with a big beard and a big family: a wife and several children, each one smaller than the next.
Various characters, extras	The action takes place on the road, in a third-class train car.

SCENE 1

[*In a train. Several characters sit, some lie stretched out, some sleep. On the racks, packages, valises. Up front, alone on a bench, close to the window, sits Menakhem-Mendel, observing his new outfit, talking to himself*]

MENAKHEM-MENDEL   Have they piled up clothes on me—like a bridegroom! All dolled up—like a bride! One problem—the pants are just a little bit too snug; and the collar . . . Oy, the collar! Just made for choking! . . . I'm traveling on a train. Do I know where I'm traveling? You will be, they said, a good agent. Your name alone, they said, will do it! Isn't it something, the name itself: Menakhem-Mendel Yakenhoz, who is known, they say, like a bad penny, everywhere—in Yehupets, in Boyberik, in Mazepevke—and where not? Travel, they said, among your little Jews, and be a success! Condemnify, they said, people to death . . . To condemnify people to death? How do you start to condemnify somebody to death? May I know such a bad supper! Though they crammed into me for two days the agent's Torah, and an "advance" they also gave me, and this is the main thing because all agents take "advances." If there were no "advances," they say, there would be no agents . . . In addition to that, they filled me up a full briefcase with constitutions—institutions, I mean—how an agent should operate when he condemnifies somebody to death. I must start in right away on the constitutions—institutions, I mean . . . [*Opens the briefcase and pulls out a letter*] Oh! Just mention Messiah—and you get a letter from Sheyne-Sheyndl! How does my mother-in-law put it: "When you look for scissors, you find a broom." . . . Still, you have to read again what she writes, your better half, may she have a long life. Anyway, it's boring on the train, nothing to do

[*Reads the letter*] "To my Honorable, Dear, Famous, Sage husband . . ." In short, "Our Teacher and Rabbi Reb Menakhem-Mendel, May his Light Illuminate. First of all, I come to inform you that we are all, thank God, in the best of health, may God let us hear the same from you, not worse, in the days to come . . ." [*Breaks off*] Thank the Almighty, blessed be He, at least in good health. [*Reads on*] "Second of all, I am writing to you that you should have as much strength, you piece of a convert . . ." [*Breaks off*] Already! She starts already with her blessings! [*Reads on*] "You should have as much strength, you piece of a convert, to wallow there in your disease, in the desolate, dark Yehupets, may it burn together with you in one fire, as much as I have strength to trip over my feet, for after all, the handsome doctor told me to lie in bed—may he lie in the cemetery next to you, as Mama says . . ." [*Breaks off*] Aha! As Mama says! [*Reads on*] " . . . as Mama says, so it'll be cozier for you on the long winter nights . . . What kind of new garbage—a new livelihood God sent down to him, my breadwinner! He will condemnify people to death! What does it mean, Mendel, that you will condemnify people to death? What for?" [*Breaks off*] She doesn't begin to understand what you write to her! [*Reads on*] "You're clean out of your mind—may you go out of your mind for all the Jews and for all the, not to put them in the same breath, Goyim, as Mama says . . ." [*Breaks off*] There she goes again with Mama! [*Reads on*] " . . . as Mama says, a horse, when you let go of the reins, lifts its tail too. It's not enough, that is, that you followed, over and over, all pagan rites, you were everything in the book: a dealer—a wheeler, a buyer—a liar, a matchmaker—a heartbreaker, a pester—a jester, so that the whole world has to deal with you—you also have to try out trading with dead living corpses, as Mama may she live says: Wait a minute, he will soon dress you up as a wet nurse some-where in Poland! . . . Wouldn't it have been a thousand times better if you should, for example, be now in the war with Jampony . . ." [*Breaks off*] Oh yes, of course! I'm flying right away! [*Reads on*] " . . . and return home in such a state, God forbid, like our Mosshe-Velvel Levi-Avrom came back, a dark night on me, with no arms and no legs and no body and no soul, as Mama says, does the bullet know who it shoots? . . . So remember, Mendel, this time I'm saying it with good wishes: May a commotion, a fire, a plague fall on you . . ."

Mark Moyseyevich Lanternshooter in Agents
by Sholem-Aleichem, 1921.

SCENE 2

[*Lanternshooter walks into the compartment with a big valise, looks for a place to sit down*]

LANTERNSHOOTER   *Permettez-moi?*

MENAKHEM-MENDEL   [*Hides the letter in his briefcase*] *Oh, pourquoi non?* [*To himself*] A fine personage with a pretty valise . . . Maybe he'll let me condemnify him to death?

LANTERNSHOOTER   [*Tends to his valise, sits down next to Menakhem-Mendel, pulls out a cigarette*] *Avez-vous du feu?*

[*To himself*] *Il faut examiner la terre*—a squeeze in the wagon.

MENAKHEM-MENDEL   Oh! *Pourquoi non?* [*Gives him a match. Talks to himself*] Better he starts first.

LANTERNSHOOTER   [*Offers him a cigarette*] *S'il vous plaît?* [*To himself*] *Un convenable subject* . . . A provincial with a new outfit . . . Maybe we can do business with him? Just a little insurance to cover expenses . . .

MENAKHEM-MENDEL   [*Takes the cigarette*] Oh! *Pourquoi non?* [*Lights the cigarette. Talks to himself*] On the face of it, a pretty solid citizen. God willing, he will condemnify himself to death.

LANTERNSHOOTER   [*To himself*] With such a jerk you can talk Yiddish. [*Starts talking Yiddish*] A pleasure to travel by train . . . Not like it used to be! When you traveled by wagon, you used to, *vous comprenez,* drag on and on and on.

MENAKHEM-MENDEL   [*Repeats after him*] Drag on and on and on.

LANTERNSHOOTER   You were in Diaspora in the hands of the carter, like clay in the Maker's hand.

MENAKHEM-MENDEL   Like clay in the Maker's hand.

LANTERNSHOOTER   He would pack a covered wagon with characters of various and sundry sorts.

MENAKHEM-MENDEL   Various and sundry sorts.

LANTERNSHOOTER   Jews, females, a sack of flour, and a cantor, and a goat, and a priest . . .

MENAKHEM-MENDEL   And a goat, and a priest . . .

LANTERNSHOOTER   And as you went uphill, he told the characters to make the effort to get out, forgive the inconvenience.

MENAKHEM-MENDEL   Forgive the inconvenience.

LANTERNSHOOTER   And today I'm a lord. I sit, *vous comprenez,* in a compartment and smoke a cigarette, *et je suis à mon aise!*

MENAKHEM-MENDEL   *A mon aise!*

LANTERNSHOOTER   The old traveling did have one advantage—your life was safe. You weren't afraid, God forbid, of an accident, a catastrophe, that is, of turning over, *vous comprenez,* and flying like dumplings, upside down.

MENAKHEM-MENDEL   Like dumplings, upside down.

LANTERNSHOOTER   It's good to be protected with several thousand rubles after your death, so your wife and children shouldn't, God forbid, *vous comprenez,* go begging in the streets.

MENAKHEM-MENDEL   Go begging in the streets . . . [*To himself*] He walks straight into it like a good horse . . .

LANTERNSHOOTER   [*To himself*] He follows me like a good colt! [*Aloud*] For, *vous comprenez,* as long as the wheel turns, it turns.

MENAKHEM-MENDEL   It turns.

LANTERNSHOOTER   And when it stops turning, it's—stop, machine!

MENAKHEM-MENDEL   Stop, machine!

LANTERNSHOOTER   [*To himself*] He follows nicely. Let's go with him straight to the stable. [*Aloud*] The problem is, not everyone can protect himself with money. Today's expenses, *vous comprenez*, with today-ay-ay-ay . . .

MENAKHEM-MENDEL   With today-ay-ay-ay . . .

LANTERNSHOOTER   So at least, *tout au moins, un petit insurance.*

MENAKHEM-MENDEL   *Un petit insurance* . . . [*To himself*] It's really something right from heaven, my word!

LANTERNSHOOTER   I just now recalled something that happened in our town. One simple citizen who never had a thousand rubles in his life, *vous comprenez*, never saw the eyes of a hundred-ruble bill, still had the good sense to insure himself in time for several thousand rubles. Now he died, traveling, may it not happen to you, in a train, so they paid his wife in our town not much but five thousand rubles cash, ruble by ruble!

MENAKHEM-MENDEL   Cash, one by one! Just the same as in our town. In our town too, something happened—not with five, but with ten thousand rubles. May God so help me wherever I turn!

LANTERNSHOOTER   [*Excited*] Ten thousand rubles?

MENAKHEM-MENDEL   Ten thousand rubles.

LANTERNSHOOTER   What did they do with such a sum of money?

MENAKHEM-MENDEL   What should they do? They opened a store, a clever store!

LANTERNSHOOTER   Really? Well? And they make some money?

MENAKHEM-MENDEL   And how! A treasure of a fortune!

LANTERNSHOOTER   [*To himself*] This is the best moment. Let's take him for a ride. [*Aloud*] What can you say, envy a dead corpse; but when you remember the living, *vous comprenez* . . . Everybody has a wife and children . . . [*Sighs*] Everybody has to do it.

MENAKHEM-MENDEL   [*Sighs*] Listen, this is what I'm talking about! [*To himself*] This is the best time. Let's rope him in.

LANTERNSHOOTER   [*Sighs*] Blessed be he who does it in time.

MENAKHEM-MENDEL   [*Sighs*] If you have good sense, you put the cart before the horse, you . . . and it's not expensive either. How much can it cost?

LANTERNSHOOTER   [*Excited*] It depends on your years. I mean, can we indeed do it here?

MENAKHEM-MENDEL   [Excited] Why not?

LANTERNSHOOTER   A doctor we can get later, submit an affidavit, *vous comprenez* . . .

MENAKHEM-MENDEL   That is my last worry. The main thing is the sum.

LANTERNSHOOTER   [*Grabs his briefcase*] The main thing isn't the sum, the main thing is the years.

MENAKHEM-MENDEL   [*Grabs his briefcase*] Normally, the years. For example, how old are you?

LANTERNSHOOTER   Me? What does it matter how old I am?

MENAKHEM-MENDEL   What do you mean what does it matter? You said yourself the main thing is the years, didn't you?

LANTERNSHOOTER   What do you mean? You want to indemnify me?

MENAKHEM-MENDEL   What else? You want to condemnify me?

LANTERNSHOOTER   Are you an agent too?

MENAKHEM-MENDEL   And how! Not just an agent, a super-agent!

LANTERNSHOOTER   [*Stands up, shakes his hand, and introduces himself politely but arrogantly*] Mark Moyseyevich Lanternshooter, Agent Acquérer Régional of "Equitable."

MENAKHEM-MENDEL   [*Stands up and introduces himself elegantly*] Menakhem-Mendel Yakenhoz, Super-agent of "Yakir."

SCENE 3

[*Bakingfish enters the compartment with two valises and looks for a place to sit down*]

BAKINGFISH   *Vous permettez?*

LANTERNSHOOTER   *S'il vous plaît.*

MENAKHEM-MENDEL   Play!

BAKINGFISH   [*Sits down opposite, spreads his valises around. He opens one valise and takes out bottles and boxes with various foods, puts the second valise upright, like a table, and starts eating*] On the road, you hear, it's good to carry everything with you because you can't get what you need at every station, and I don't eat everything they give me. I'm afraid for my stomach. That is, God forbid, that I have a sick stomach, may it go on forever, but I'm afraid not to spoil it. The stomach, you hear, is a kettle. If, God forbid, the kettle stops cooking, then the whole machine is kaput. [*Opens a bottle and pours himself a drink*] L'Chaim, Jews, to your health. [*Pours another drink and offers it to*

Menakhem-Mendel] Forgive me, will you have a little sip? My own home brew from orange peels.

MENAKHEM-MENDEL   [*To himself*] A real friendly person. Maybe we could condemnify him to death? [*Aloud*] Thank you! Better offer it to him. [*Points to Lanternshooter*]

LANTERNSHOOTER   [*To Menakhem-Mendel*] Drink up. [*To himself*] A friendly subject. We could indemnify him, to cover expenses . . .

BAKINGFISH   [*Has another drink and offers one to Lanternshooter*] Have a sip, I beg you, of a good little drink and wash it down with these sardelles. Exquisite sardelles. Hah? What do you say? Aren't they good sardelles? Aren't they fresh? I don't move without sardelles. Don't ask, who knows what may happen on the road. On the road, you have to watch out for your food, because your health, you hear, is the most precious thing in the world. [*Opens a bundle of kishke (stuffed derma), eats, and offers them some*] Since you already tasted my sardelles, you have to taste my dried kishke too. Don't be scared, it's fresh and kosher, too. I, if I buy kishke, I don't buy just any old kishke. Health, you hear, is the most precious thing in the world. Because, if you think about death, you're not sure of your life, and especially if you left at home a wife with two little kids like two eyes in your head.

LANTERNSHOOTER   [*Eats*] No more than two?

MENAKHEM-MENDEL   Only two?

BAKINGFISH   [*Chewing*] Not enough? And if, God forbid, you pick yourself up and drop dead?

LANTERNSHOOTER   [*Eats*] With your complexion?

MENAKHEM-MENDEL   [*Eats*] Kenna-hora, no evil eye should see it, with your looks?

BAKINGFISH   [*Chewing*] Don't look at me that I'm so . . . If I hadn't supported myself with food, I would already have—Eh-heh-heh! [*Opens another bundle*] Come on, will you taste, forgive me, the soaked meat! It's cold but fresh. I, when I buy meat, I don't buy just any old meat. Why don't you have a pickle? It's an etrog, not a pickle. My wife, may she live long, before I leave home, when she starts to pack, she packs and packs and packs and packs . . . Take, I beg you, a glass of cherry brandy. It's our own cherry brandy, my wife's specialty.

LANTERNSHOOTER   [*Drinks*] A loyal wife you have.

MENAKHEM-MENDEL   [*Drinks*] You have a loyal wife.

BAKINGFISH   A rarity. One in a whole guberniya! What do you know?

LANTERNSHOOTER   It's not a wife, *vous comprenez*, but a treasure!

MENAKHEM-MENDEL   A treasure, not a wife!

BAKINGFISH   What do you know? What do you know?

LANTERNSHOOTER   [*To himself*] Stepped on the right spot . . . It looks like it'll go the right way . . . [*Aloud*] Such a wife, you must appreciate.

MENAKHEM-MENDEL   [*To himself*] He takes him in the right way . . . [*Aloud*] Such a wife, you have to respect, such a wife!

BAKINGFISH   [*Peels an orange*] What do you know? What do you know? Take, I beg you, a piece of orange. Good oranges. I, when I go to buy oranges, I don't buy just any old oranges. This, too, she packed for me, my wife, I mean . . .

LANTERNSHOOTER   [*Peels an orange*] A wife like yours, you must not leave just like that, with no protection, God forbid, for in case of the worst case, in case, Heaven forfend, of a catastrophe. *Vous comprenez?* My way of doing it, that, *en principe*, a wife must be protected, let alone children, and let alone people like us, *vous comprenez*, road people . . .

MENAKHEM-MENDEL   [*To himself*] Not bad, not bad, on my word! [*Aloud*] We are, after all, road people, aren't we!

BAKINGFISH   My way of doing it too, that a wife you must protect, insure at least with a capital of some ten thousand rubles. There is only one recipe for that.

LANTERNSHOOTER   [*Excited*] To indemnify yourself?

MENAKHEN-MENDEL   [*Excited*] To condemnify yourself to death?

BAKINGFISH   How did you guess what I mean? You took the words right out of my mouth!

LANTERNSHOOTER   Good sense. For how else could people like us, *vous comprenez*, protect our wives?

MENAKHEM-MENDEL   Simple good sense!

BAKINGFISH   Absolutely right. If you can pay a little at a time, and it doesn't cost much . . . Which one of you would like to make a deal?

LANTERNSHOOTER   [*Grabs his briefcase*] Me, naturally. [*Looks down at Menakhem-Mendel*]

MENAKHEM-MENDEL   [*Grabs his briefcase*] Naturally, me.

BAKINGFISH   You mean, both of you? My pleasure, even better. [*Bends down for his briefcase*] About a doctor, I think, there won't be any problem.

LANTERNSHOOTER   From a doctor, we can bring an affidavit later. The main thing is the years.

MENAKHEM-MENDEL   A paper from a doctor you can furnish later. How old are you—this is the main thing.

BAKINGFISH   Me?

LANTERNSHOOTER   Who else?

MENAKHEM-MENDEL   Who else, me?

BAKINGFISH   What do you mean? Didn't you want me to in—

LANTERNSHOOTER   You should us? We thought you!

MENAKHEM-MENDEL   You, we thought!

BAKINGFISH   You? Me? Are you age—?

LANTERNSHOOTER   Of course, agents! And you?

MENAKHEM-MENDEL   Agents, naturally! And you, who are you?

BAKINGFISH   [*Stands up, dusts off the food. Stretches out his hand*] I have the honor to introduce myself: Akim Isaakovich Bakingfish, Inspector-Organizer of "New York."

LANTERNSHOOTER   Really? Our brother's keeper! Mark Moyseyevich Lanternshooter, Agent Acquéreur Régional of "Equitable." [*Looks down at Menakhem-Mendel*]

MENAKHEM-MENDEL   Are you really, indeed, one of us?! [*Elegantly*] Menakhem-Mendel Yakenhoz, Super-agent of "Yakir."

SCENE 4

[*Turtledove enters the train with his clan, lots of suitcases, packages, and baskets covered with shawls. Looks for a place for himself and his family*]

TURTLEDOVE   *Est-ce que je peux entrer?*

BAKINGFISH   *Je vous en prie.*

LANTERNSHOOTER   *Enchanté.*

MENAKHEM-MENDEL   *Dans chanté.* [*The new character sits down with his wife and children, and they begin spreading their packages around. Commotion, tumult. One screams "Dinner! Mama, dinner!" Another wants a drink. The mother cracks nuts and puts them into a little child's mouth; she holds another baby at her breast. The older ones push to the window, elbow each other aside. The father honors them—one with a slap, one with a poke, one with a smack on the back*]

BAKINGFISH   [*To himself*] Such a head of a family surely would need to be insured. [*Aloud*] No good with children on the road?

LANTERNSHOOTER   [*To himself*] *Un convenable* subject to indemnify himself with the children! [*Aloud*] On the road with children must, I'm sure, be hard?

MENAKHEM-MENDEL   [*To himself*] Maybe this character would condemnify himself to death, maybe? [*Aloud*] It's hard, I'm sure, with children on the road?

TURTLEDOVE   As hard as death.

BAKINGFISH   They're jittery, your kids, aren't they?

LANTERNSHOOTER   You spoil them?

MENAKHEM-MENDEL   Are they spoiled, your kids?

TURTLEDOVE   [*Pokes the oldest to move him away from the window*] Not so jittery as dear.

BAKINGFISH   Fine children you have.

LANTERNSHOOTER   No evil eye turned out well, *vous comprenez?*

MENAKHEM-MENDEL   Turned out well, no evil eye.

TURTLEDOVE   Not bad. Learn very well. Well-bred. Breeding is the main thing. [*Calls the oldest one*] Abrasha, come here! Give the uncle a hand. So, Abrasha! [*Abrasha doesn't want to come and gets a slap from father*] You see this brat? [*Points to the second one*] What a head! A genius, I'm telling you! But a hooligan! Oy, a hooligan! You argue with him, he'll mix you with mud . . . And that snot-nosed boy, you see?—A sage! Listens to his mother like a tomcat. But for me they have some respect. That is, they wouldn't listen to me either, but I have a whip and I lash, oy do I lash! Children, you hear, have to be taught, educated. Education is the main thing. You see this little squirrel, whose mother feeds him nuts? A big mouth! Not yet four years old and talks every word, every word like an old man. Davidke! Come here, Davidke! [*The squirrel called Davidke doesn't want to get out of his mother's arms, turns his head to father*] Tell me, Davidke, what's your name? [*Davidke answers "Tye, tye, tye."*] How old are you, Davidke? [*Davidke answers "Tye, tye, tye."*] Davidke! Ask your mother to give you jam. [*Davidke turns his head to his mother: "Tye, tye, tye!"*] What do you say to that? Every word, every word, like an old man!

BAKINGFISH   [*Enthusing*] For such children, you got to have a lot.

LANTERNSHOOTER   For them, *vous comprenez*, you got to gird your loins.

MENAKHEM-MENDEL   Gird your loins, you got to.

TURTLEDOVE   What's to be amazed! You see my gray hair? [*Points to his beard*] Not yet fifteen years after the wedding.

BAKINGFISH   [*Shakes his head*] Ay-yay-yay!

LANTERNSHOOTER   No evil eye, such a company!

MENAKHEM-MENDEL   Such a company, no evil eye!

TURTLEDOVE   To nourish, clothe, shoe, teach, educate! Education is the main thing. That is, I'm not complaining, God forbid. Thank God I have a fine job, I work out my few thousand rubles with these ten fingers. [*Shows them his fingers*] But as I take a look at my tribe, no evil eye, and it occurs to me, if, heaven forfend, may God watch over, the hour should never come . . . You understand? As long as the head serves, and the hands work . . . You understand?

BAKINGFISH   Oh! We understand very well. We are also family men. We know the taste of raising children.

LANTERNSHOOTER   To protect children is, *vous comprenez*, one of the big things!

MENAKHEM-MENDEL   A big thing to protect children, to protect!

TURTLEDOVE   I argue it all the time with my wife, and with everybody separately, wherever I come, I argue the same: What would people like us have done, middle-class people, if there were no means to—

BAKINGFISH   [*Takes the words out of his mouth*] To insure yourself?

LANTERNSHOOTER   To indemnify yourself, *pour le cas de mort*?

MENAKHEM-MENDEL   To condemnify yourself to death?

TURTLEDOVE   [*Excited*] I see on your faces that you all understand it very well, and that you are all ready to make a deal? So I can only congratulate you—you're doing a good thing.

BAKINGFISH   [*Very agitated*] We do what our duty tells us to do.

LANTERNSHOOTER   What our conscience dictates, *vous comprenez*.

MENAKHEM-MENDEL   We are doing the just thing, we are.

TURTLEDOVE   May God help you, as you wish it for yourself, may you have long days and years, may God give you pleasure as you have given me pleasure, along with my wife and children; they, poor things, are looking for this, for I am their only breadwinner. [*Pulls out a briefcase*] How much do you want to make? For instance, what kind of a sum, that is?

BAKINGFISH   [*Busies himself with his briefcase*] How can we know what kind of a sum?

LANTERNSHOOTER   [*Busies himself with his briefcase*] Can we, *vous comprenez*, give you any advice?

MENAKHEM-MENDEL   What do you mean, we should give you advice, we?

TURTLEDOVE   [*Amazed*] What do you mean, you me? It's I who want you—

BAKINGFISH   [*Beside himself*] You want to make the spiel to us?

LANTERNSHOOTER   You want to indemnify us, *en cas de mort*?

MENAKHEM-MENDEL   You want to condemnify us to death? *You?*

TURTLEDOVE   What else? *You—me?* Are you agents too?

BAKINGFISH   Ha-ha-ha! Of course, agents. And how about you?

LANTERNSHOOTER   Agents, *vous comprenez.* And who are you?

MENAKHEM-MENDEL   Agents, you bet! And you?

TURTLEDOVE   [*Elegantly*] Lazar Konstantinovich Turtledove, Inspector General and Agent Organizer of "Urban."

BAKINGFISH   [*Elegantly*] Akim Isaakovich Bakingfish, Inspector-Organizer of "New York."

LANTERNSHOOTER   Mark Moyseyevich Lanternshooter, Agent Acquéreur Régional of "Equitable." [*Looks down at Menakhem-Mendel*]

MENAKHEM-MENDEL   [*Elegantly*] And I am Menakhem-Mendel Yakenhoz, am I, Super-agent of "Yakir." [*All four shake hands and exchange cards. Only Menakhem-Mendel pats all his pockets*] Oh dear! I haven't got any cards yet, I haven't!

TURTLEDOVE   [*Sighs*] A hard way to make a living. Eh?

BAKINGFISH   [*Sighs*] Like crossing the Red Sea! You travel, you sniff, you think—maybe?

LANTERNSHOOTER   [*Looks down at Menakhem-Mendel*] *Vous comprenez?* Maybe it would not have been so bad if there weren't so many agents. *Vous comprenez,* competition . . .

MENAKHEM-MENDEL   What do I need competition-shmompetition? Say it in simple Yiddish: You lay in the ground and bake bagels.

CURTAIN

It's a Lie! Dialogue in Galicia   1906, Yiddish[*]

"You're going, it seems, to Kolomea?"

"How do you know to Kolomea?"

"I heard you talking to the conductor. Are you really from Kolomea, or are you just going to Kolomea?"

"Really from Kolomea. So what?"

"Nothing. I'm just asking for no reason. A really nice town, Kolomea?"

"So what if it's a nice town? A town, like any other town in Galicia. A pretty town, a very pretty town! . . ."

[*] *Ale verk fun Sholem Aleykhem,* vol. 4 (New York, 1944).

Scene from It's a Lie!
Dialogue in Galicia
by Sholem-Aleichem, 1923.

"I mean, you've got some fine people, rich people there?"

"There's all kinds: there's rich ones, there's beggars. The usual, more beggars than rich ones."

"The same thing we've got. For every rich man—no evil eye, a thousand beggars. With you in Kolomea, there must be a rich man Finkelstein?"

"There's a rich man Finkelstein. So what? You know him?"

"Know him I don't, but I heard. Isn't his name Reb Shaya?"

"Reb Shaya. So what?"

"Nothing. I'm just asking for no reason. Is he really as rich as they say, this Reb Shaya?"

"Do I know? I didn't count his money. What are you asking me so much? You need to know because of credit?"

"No, no good reason. He has, they say, a daughter."

"He has three daughters. Maybe because of a match? How much—did they tell you?—he's giving his daughter as a dowry?"

"This has nothing to do with a dowry, understand. We're talking here about a house: What kind of house does Reb Shaya Finkelstein have? What kind of conduct, that is?"

"What kind of house? A house like all houses. A Jewish house, a fine house, a Hasidic house, a very handsome house! They even say that, for Jewishness with him lately . . . But it's a lie!"

"What's a lie?"

"Whatever they say, it's a lie. Kolomea, you should know, is a town where everybody's a liar."

"So, just because of that, it's good to know what they say, for instance, about his house?"

"They say that it's not what it used to be. For instance, that they used to eat there on Passover superkosher matzo, shmura . . . He himself used to go twice a year to the Rebbe. And now . . . Now that's not it . . ."

"And that's all?"

"What did you want? They should throw out beards and sidelocks and eat pork in public?"

"You say 'they say,' so I thought, Who knows what they say! So the important thing is whether the human being himself is a human being. That is, I mean, whether he, this Reb Shaya Finkelstein, I mean, is a fine man, a decent one? That's what I mean."

"So what if he's a decent man? A man like any other man. A fine man. What should I say? An extremely fine man! In our town they even say that he's a little . . . But it's a lie!"

"What's a lie?"

"Everything they say about him, it's a lie; Kolomea is that kind of town, where they love to talk about each other; so I don't want to repeat it, 'cause that's what's called slander."

"If you know it's a lie, it's not slander anymore."

"They say that he's . . . a little . . . a spinning top."

Scene from It's a Lie!

"A spinning top? Every Jew's a spinning top. A Jew spins. You don't?"

"A spinning top and a spinning top, it's not the same thing. About him they say, you understand . . . But it's a lie!"

"What, in fact, do they say about him?"

"Why, I'm telling you, it's a lie!"

"I want to know the lie they say."

"They say he already went bankrupt three times. But it's a lie! I know only about once."

"That's all? Where did you see a dealer not go broke? A dealer deals until he deals himself out. A dealer, if he dies without going broke, it's a sign that he died too soon. What? Isn't it?"

"With you, everything's called going broke? About him they say that he went broke in an ugly way, he dropped his pants and gave the world the finger. Get it?"

"No dummy, apparently. Well, and outside of that, nothing?"

"What else did you want? He should slaughter somebody? Commit a crime? In our town, they even tell a story that's not so nice . . . But it's a lie!"

"That is, what kind of story?"

"A story with a landlord . . . A cock and bull story!"

"What kind of story with a landlord?"

"Some landlord there . . . Receipts . . . Do I know what Kolomea can make up? It's a lie! I know it's a lie!"

"So you know it's a lie, so that won't hurt him."

"He dealt, they say, with a landlord, a very rich landlord, that he was a very important man with the landlord, a very important man. Meantime, the landlord died, so he submitted a few receipts from him; so a shout came up in the town: Where did he get those receipts, since the landlord didn't sign any paper when he was alive? . . . Kolomea, you should know, is a town where they pay attention . . ."

"Well?"

"Well, well! So he had a bundle on him . . ."

"That's all? Every Jew's got a bundle. Did you ever see a Jew without a bundle?"

"But that one, they say, had three bundles."

"Three bundles? That is, what kind of bundles did he, do they say, have on him?"

"With a mill, they say, he had something to do . . . But that's surely a lie!"

"It burned down, probably, and they said he himself made the blessing—"Blessed be He who created Light by means of fire"—because the mill was old, so he insured it properly so he could build a new one afterward."

"How do you know that was the story?"

"Know it I didn't, but I supposed that had to be the story."

"That, that is, is how they talk in our town of Kolomea, but it's a lie. I can swear to you that it's a lie!"

"I don't care if it's the truth. What other bundle did you say he carried on him?"

"I say? The town says. But that's just nitpicking, a frame-up, a pure frame-up."

"A frame-up? False coin?"

"Even worse."

"What could be worse?"

"A shame to tell what Kolomea can make up! Empty people . . . Do-nothings . . . And maybe it was something concocted so they could suck out money? You don't know? A small town, and rich and has enemies . . ."

"He had something to do, of course, with a servant maid? . . ."

"How do you know? They already told you?"

"Told me did nobody, but I already guessed. That must have cost him a few good kreuzers, that frame-up?"

"I wish for both of us that we would earn every week, I'm not your enemy, what that cost him, if he was not guilty of that. A small town . . . A rich Jew . . . If things are good for him . . . they don't wish him well . . . They simply don't wish him well! . . ."

"Could be. Has he got fine children, decent? Three daughters, you, I think, said."

"Three. Two married and one single. Fine children, very fine children . . . About the oldest one they even say that . . . But it's a lie!"

"That is, what do they say about her?"

"But I told you, it's a lie."

"I know it's a lie. But I want to know the lie."

"If you want to hear all the lies that are going around in our town of Kolomea, three days and three nights won't be enough for you . . . About the oldest one, they say that she walks around with her own hair. I'm here to tell you that that's a lie 'cause she's not so educated that she should wear her own hair. And about the second daughter, they simply made that up when she was still a girl . . . But what Kolomea can make up! It's a lie!"

"It's worthwhile to hear what they can make up in your town of Kolomea."

"Well, I told you that everybody in Kolomea is a liar, a slanderer, and a long-tongued gossip. You don't know? In a little town, if a girl goes out walking alone at night in the street in the dark with a fellow, they set up a ruckus: What does a girl have to go walking around in Kolomea at night alone with a druggist?

"That's the whole thing?"

"What else did you want? She should run away with him in the middle of Yom Kippur to Czernowicz like, they say, the trick the younger one played?"

"What kind of trick did the younger one play?"

"Never mind, really, to repeat all the nonsense going around in our town of Kolomea—I hate repeating a lie! . . ."

"You already told a whole lot of lies. Tell this lie too."

"I don't tell my own lies, Reb Jew, I tell those of others! . . . And I really don't understand why you're asking so much about every one separately, like a prosecutor? You, it seems to me, a Jew, who likes only to grope around, interrogate, drag out of everybody the marrow of his bones, and you yourself are scared to let a word escape from your mouth . . . Don't attack me for telling you the truth and nothing but the truth. You, it seems to me, are a Russian Jew, and the Russians have in them an ugly nature: they like to get right into your heart with their boots . . . The Russians, it turns out, are no little slanderers . . . By the way, Kolomea's coming up . . . The time has come to take the bundles . . . Ex-c-cuse me!"

Notes

CHAPTER 1. THE YIDDISH ART THEATER

1. See Chapter 4.
2. In the Soviet Yiddish spelling, "Yiddish" is spelled with an alef אידיש and the word is pronounced "Idish"; and "theater" is spelled as in Russian, "Teatr," rather than as the generally accepted Yiddish "Teater."
3. See Harshav, *Language in Time of Revolution.*
4. Jewish immigrants in America referred to their language as "Jewish."
5. Huntley Carter, in *Leningradskaya krasnaya gazeta*, Aug. 30, 1926.
6. Kerr, "Moscow Yiddish Theater (1928)." (The essay is translated in full in Chapter 5.)
7. *Kultur-Lige*, pp. 1–3.
8. See Chapter 4.
9. Levidov, "Jewish Theater Society and the Chamber Theater." (See the translated essay in Chapter 4.)
10. See Chapter 4.
11. Orshansky, *Teatr-shlakhtn.*
12. See Chapter 3.
13. See Chapter 3.
14. See Chapter 4.
15. Mikhoels, "In Our Studio," p. 22. (See the translated essay in Chapter 4.)
16. Ibid.
17. Ibid.
18. Ibid.
19. See Chapter 7.
20. See Chapter 4.
21. See Chapter 6.
22. Markov, *Soviet Theatre*, pp. 165–166.
23. On the concept of a fictional world, see Pavel, *Fictional Worlds*; and Harshav, "Fictionality and Fields of Reference."
24. On the role of fictional worlds and the Chagallian fictional universe in his art, see Harshav, *Marc Chagall and the Lost Jewish World.*
25. See Chapter 5.
26. See Chapter 9.

27. For one version of *Benjamin the Third*, see *The Travels of Benjamin the Third* by Mendele Moykher Sforim, adapted for the stage by Yikhezkel Dobrushin, a literary theater script published by Benjamin Harshav and Yosef Schein and included in *The Flowering of the Moscow Yiddish Theater*, edited and introduced by Benjamin Harshav, pp. 1–40.

28. Mikhoels, "Mikhoels Vofsi on the Theater."

29. Ibid.

30. Mikhoels, "Our Comedians' Parade."

31. Van Gyseghem, *Theatre in Soviet Russia*, p. 174.

32. See Chapter 5.

33. Osborn, "Marc Chagall," p. 13.

34. Ibid.

35. On Chagall's life, see Harshav, *Marc Chagall and His Times*.

36. See Chapter 8.

37. Chagall, "My Work in the Moscow Yiddish Theater."

38. In the *New York Times* of December 14, 1926, the influential drama critic J. Brooks Atkinson wrote of *The Dybbuk*, "The effect is astonishing, as unreal as the mystic legend of the play."

39. The Labor Zionists won the Jewish vote in the only free elections in Soviet Russia, the 1918 elections to the Constitutional Assembly, which was forcibly dispersed by the Bolsheviks. Those Zionist voters were still alive six years later. The "Jewish rich man" is an allusion to the nouveaux riches of the NEP, the liberal New Economic Policy that enabled the temporary emergence of a new entrepreneurial class. Both the Zionists and the nouveaux riches were quite recent and soon liquidated.

40. Abram, "No Doubt!"

41. *Idisher kamer teatr* (1924).

42. Toller, Roth, and Goldschmidt, *Das Moskauer Jüdische Akademische Theater*. The book is translated in this volume; see Chapter 6.

43. Burko, *Soviet Yiddish Theatre in the Twenties*, p. 81.

44. Schein, *Arum moskver yidishn teater*.

45. The papers of the commission were kept in TsGALI (Central State Archive for Literature and Art, today named RGALI, Russian State Archive for Literature and Art), Moscow, fond. 2307, opis' 1, unit 81: "Acts of Documentary Control of the Financial-Economic Activity of the Liquidation Commission of the Moscow State Yiddish Theater" (1950; 66 pp.); and units 82–83: "Acts and Powers of Attorney for the Transfer and Acceptance of Property of the Moscow State Yiddish Theater" (1950; vol. 1, 206 pp.; vol. 2, 179 pp.). In 1976, however, these files were extracted from the archive and sent for destruction as scrap paper (*vydeleny v makulaturu*). Unit 3 is also missing. According to some sources, the commission's papers must be preserved somewhere, perhaps by the KGB (the fate of similar files sent as "scrap paper"). (This note was written in 1992. Better information may be obtainable now. Most papers on this theater and its liquidation are in the archives of the Ministry of the Interior, the former KGB.)

46. See Kovaliev, "Report on the Restoration of the Murals," p. 134.

CHAPTER 2. CHAGALL'S THEATER MURALS

1. This chapter is based on two books on Chagall: on his life, Harshav, *Marc Chagall and His Times*; and on his art, Harshav, *Marc Chagall and the Lost Jewish World*. The readers may find there further stories, discussions, and bibliographies.

2. See Chapter 3.

3. See Chapter 3.

4. See Chapter 3.

5. "Realization of a metaphor" is a concept of the Russian Formalists: an image introduced in the text through a metaphor becomes a real figure or object in the fictional reality of the poem. It is a major device of modern poetry and is typical of Kafka's and Chagall's works.

6. Malevich, "Non-Objective World," in Chipp et al., *Theories of Modern Art*, pp. 341–342.

7. Chagall apparently ran out of paint, as he claimed years later, explaining to his Russian hosts in 1973 why he left the Soviet Union in 1922.

8. It is interesting to note that at the time Bakhtin lived in Vitebsk and his pupil Pavel Medvedev was head of the City Culture Department and collaborated with Chagall. The Bakhtinian concepts of carnival, polyphony, and dialogical discourse fit Chagall very well.

9. See Chapter 3.

10. This iconography is a development from my earlier descriptions of the long wall, notably: (1) Harshav, "Chagall: Postmodernism and Fictional Worlds"; and (2) Harshav, "L'Introduction au Théâtre juif."

    Several scholars contributed to the interpretation of the *Introduction*, notably Ziva Amishai-Maisels, in "Chagall's Murals for the State Jewish Chamber Theater." I learned from Professor Amishai-Maisels and others, but there is no space here to rehearse critical arguments about diverse interpretations.

11. Chagall, *My Life*.

12. Chagall, "Chagall's First Autobiography."

13. The identity of the player as the leading actor Solomon Mikhoels has been questioned, but is recorded by Franz Meyer in Chagall's name and matches Chagall's memoirs on Mikhoels's puzzled admiration for Chagall and his conversion to the painter's modern art, which carried along the whole ensemble.

14. Chagall wrote this long name from left to right, i.e., from the end backward, for in Hebrew a vowel marked under a letter comes after the consonant. If he had written it in the Yiddish direction, right to left, it would come out IKISVNORAG and would make no sense either way we read it.

15. It seems that Chagall started to write this name from left to right, then stumbled for some reason (perhaps because, instead of the Yiddish "O," he wrote "V," as the letter would be in Hebrew). Then he started with small letters from the right, slowly moving up toward the size of the left-hand letters, intending to spell IKS, but discovered the graphically similar IKT, the name of the theater, and repeated it in order to fill the void. There is clearly a leap upward from the right to the "U" on the left.

16. See Chapter 4.

17. Some read this as "Yiddish Chamber Theater Movement" (here, "K" stands for "*kamer*"), but this is wrong, because "*Yidishe*" is feminine, while "theater" is masculine. Apart from "*kultur*," only "movement" is feminine; if correct, the alternative could only mean "the Yiddish movement of chamber theaters," but there was no such movement and a chamber theater with ninety seats hardly makes

one. The trap lies in the letter "к," which elsewhere alludes to "K[amer]" (Chamber) but may also allude to "K[ultur]," or to "K[ultur-Lige]," i.e., the Yiddish culture movement.

18. The Yiddish reflexive *ikh bàlave zikh* or, in colloquial Yiddish, *ikh bàlavezekh* ("I entertain myself," from the Russian *balovat'sia*) is written here in one word, as in Russian—yet another example of Chagall's use of Russian spelling habits in Yiddish. The repeated *ikh* (I) at the beginning and end of the phrase is a form of folk grammar, a way to show emphasis. Ziva Amishai-Maisel's translation of this expression as "I love you" (whom?) has no basis in either Yiddish or Russian.

19. Chagall, "Leaves from My Notebook," pp. 38–40.

20. Chagall, "My Work in the Moscow Yiddish Theater."

21. Chagall, "Chagall's First Autobiography."

Glossary of Names

This list is intended to be helpful rather than comprehensive. It does not include every name mentioned in the book, nor the names of some generally well-known people.

Abramovich, Sh. Y. *See* Mendele Moykher Sforim

Akhron, Yosef (1886–1943), music composer for the Moscow Yiddish theater.

Aleichem, Sholem. *See* Sholem-Aleichem.

Altman, Natan (1889–1970), Soviet painter and stage designer. After Chagall's departure, became a regular set designer at the Moscow Yiddish theater.

An-sky, Solomon, pseudonym of Shloyme-Zanvl Rapoport (1863–1920), scholar, folklorist, writer, author of *The Dybbuk*. Born in Vitebsk Province.

Asch, Sholem (1880–1957), prominent Yiddish novelist.

Baal-Makhshoves ("The Thinker"), pseudonym of Dr. Israel Isidor Elyashev (1873–1924), a major Yiddish literary critic.

Ben-Gurion, David (1886–1973), Labor Zionist leader in Palestine; first prime minister of Israel.

Bergelson, Dovid (1884–1952), major Yiddish Soviet novelist who lived in Germany in the 1920s. Shot on Stalin's orders.

Blok, Aleksandr (1889–1921), major Russian Symbolist poet.

Chagall, Marc (1887–1985), major Jewish modern painter.

Dimandshteyn, Semen (1886–1937), leader of the Yevsektzia (Jewish section of the Communist Party); liquidated in the Great Purges.

Dobrushin, Yikhezkel (1883–1952), dramaturge of the Yiddish theater who adapted most classical Yiddish works to the new Soviet reality.

Dobuzhinsky, Mstislav (1875–1957), a Russified Lithuanian aristocrat, art teacher, set designer; a leading figure in the Russian World of Art movement. Drew the first logo of the Moscow Yiddish theater in Petrograd.

Efros, Abram (1898–1954), art critic, professor of art history, poet, and translator; literary director of the Moscow Yiddish theater.

Evreinov, Nikolay (1879–1953), theater director, theoretician, innovator in the avant-garde theater.

Falk, Robert (1886–1958), painter, artist of Granovsky's Yiddish theater.

Fefer, Itsik (1900–1952), major Soviet Yiddish poet. Shot on Stalin's orders.

Frug, Semen (Shimen) (1860–1916), Russian and Yiddish poet.

Goldfaden, Abraham (1849–1908), playwright, theater director, pioneer of the Yiddish popular stage.

Goldschmidt, Alfons (dates unknown), German theater critic.

Granovsky, Aleksey or Aleksandr (Abraham Azarkh) (1890–1937), founder and original theater director of the Yiddish theater in Petrograd and Moscow until 1928.

Gutzkow, Karl (1811–1878), German playwright, author of *Uriel Acosta*.

Hirshbeyn, Perets (1881–1948), Yiddish playwright.

Kaganovich, Lazar (1893–1991), Soviet leader close to Stalin; a central member of the Politburo.

Kerr, Alfred (1867–1948), a leading Berlin theater critic.

Krein, Aleksandr (1883–1951), music composer; worked for the Yiddish and other theaters.

Kulbak, Moyshe (1896–1940), Yiddish poet and fiction writer. Liquidated in the purges.

Kurbas, Les (1887–1937), avant-garde Ukrainian theater director; studied with Max Reinhardt. Arrested and executed in 1937.

Levidov, Lev (dates unknown), chairman of the Jewish Theater Society in Petrograd.

Lissitzky, El (Eliezer) (1890–1941), major Suprematist and Constructivist artist.

Litvakov, Moyshe (1880–1939), prominent Jewish cultural leader in the Soviet Union; editor of the Yiddish party newspaper *Der emes* (The Truth). Liquidated.

Lunacharsky, Anatoly (1875–1933), first Soviet commissar of enlightenment (culture and education). Had a decisive role in transforming Russian culture after the Revolution.

Lyubomirsky (Lubomirsky), Y. (Yosef/Osip) (1884–1977) literary critic; wrote books on the Yiddish theater and on Mikhoels.

Malevich, Kazimir (1878–1935), painter, founder of Suprematism, promoter of "Non-Objective" abstract painting.

Mandelshtam, Y. (Osip) (1891–1938), major Russian poet. Liquidated.

Markish, Perets (1895–1952), major Yiddish Expressionist and Soviet poet. Shot on Stalin's orders.

Mayakovsky, Vladimir (d. 1930), major Futurist and Communist poet.

Mazeh, Jacob (1859–1924), Chief Rabbi of Moscow.

Mendele Moykher Sforim, or Mendele the Bookseller, pseudonym of Sh. Y. Abramovich (1835–1917), founding writer of modern Yiddish and Hebrew fiction.

Meyerhold, Vsevolod (1874–1940), major avant-garde innovator of Russian and Soviet theater.

Mikhoels, Solomon, pseudonym of Shloyme Vovsi/Vofsi (1890–1948), brilliant actor and theater director of the Moscow Yiddish theater.

Orshansky, Ber (1884–1945), activist in Soviet Jewish culture; chair of the Enlightenment Department of the Jewish Commissariat.

Pen, Yehuda (Yury) (1854–1937), painter of the Russian naturalistic school and Chagall's first art teacher.

Peretz, Itskhok-Leybush (Y.-L.) (1852–1915), Yiddish modern short-story writer and center of the young writers' movement in the beginning of the twentieth century.

Pinsky, Dovid (1872–1959), Yiddish fiction writer and playwright.

Pulver, Lev (1883–1970), musician and composer of the Yiddish theater.

Rabichev, Itshak (1896–1957), young artist of the Yiddish theater.

Rabinovich, Itshak (1894–1961), young artist of the Yiddish theater.

Radlov, Sergey (1898–1964), theater director.

Reinhardt, Max (1873–1943), innovative German theater director.

Rivesman, Mark (1868–1924), literary director of the Yiddish Chamber Theater.

Romains, Jules (1885–1972), French writer.

Roth, Joseph (1894–1939), major Jewish-German fiction writer in the early twentieth century.

Schein, Yosef (1919–unknown), one of the last students of Mikhoels's theater studio in Moscow; lived in Paris after World War II.

Segal, Chaim ben Yitshak from Slutsk (dates unknown), eighteenth-century artist; painted images in the synagogue in Mohilev. Chagall believed that Chaim Segal was his ancestor.

Shklovsky, Viktor (1893–1984), prominent Russian Formalist; modernist writer; theoretician of prose.

Sholem-Aleichem (meaning "How do you do?") (1859–1916), highly popular classical writer of Yiddish literature who wrote plays, novels, and short stories; master of humor combined with a profoundly critical view of Jewish existence.

Shtif, Nokhem (1879–1933), Yiddish scholar and cultural activist.

Stanislavsky, Konstantin (1863–1938), director of MKhAT (Moscow Academic Art Theater); staged all of Chekhov's plays. Theoretician of realist-psychological theater based on the actor's empathy with a real-life character, the "Stanislavsky method."

Tairov (Kornblit), Aleksandr (1885–1950), innovator and avant-garde director of the Moscow Chamber Theater, the "Little" Theater (Maly).

Toller, Ernst (1893–1939), German poet and Communist activist.

Tyshler, Aleksandr (1898–1964), prominent Russian stage designer and artist; last artist of the Moscow State Yiddish Theater.

Vakhtangov, Evgeny (1883–1922), prominent Russian theater director, disciple of Stanislavsky, director of the Hebrew theater HaBima.

Vayter, A. (Devenishsky) (1879–1919), Yiddish writer and cultural activist.

Yehoash, pseudonym of Solomon Blumgarten (1872–1927), major American Yiddish poet; translated the Bible into Yiddish.

Zemach (Tsemakh), Nakhum (1887–1939), founder and director of HaBima. Settled in the United States.

Zuskin, Benjamin (1899–1952), actor of the Yiddish theater, ranked second after Mikhoels. Shot on Stalin's orders.

Bibliography

Abram, L. "No Doubt!" In *Idisher kamer teatr* (1924). [Yiddish]

Altman, Natan. "The State Yiddish Chamber Theater (After the Premiere)." *Der emes*, Sept. 29, 1921. [Yiddish]

Altshuler, Mordechai, ed. *The Jewish Theater in the Soviet Union: Studies—Essays—Documents.* Jerusalem: Center for Research and Documentation of East European Jewry, The Hebrew University, 1996. [Hebrew]

Amiard-Chevrel, Claudine. *Le théâtre artistique de Moscou (1898–1917).* Paris: Centre national de la recherche scientifique, 1979. [French]

Amishai-Maisels, Ziva. "Chagall and the Jewish Revival: Center or Periphery?" In Apter-Gabriel, *Tradition and Revolution*, pp. 71–100. [English]

———. "Chagall's Murals for the State Jewish Chamber Theater." In Vitali, *Marc Chagall*, pp. 107–128. [English]

Apter-Gabriel, Ruth, ed. *Tradition and Revolution: The Jewish Renaissance in Russian Avant-Garde Art, 1912–1928.* Jerusalem: The Israel Museum, 1987. [English]

———. *Chagall: Dreams and Drama: Early Works and Murals for the Jewish Theatre.* Jerusalem: The Israel Museum, 1993. [English]

Atkinson, J. Brooks. "The Play" [review of *The Dybbuk*]. *New York Times*, Dec. 14, 1926. [English]

B. "The Opening of the Yiddish Chamber Theater." *Pravda*, Oct. 5, 1923. [Russian]

Bablet, Denis. *The Revolutions of Stage Design in the Twentieth Century.* Paris: Léon Amiel, 1977. [English]

Ben-Ari, R. *HaBima.* Chicago: L. M. Shteyn, 1937. [Yiddish]

Ben-Gurion, David. "Diary." In Norman, *Be-reyshit Ha-Bima.* [Hebrew]

Berezkin, V. I. *Sovetskaya stsenografiya* [Soviet Stage Design]. Moscow: Nauka, 1990. [Russian]

Bergelson, Dovid. "Dovid Bergelson on the Theater." *Literarishe bleter* (Warsaw), 5, no. 17 (Apr. 27, 1928). [Yiddish]

Bowlt, John E. *Russian Stage Design: Scenic Innovation, 1900–1930.* Jackson: Mississippi Museum of Fine Arts, 1982. [English]

———. *Khudozhniki russkogo teatra 1880–1930: Sobraniye Nikity i Niny Lobanovykh-Rostovskikh* [Artists of the

Russian Theater, 1880–1930: The Nikita and Nina Lobanov-Rostovsky Collection]. Moscow: Iskusstvo, 1990. [Russian]

Brockett, Oscar G. *Modern Theatre: Realism and Naturalism to the Present.* Boston: Allyn and Bacon, 1982. [English]

Buber, Martin. "Jüdische Renaissance" [The Jewish Renaissance]. In Buber, *Die jüdische Bewegung.* Berlin: Jüdischer Verlag, 1916. Originally published in *Ost und West,* 1901. [German]

———. "Von jüdischer Kunst" [On Jewish Art]. In Buber, *Die jüdische Bewegung.* Berlin: Jüdischer Verlag, 1916. Originally published in *Die Welt,* Jan. 17, 1902. [German]

Burko, Faina. *The Soviet Yiddish Theatre in the Twenties.* Ph.D. diss., Southern Illinois University, Carbondale, 1978. [English]

Carter, Huntley. Interview. *Leningradskaya krasnaya gazeta* [Leningrad Red Gazette], Aug. 30, 1926.

———. *The New Theater and Cinema of Soviet Russia.* New York: International Publishers, 1935. [English]

———. *The New Spirit in the Russian Theater: 1917–28.* New York: Benjamin Blom, 1970. [English]

Chagall, Marc. "Eygns" [My World; this is the original autobiography, written in 1922–1924]. *Tsukunft,* 30 (1925), pp. 158–162, 290–293, 359–361, 407–410. [Yiddish]

———. "My Work in the Moscow Yiddish Theater." *Di yidishe velt: Monthly for Literature, Criticism, Art, and Culture,* no. 2 (Vilna, Poland: B. Kletskin Publishing House, 1928). [Yiddish]

———. "My First Meeting with Solomon Mikhoels." *Yidishe kultur: Monthly of the Jewish World Culture Union* (New York), 6, no. 1 (1944). [Yiddish]

———. *Ma vie* [My Life]. Translated [from the Russian?] by Bella Chagall. Paris: Stock, 1932. Reprint, 1972. [French]

———. "Chagall's First Autobiography" [translation of "Eygns"]. In Harshav, *Marc Chagall and His Times,* pp. 70–166. [English]

———. "Leaves from My Notebook" [published in Yiddish in 1922]. In Harshav, *Marc Chagall on Art and Culture.* [English]

Chipp, Herschel B., with Peter Selz and Joshua C. Taylor. *Theories of Modern Art: A Source Book by Artists and Critics.* Berkeley: University of California Press, 1968. [English]

Compton, Susan. "Chagall's Auditorium: 'An Identity Crisis of Tragic Dimensions.'" In Guggenheim Museum, *Marc Chagall and the Jewish Theater,* pp. 1–13. [English]

Deytsh, Aleksandr. *Maski evreyskogo teatra* [Masks of the Yiddish Theater]. Moscow: Russkoe teatral'noe obshtshestvo, 1927. [Russian]

———. "The Paths of GOSET." *Teatral'naya dekada,* no. 5 (1935), pp. 4–10. [Russian]

———. *The Voice of Memory.* Moscow: Iskusstvo, 1966. [Russian]

Dobrushin, Yikhezkel. "From Cloud to Fire." *Der emes,* Jan. 21, 1923. [Yiddish]

———. "The German Press about the Guest Performances of the Moscow State Yiddish Theater." *Der emes,* May 10, 1928. [Yiddish]

————. *Mikhoels der aktyor* [Mikhoels the Actor]. Moscow: Der emes, 1941. [Yiddish]

————. *The Yiddish Chamber Theater: On the Hundredth Performance of "The Sorceress." Krasnaya niva.* [Russian]

Efros, Abram. "Remarks about Art: Chagall, Altman, Falk." *Novy put',* no. 48–49 (1916), pp. 58–64. [Russian]

————. "The Artist and the Stage." *Kultura teatra,* no. 1 (Feb. 1, 1921), pp. 11–12. [Russian]

————. "Before the Opening Curtain: The New Season at the Jewish Theater." *Teatr i muzyka* (Moscow), no. 9 (November 1922), pp. 110–111. [Russian]

————. "On the Rise: The Jewish Chamber Theater." *Novaya rossiya,* no. 1 (1924), pp. 18–19. [Russian]

————. "The Artists of Granovsky's Theater." *Iskusstvo* (Moscow), 4 (1928), books 1–2, pp. 63–74. Reprinted in *Kovtsheg: Almanakh evreyskoy kul'tury* [The Ark: Almanac of Jewish Culture]. Jerusalem: Tarbut; Moscow: Khudozhestvennaya literatura, 1991. [Russian]

————. *Profili* (Profiles). Moscow: Federatsiya, 1930. [Russian]

Evreyskoe schastye [Jewish Luck; film with Menakhem-Mendel]. Produced by the First Goskino Factory, 1925. Kinokomedya in 7 parts. Director, Al. Granovsky; operator, Ed. Tisse; Artist, Natan Altman; Music, Lev Pulver; Subtitles, I. Babel. [Russian]

Evreyskoe schastye [brochure for the eponymous film]. Moscow: Kino-petshat' [Kino-Izdatelstvo RSFSR], 1925. Artistic design, Natan Altman; Text, Viktor Shklovsky. [Russian]

Felitsin, Y. "The Moscow State Yiddish Chamber Theater: On Its Fifth Anniversary." *Literarishe bleter* (Warsaw), no. 12 (1924). [Yiddish]

Freydkina, L. *King Lear in the Moscow State Yiddish Theater.* Moscow: Der emes, 1935. [Russian]

Frost, Matthew. "Marc Chagall and the Jewish State Chamber Theater." *Russian History,* 8 (1981), parts 1–2, pp. 90–107. [English]

Geyser, M. *Solomon Mikhoels.* Moscow: Prometheus, 1990. [Russian]

————. *Mikhoels: Zhizn' i smert'* [Mikhoels: Life and Death]. Moscow: Journalist Agency "Glasnost'" of the Union of Journalists of the Russian Federation, 1998. [Russian]

Gnessin, M. *Darki im ha-teatron ha-ivri* [My Road with the Hebrew Theater]. Tel Aviv: Hakibuz hameuchad, 1946. [Hebrew]

Goldschmidt, Alfons. "The Yiddish Theater in Moscow." In Toller, Roth, and Goldschmidt, *Das Moskauer Jüdische Akademische Theater.*

GOSET [State Yiddish Theater]. *Moscow State Jewish Theater.* Playbill for GOSET's 1926 tours to Minsk, Kiev, Homel, Odessa, and Leningrad; includes short play reviews. Artistic director, Al. Granovsky. [Russian and Yiddish]

Granach, Aleksander. "Granovsky, Mikhoels, and Zuskin—Congratulations!" *Literarishe bleter* (Warsaw), no. 20 (1928), p. 390. [Yiddish]

Granovsky, Aleksey [Aleksandr]. "Our Goals and Objectives." In *Dos idishe kamer teatr* (1919). [Yiddish]

————. "The Yiddish Theater." *Zvezda* (Minsk), July 31, 1923. [Russian]

————. "Our Theater." *Literarishe bleter* (Warsaw), 5, no. 17 (Apr. 27, 1928). [Yiddish]

Green, Christopher. "Les cubismes de l'école de Paris." In *L'école de Paris 1904–1929: Le part de l'autre*, pp. 58–70. Musée d'art moderne de la Ville de Paris exhibition, 2000–2001. Paris: Paris musées, 2001. [French]

Gregor, Joseph, and René Fülop-Miller. *Das russische Theater* [The Russian Theater]. Vienna: Amaltheat-Verlag, 1927. [German]

Grinbald, Y. *Mikhoels.* Moscow: OGIZ, 1948. [Russian]

Guggenheim Museum. *Marc Chagall and the Jewish Theater.* Edited by Jennifer Blessing et al. New York: Guggenheim Museum, 1992. [English]

Harshav [Hrushovski], Benjamin. *The Meaning of Yiddish.* Berkeley: University of California Press, 1990. [English]

————. "Chagall: Postmodernism and Fictional Worlds in Painting." In Guggenheim Museum, *Marc Chagall and the Jewish Theater*, pp. 15–64, 200–204. [English]

————. *Language in Time of Revolution.* Los Angeles: University of California Press, 1993; Stanford, Calif.: Stanford University Press, 2000; Cambridge: Cambridge University Press, 2000. [English]

————. "Marc Chagall: Painting, Theater, World." *Alpayim,* no. 8 (Fall 1993), pp. 9–97. [Hebrew]

————. "The Role of Language in Modern Art: On Texts and Subtexts in Chagall's Paintings." *Modernism/Modernity,* 1, no. 2 (April 1994), pp. 51–87. [English]

————. "Le postmodernisme et l'art du carnaval." In *Marc Chagall: Les années russes, 1907–1922,* pp. 18–39. [French]

————. "L'introduction au théâtre juif." In *Marc Chagall: Les années russes,* pp. 200–223. [French]

————. "El Teatro Judio." In *Marc Chagall: Tradiciones Judias,* pp. 26–53. Barcelona: Fundacion Juan March and Fundacio Caixa Catalunya, 1999. [Spanish]

————. "El Teatre Jueu." In *Marc Chagall: Tradicions Jueves,* pp. 26–53. Barcelona: Fundacion Juan March and Fundacio Caixa Catalunya, 1999. [Catalan]

————. *Marc Chagall and His Times: A Documentary Narrative.* Stanford, Calif.: Stanford University Press, 2004. [English]

————. *Marc Chagall and the Lost Jewish World: The Nature of Chagall's Art and Iconography,* New York: Rizzoli, 2006. [English]

————. "Fictionality and Fields of Reference." In Benjamin Harshav, *Explorations in Poetics.* Stanford, Calif.: Stanford University Press, 2007. [English]

Harshav, Benjamin, ed. *The Moscow Yiddish Theater.* Special issue of *Di pen* (Oxford), nos. 28–29 (November–December 1996), including Benjamin Harshav, "The Flowering of the Moscow Yiddish Theater," and publication (with Yosef Schein) of Mendele Moykher Sforim, *Masoes Binyomin ha-Shlishi* (The Travels of Benjamin the Third), a literary theater script by Yikhezkel Dobrushin, pp. 1–40. [Yiddish]

————. *Marc Chagall on Art and Culture*. Texts and documents translated from several languages by Barbara and Benjamin Harshav. Stanford, Calif.: Stanford University Press, 2004. [English]

Harshav, Benjamin, and Barbara Harshav, trans. "Texts and Documents." In Guggenheim Museum, *Marc Chagall and the Jewish Theater*, pp. 133–199. [English translations from Russian and Yiddish]

Hermann, Frank, and Heinke Schmitz. *DerVerlag Die Schmiede, 1921–1929: Eine kommentierte Bibliographie*. Morsum/Sylt, Germany: Cicero Presse, 1996. [German]

Hume, Samuel A., and Walter Rene Fuerst. *XXth Century Stage Decoration*. Vol. 1. New York: Alfred A. Knopf, 1929. [English]

Idishe kamer teatr, Dos [The Yiddish Chamber Theater, on Its Opening in July 1919]. Petrograd: Jewish Theater Society, 1919. [Yiddish]

Idisher kamer teatr [The Yiddish Chamber Theater]. Kiev: Kultur-Lige, 1924. [Yiddish]

"Invitation to the XXIII Exhibition of the Central Section of IZO NARKOMPROS" [included in Chagall's collage *Tsedek*]. June 1921. [Russian]

Jiddisch: Monatsschrift für jüdische Kultur in Wien [special issue on the Moscow Yiddish theater], 1, nos. 5–6 (August–September 1928). Includes "Biographical Note on the Moscow Artists." [Yiddish]

Jouffrey, Alain. "Theater and Revolution." In G. di San Lazzaro, ed., *Chagall Monumental Works*. Special issue of *XXe siècle Review*. New York: Tudor, 1973. [English]

Kamensky, Aleksandr. *Chagall: The Russian Years, 1907–1922*. Translated from the French by C. Phillips. New York: Rizzoli, 1989. [English]

Kampf, Avram. "In Quest of Jewish Style in the Era of the Revolution." *Journal of Jewish Art*, 5 (1978), pp. 48–75. [English]

————. "Art and Stage Design: The Jewish Theaters of Moscow in the Early Twenties." In Apter-Gabriel, *Tradition and Revolution*, pp. 125–142. [English]

————. *Chagall to Kitaj: Jewish Experience in Twentieth Century Art*. London: Lund Humphries, with the Barbican Art Gallery, 1990. [English]

————. "Chagall in the Yiddish Theatre." In Vitali, *Marc Chagall*, pp. 94–106. [English]

Kann, E. "Music at GOSET." *Teatral'naya dekada*, no. 5 (1935), p. 10. [Russian]

Kasovsky, Grigori. "Chagall and the Jewish Art Programme." In Vitali, *Marc Chagall*, pp. 53–60. [English]

Kerr, Alfred [K...r]. "The Moscow Yiddish Academic Theater in Theater des Westens." *Berliner Tageblatt*, Apr. 12, 1928. [German]

————. "The Moscow Yiddish Theater ([October 10,] 1928)." In Hugo Fetting, ed., *Mit Schleuder und Harfe: Theaterkritiken aus drei Jahrzehnten*. Berlin: Henschelverlag, 1981. [German]

Kornhendler, Yikhezkel. "About the Moscow Yiddish Chamber Theater." *Fraye arbeyter shtime* (New York), Aug. 24, 1928. [Yiddish]

Kovaliev, Aleksei. "Report on the Restoration of the Murals for the Jewish Kamerny Theatre in Moscow." In Vitali, *Marc Chagall*, pp. 134–139. [English]

Kultur-Lige: A sakh-hakl [The Culture League: A Stock Taking; a publication of the Central Committee]. Kiev: November 1919. [Yiddish]

Levidov, Lev. "The Jewish Theater Society and the Chamber Theater." In *Dos idishe kamer teatr* (1919). [Yiddish]

Levy, Emanuel. *Ha-teatron ha-leumi Ha-Bima: Korot ha-teatron ba-shanim 1917–1979* [The National Theater HaBima: History of the Theater in the Years 1917–1979]. Tel Aviv: Eked, 1981. [Hebrew]

Lirov, M. "The Jewish State Chamber Theater." *Prozhektor*, Dec. 31, 1924. [Russian]

Litvakov, M. "Of the October Miracles." *Der emes*, Apr. 13, 1922. [Yiddish]

———. "*The Sorceress* in the Yiddish Chamber Theater." *Der emes*, Dec. 16, 1922. [Yiddish]

———. "Sholem-Aleichem in the Yiddish Chamber Theater." *Der emes*, Jan. 21, 1923. Also in *Literarishe bleter* (Warsaw), no. 4 (1924). [Yiddish]

———. *Finf yor melukhisher yidisher kamer-teatr: 1919–1924* [Five Years of the State Yiddish Chamber Theater: 1919–1924]. Moscow: Shul un bukh, 1924. [Yiddish]

Lozowick, Louis. "Moscow Theatre, 1920s." *Russian History*, 8, nos. 1–2 (1981), pp. 140–144. [English]

Lyubomirsky, Y. [Yosef/Osip] *Der revolutsyonerer teatr* [The Revolutionary Theater]. Moscow: Shul un bukh, 1926. [Yiddish]

Lyubomirsky, O. [Osip/Yosef]. *Mikhoels*. Moscow: Iskusstvo, 1938. [Russian]

Malevich, Kazimir. "The Non-objective World." In Chipp, *Theories of Modern Art*. [English]

Mandelshtam, Y. [Osip]. "The Moscow State Yiddish Theater." In *Vechernaya krasnaya gazeta* [The Red Evening Gazette] (Leningrad), Aug. 10, 1926. [Russian]

———. "Mikhoels (1926)." In G. P. Struve and B. A. Filipoff, eds., *Sobraniye sochineny v trekh tomakh*, vol. 3 (New York: Inter-Language Associates, 1969), p. 106. [Russian]

Manteyfel, A. N. "The First Theater of the Revolution." *Moskva*, no. 1 (1968), pp. 192–194. [Russian]

———. "The Theater of Revolutionary Satire (TEREVSAT)." *Teatral'noe iskusstvo*, pp. 182–190. [Russian]

Marc Chagall: Les années russes, 1907–1922. Paris: Musée d'art moderne de la Ville de Paris, 1995. Paris: Paris musées, 1995. [French]

Margolin, S. [S. M.] "Tragic Carnival: 'A Night at the Old Market' at the Jewish State Theater." *Vsemirnaya illyustratsiya*, no. 3 (1925). [Russian]

———. *Night in the Old Marketplace*. 1925. [Russian]

———. "The Artist and the Theater: GOSET Performances." *Teatral'naya dekada*, no. 5 (1935), pp. 8–9. [Russian]

Markov, P. A. *The Soviet Theatre*. New York: G. P. Putnam's Sons, 1935. [English]

Mayzel, Nakhman. "Five Years of the Yiddish Chamber Theater in Russia." *Literarishe bleter* (Warsaw), no. 46 (Mar. 20, 1925). [Yiddish]

———. "The Great Stage Miracle." *Literarishe bleter* (Warsaw), 5, no. 17 (Apr. 27, 1928). [Yiddish]

Meyer, Franz. *Marc Chagall: Life and Work.* New York: Harry N. Abrams, 1963. [English]

Mikhoels, S. "In Our Studio." In *Dos idishe kamer teatr* (1919). [Yiddish]

———. "The New Jewish Comedian." *Der veker* (Minsk), July 19, 1923. [Yiddish]

——— [Vofsi-Mikhoels]. "Our Comedians' Parade in Ukraine." In *Idisher kamer teatr* (1924), p. 10. [Yiddish]

———. "Mikhoels Vofsi on the Theater" [interview]. *Literarishe bleter* (Warsaw), 5, no. 17 (Apr. 27, 1928). [Yiddish]

———. "What a Question!" [interview]. *Jiddisch*, 1, nos. 5–6 (August–September 1928). [Yiddish]

———. *Stat'i, besedy, retshi* [Articles, Conversations, Lectures]. Moscow: Iskusstvo, 1965. [Russian]

Mikhoels: 1890–1948 [collection about Mikhoels, on his death]. Moscow: Der emes, 1948. [Yiddish]

Mikhoels, S., and Y. Dobrushin. "Yiddish Theater Culture in the Soviet Union." In S. Dimandshteyn, ed., *Yidn in FSSR* [Jews in the USSR: A Symposium], pp. 149–162. Moscow: Mezhdunarodnaya kniga and Emes, 1935. [Yiddish]

Milhau, Denis. *Chagall et le théâtre.* Toulouse: Musée des Augustins, 1967. [French]

———. "Chagall and the Theater." In G. di San Lazzaro, ed., *Homage to Marc Chagall.* New York: Tudor, 1969. [English]

Neklyudova, M. G. *Traditsii i novatorstvo v russkom iskusstve kontsa XIX–natshala XX veka* [Tradition and Innovation in Russian Art from the End of the Nineteenth to the Beginning of the Twentieth Century]. Moscow: Isskustvo, 1991. [Russian]

Norman, Itzhak, ed. *Be-reyshit Ha-Bima: Nahum Zemach meyased Ha-Bima be-hazon u-ve-ma'as* [The Birth of HaBima: Nakhum Zemach, Founder, HaBima in Vision and Practice]. Jerusalem: Ha-Sifriya ha-Zionit [The Jewish Agency], 1966. [Hebrew]

Orshansky, B. *Teatr-shlakhtn* [Theater Battles]. Minsk, 1931. [Yiddish]

Osborn, Max. "Marc Chagall." *Zhar-ptitsa* (Berlin), no. 11 (1923). [Russian]

Pavel, Thomas G. *Fictional Worlds.* Cambridge: Harvard University Press, 1986. [English]

Payne, Darwin Reid. *The Scenographic Imagination.* Carbondale: Southern Illinois University Press, 1981. [English]

Picon-Vallin, Béatrice. *Le théâtre juif soviétique pendant les années vingt* [The Soviet Jewish Theater in the Nineteen-Twenties]. Lausanne: La Cité, 1973. [French]

Reifenscheid, Beate, *Chagall und die Bühne* [Chagall and the Stage]. Bielefeld: Kerber Verlag, 1996. [German]

Rischbieter, Henning, ed. *Art and the Stage in the Twentieth Century.* Translated from the German by Michael Bullock. Greenwich, Conn.: New York Graphic Society, 1978. [English]

Rivesman, M. "The Past and the Future of Yiddish Theater." In *Dos idishe kamer teatr* (1919). [Yiddish]

Romm, Aleksandr. "Marc Chagall." Unpublished manuscript. [Russian]

Roose-Evans, James. *Experimental Theatre: From Stanislavsky to Today.* New York: Universe Books, 1970. [English]

Roth, Joseph. "The Moscow Yiddish Theater." In Toller, Roth, and Goldschmidt, *Das Moskauer Jüdische Akademische Theater.*

Rudnitsky, Konstantin. *Meyerhold the Director.* Translated by George Petrov. Ann Arbor, Mich.: Ardis, 1981. [English]

———. *Istoriya russkogo sovetskogo dramatitcheskogo teatra* [History of the Russian Soviet Dramatic Theater]. Vol. 1: 1917–1945. Moscow, 1984. [Russian]

———. *Russian and Soviet Theater, 1905–1932.* Translated from the Russian by Roxane Permar. New York: Harry N. Abrams, 1988. [English]

Russian Painters and the Stage: 1884–1965 [a loan exhibition of stage and costume designs from the collection of Mr. and Mrs. Nikita D. Lobanov-Rostovsky]. Austin: University of Texas Art Museum, 1978. [English]

Sandrow, Nahma. *Vagabond Stars: A World History of Yiddish Theater.* New York: Harper and Row, 1977. [English]

Schein, Yosef. *Arum moskver yidishn teater* [Around the Moscow Yiddish Theater]. Paris: Les éditions polyglottes, 1964. [Yiddish]

Schneider, Pierre. *Marc Chagall.* Paris: Flammarion, 1995. [French]

Semenovsky, V. "About Granovsky." *Moskovsky nablyudatel,* no. 2 (January 1991), pp. 50–52. [Russian]

Shatskich, Alexandra [Aleksandra Shatskikh]. "Marc Chagall and the Theater." In Vitali, *Marc Chagall,* pp. 76–89. [English]

———. "Copies of Mark Chagall's Theatrical Sketches in the Bakhrushin Museum." Unpublished manuscript. [Russian]

———. "Mark Chagall and the Jewish Chamber Theater." Unpublished manuscript. [Russian]

———. "The Theatrical Phenomenon of Mark Chagall." Unpublished manuscript. [Russian]

Shklovsky, Viktor. "Jewish Luck." In *Evreyskoe schastye* [brochure]. [Russian]

Sholem-Aleichem. *Ale verk fun Sholem Aleykhem* [Complete Writings of Sholem-Aleichem]. Vol. 4. Forverts edition. New York, 1944. [Yiddish]

Swett, Herman. "German Jews, German Press, and the Granovsky Theater." *Literarishe bleter* (Warsaw), 5, no. 17 (Apr. 27, 1928). [Yiddish]

———. "The Theater World in Berlin." *Literarishe bleter* (Warsaw), no. 41 (1928). [Yiddish]

———. "Meyerhold and Granovsky." *Literarishe bleter* (Warsaw), no. 19 (1930), p. 344. [Yiddish]

Tairov, Aleksandr. *Zapiski rezhisera* [Notes of a Theater Director]. Moscow: Kamernyi Teatr, 1921. [Russian]

Tarabukhin, Nikolai. "Art Exhibitions: Altman, Chagall, Shterenberg." *Vestnik isskustv,* no. 5 (1922), pp. 27–28. [Russian]

Teatral'naya moskva [a guide to theater, music, and film that includes entries on the Moscow State Yiddish Theater and HaBima]. 1926. [Russian]

Teatral'naya zhizn' [special issue on GOSET], no. 10 (1990), p. 764. [Russian]

Toller, Ernst. "A Salute to the Yiddish National Theater." In Toller, Roth, and Goldschmidt, *Das Moskauer Jüdische Akademische Theater.*

Toller, Ernst, Joseph Roth, and Alfons Goldschmidt. *Das Moskauer Jüdische Akademische Theater* [The Moscow Jewish Academic Theater]. Berlin: Verlag Die Schmiede, 1928. [German]

Van Gyseghem, André. *Theatre in Soviet Russia.* London: Faber and Faber, 1943. [English]

Van Norman Baer, Nancy, ed. *Theater in Revolution: Russian Avant-Garde Stage Design, 1913–1935.* New York: Thames and Hudson / The Fine Arts Museum of San Francisco, 1991. [Russian]

Veidlinger, Jeffrey. *The Moscow State Yiddish Theater: Jewish Culture on the Soviet Stage.* Bloomington: Indiana University Press, 2000. [English]

Vetrov, A. [David Arkin]. "Exhibition of Three." *Ekran,* no. 28 (1921). [Russian]

———. "On Chagall." *Ekran,* no. 7 (1921). [Russian]

Vevyorke, A. "A Jewish Theater Style: On the Sholem-Aleichem Evenings in M.Y.C.T. [Moscow Yiddish Chamber Theater]." *Der emes,* no. 78 (1921). [Yiddish]

———. "A Holiday." *Der emes,* Apr. 13, 1922. [Yiddish]

Vitali, Christoph, ed. *Marc Chagall: The Russian Years, 1906–1922.* Frankfurt: Schirn Kunsthalle, 1991. [English]

Vlasova, R. I. *Russkoe teatral'no-dekoratsionnoe iskusstvo natshala XX veka* [Russian Theatrical Design of the Early Twentieth Century]. Leningrad: Khudozhnik RSFR, 1984. [Russian]

Vofsi-Mikhoels, Natalia. *Avi Shlomo Mikhoels* [My Father Shlomo Mikhoels]. Tel Aviv: Hakibutz hameuchad, 1982. [Hebrew]

Walden, Herwarth. "The Moscow Yiddish Chamber Theater." *Der Sturm,* vols. 2–3 (1928–1929), p. 229. [German]

Worrall, Nick. *Modernism to Realism on the Soviet Stage: Tairov-Vakhtangov-Okhlopov.* Cambridge: Cambridge University Press, 1989. [English]

Zagorsky, M. *Mikhoels.* Moscow and Leningrad: Kinopetshat', 1927. [Russian]

———. "Mikhoels." *Teatral'naya dekada,* no. 5 (1935), p. 7. [Russian]

Zingerman, B. "Russia, Chagall, Mikhoels, and Others." *Teatr,* 2 (1990), pp. 35–53. [Russian]

———. "About Mikhoels." *Moskovsky nablyudatel',* no. 2 [in section Panl'eon] (January 1991), pp. 53–57. [Russian]

Znosko-Borovsky, Evg. *Russky teatr natshala XX veka* [Russian Theater in the Early Twentieth Century]. Vol. 1. Prague: Plamya Press, 1923. [Russian]

Zrelishtsha [special issue on the fifth anniversary of GOSET], no. 89 (1924). [Russian]

Zuskin, B. "Actor B. Zuskin on the Theater" [interview]. *Literarishe bleter* (Warsaw), 5, no. 17
    (Apr. 27, 1928). [Yiddish]

Zylbercwaig, Zalman. *Leksikon fun yidishn teater* [Lexicon of the Yiddish Theater]. [Yiddish]
    Vol. 1. Warsaw: Elisheva, 1934 [includes entry on Granovsky, pp. 516–517].
    Vol. 2. Warsaw: Elisheva, 1934 [includes entries on the Moscow State Yiddish Theater, pp.
    1227–1239 (with an extensive bibliography), and Mikhoels, pp. 1312–1314]
    Vol. 4. New York: Elisheva, 1963 [includes entry on Sholem-Aleichem and descriptions of
    stage productions, pp. 3309–3578].

Illustration Credits